PENGUIN BOOKS

A FINE MESS

T. R. Reid is a longtime correspondent for *The Washington Post* and a former chief of its Tokyo and London bureaus. He is a commentator for National Public Radio and has been a correspondent for several PBS documentaries. His bestselling books include *The Healing of America*, *The United States of Europe*, *The Chip*, and *Confucius Lives Next Door*.

ALSO BY T. R. REID

The Healing of America

The United States of Europe

Confucius Lives Next Door

Heisei Highs and Lows

Tomu no Me, Tomu no Mimi

Ski Japan!

The Chip

Congressional Odyssey

A FINE MESS

A GLOBAL QUEST FOR A SIMPLER, FAIRER, AND MORE EFFICIENT TAX SYSTEM

T. R. REID

Penguin Books

PENGUIN BOOKS

An imprint of Penguin Random House LLC

375 Hudson Street

New York, New York 10014

penguin.com

First published in the United States of America by Penguin Press,
an imprint of Penguin Random House LLC, 2017
This edition with a new afterword published in Penguin Books 2018

Cartoon by Jeff MacNelly, courtesy of Gallery on Greene

ISBN 9781594205514 (hardcover)
ISBN 9780143111146 (paperback)
ISBN 9780735223967 (e-book)

Printed in the United States of America
1   3   5   7   9   10   8   6   4   2

DESIGNED BY MEIGHAN CAVANAUGH

Filio filiabusque in amore dedicatus

CONTENTS

Prologue: Every Thirty-Two Years   *1*

1. Policy Laboratories   *5*

2. "Low Effort, Low Collection"   *13*

3. Taxes: What Are They Good For?   *27*

4. BBLR   *49*

5. Scooping Water with a Sieve   *71*

6. Flat Broke   *93*

7. The Defining Problem; the Taxing Solution   *115*

8. Convoluted and Pernicious Strategies   *141*

9. The Single Tax, the Fat Tax, the Tiny Tax,
    the Carbon Tax—and No Tax At All   *171*

10. The Panama Papers:
    Sunny Places for Shady Money   *197*

11. Simplify, Simplify   *209*

12. The Money Machine   *227*

    Epilogue: The Internal Revenue
    Code of 2018   *249*

    Afterword: The Tax Cuts and Jobs Act   *259*

    Thanks   *267*
    Notes   *271*
    Index   *279*

A FINE MESS

PROLOGUE:
EVERY THIRTY-TWO YEARS

The members of the U.S. Senate rose to their feet and erupted into cheers, handshakes, and hugs on September 7, 1913, to celebrate final passage of the Underwood–Simmons Tariff Act—the statute that created America's federal income tax. Determined to milk the moment for maximum political benefit, President Woodrow Wilson held a formal signing ceremony at the White House and told the assembled reporters he was proud to be present at the creation of this highly popular tax.

Back then, the newly minted federal income tax was popular with almost all Americans because hardly any had to pay it. The tax we love to hate today was initially aimed squarely at the silk-suit-and-satin-gown set—the Astors and Vanderbilts, the Morgans and Rockefellers. Only the richest smidgen of the population had to file a return, and even for them the top tax rate was just 7%. Over the next nine years, Congress tinkered with the tax regime, each year passing a new internal revenue code with exemptions and exclusions; the deduction for charitable contributions, for example, was added in 1917. The top rate went up sharply to pay for World War I and then came down again. Eventually, in the Internal Revenue Code of 1922, the structure of the federal income tax was essentially set. There were new revenue acts every few years—1932, 1939, 1946—but the basic system stayed in place for three decades.

By the 1950s, everyone agreed that the Internal Revenue Code was a complex, confusing, contradictory mess. The new president, Dwight Eisenhower, demanded reform—and Congress obliged with a complete rewrite: the Internal Revenue Code of 1954. Among much else, it set the deadline for filing your income tax return on April 15. This code stayed in place for three decades, but almost every year Congress, of course, added exclusions and credits and allowances in a haphazard fashion.

By the mid-1980s, the code was such a voluminous, complicated monster that a conservative Republican president and a liberal Democratic Speaker of the House agreed to another complete rewrite: the Internal Revenue Code of 1986. The economists loved this one; it was a comprehensive revision based on the most fundamental principle of sound tax writing.

There's a pattern here. In the thirty-two years from 1922 to 1954, the Internal Revenue Code became such a chaotic muddle that it had to be replaced. In the thirty-two years from 1954 to 1986, history repeated itself, and once again the Internal Revenue Code had to be rewritten.

It has now been three decades since the last revision. Everyone agrees once again that our nation's basic tax law has become a fine mess: so absurdly complex, so byzantine, that it has to be completely revised. Following the historical pattern—every thirty-two years—the next major revision should come in 2018. Recognizing that, the White House and Congressional Republicans in the fall of 2017 proposed a sweeping set of tax changes. (This plan is described in the Afterword to this book.)

But what should be in this new tax code? Can we make the U.S. tax system simpler, fairer, and more efficient? The answers: yes, yes, and yes. Could we cut tax rates and still bring in more revenue? Yes. We know this because there are good models all over the world to show us how to do it. Other rich countries like ours—advanced, high-tech, free-market democracies—have devised tax regimes that are equitable, effective, and easy on the taxpayer (although they've made some serious blunders as well). By looking at tax systems around the world, we can learn what the United States should and shouldn't do in writing the Internal Revenue Code of 2018.

1.

POLICY LABORATORIES

During one of its periodic bursts of anger at the Internal Revenue Service, the U.S. Congress passed a strict new law requiring the Treasury Department to reduce the complexity of America's income tax system. In standard congressional fashion, this mandate for simplicity—it's known as the "anti-complexity clause"—was included in a massively complex piece of legislation that added some thirty thousand words and scores of complicated new deductions, exemptions, and credits to the bloated multivolume corpus of the nation's tax law. If you happen to be browsing through the statute books some restless night, you can find the anti-complexity clause in Subsection IX of subpart (ii) of Section 7803(c)(2)(B) of the Internal Revenue Code.

It's classic: Congress decides to reduce the complexity of our tax code by making it even more complex. It might be funny if the whole taxpaying process in America weren't so maddeningly expensive, inefficient, and time-consuming. At the same time Congress took that principled stand in favor of simplicity, it also added a clause—that would be Section 7803(c)(2)(B)(ii)(III)—requiring that Treasury file a report each year on the overall cost of the income tax regime. The reported burden on U.S. taxpayers turns out to be no laughing matter.

In 2015, the government estimates, American taxpayers spent just over six billion hours preparing and filing their income tax returns.

They paid $10.1 billion in fees to the booming tax-preparation industry and another $2 billion for tax software programs (programs that still require hours of work for the typical taxpaying household). For an American household earning the median family income—about $55,000—the average is more than thirty hours per year gathering documents and filling out forms. Tens of millions of Americans have to spend the weekend before April 15—a lovely spring interlude when they should be out on the golf course or at the kids' soccer game— tearing their hair out over instructions like this gem from IRS Form 1041: "Go to Part IV of Schedule I to figure line 52 if the estate or trust has qualified dividends or has a gain on lines 18a and 19 of column (2) of Schedule D (Form 1041) (as refigured for the AMT, if necessary)."

THE CARTOONIST JEFF MACNELLY used to offer a satire of this process every April 15:

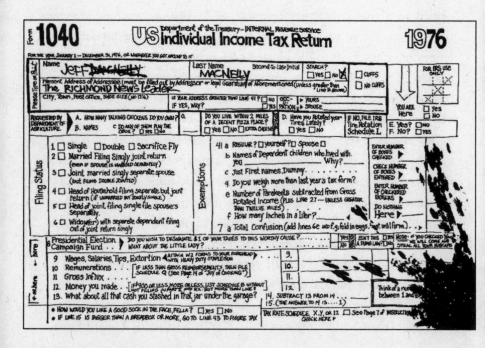

It doesn't have to be this way.

If you walk down the street in London, Tokyo, Paris, or Lima, you won't see an office of H&R Block or any similar firm; in other nations, people don't need a tax-preparation industry to file their returns. Parliaments and tax collection bureaus all over the world have done what the U.S. Congress seems totally unable to do: they've made paying taxes easy.

In the Netherlands, for example, the Algemene Fiscale Politiek (in essence, the Dutch IRS) has a slogan: "We can't make paying taxes pleasant, but at least we can make it simple." It is certainly simple for my friend Michael, a successful Dutch executive with a six-figure income and all the economic complications that come with his family's upper-bracket lifestyle. An American in the same situation would have to fill out at least a dozen different forms, some of them six pages long (or pay somebody to do it for her). Michael, in contrast, told me that he sets aside fifteen minutes per year to file his federal and local tax returns, and that's usually enough. But sometimes, he said, he needs to check some line item on the return, and that can be time-consuming. At this point, Michael was getting downright indignant. "I mean, some years, it takes me nearly half an hour just to file my tax returns!"

AMERICA COULD LEARN SOMETHING from the Netherlands, and from other countries, about how to make the taxpaying process simple. And it's not just the complexity problem that we could solve by taking a look at other countries. Almost every government on earth collects taxes (as we'll see, there are a few lucky nations that get by just fine without taxing their citizens). Many of the developed countries have come up with tax systems that are simpler, fairer, and more efficient than ours. They can show us what to tax, how much to tax it, and how to collect the money that's due.

I traveled the globe looking at tax systems that work better than ours (and some that are worse). I found useful lessons for the United States all over the world. Other countries can show us how to get the same amount of revenue with lower tax rates and how to use the tax code to deal with important national problems, such as the growing inequality of wealth between the richest Americans and everybody else.

Just about every economist and political figure in America agrees these days that our tax code has to be reformed. As Americans elected a new Congress and president in 2016, it appeared that our body politic was finally ready to take on this challenge.

One of the benefits of a comparative study of taxes is that the other countries can serve as policy laboratories for us. In fact, just about every idea that anybody, left or right, has proposed to "fix" the U.S. tax system has already been tried somewhere. For example:

- From the right, there have been repeated proposals for a flat-rate income tax, with everybody paying the same rate—about 18%—of their income in tax. Several Republican presidential candidates in the 2012 election, and at least four more in 2016—that would be Ben Carson, Rand Paul, Ted Cruz, and Rick Perry—have backed the flat tax. (Steve Forbes, the publisher who ran for president twice, has been the most prominent advocate of this idea.) Would it work? As it happens, about a dozen countries have actually tried this innovation.

- From the left, there have been repeated proposals for a carbon tax, designed to reduce fossil fuel emissions and thus encourage development of "green" forms of energy. As it happens, Australia actually tried this innovation—and quickly gave up on it.

- Virtually all economists agree that two of the most widely used deductions in the federal income tax code—the deduction for mortgage interest and the deduction for charitable contributions—cut government revenues by billions of dollars but provide almost no economic benefit. The logical response would be to eliminate them. There are all sorts of proposals floating around Washington, but

Congress has never found a politically palatable way to take away these popular write-offs. As it happens, many rich countries have come up with intelligent ways to get rid of these deductions, with minimal impact on home ownership or charitable giving.

• The United States provides tax breaks for savings plans, to encourage Americans to put away money for retirement. As with everything else in our tax code, this straightforward idea has become absurdly complex. There's a bewildering variety of different plans, with names that sound like secret code—the 401(k), the 403(b), the 457(b), the SEP, the SARSEP, the ESOP, and so on. There's an IRA, and there's a Roth IRA, which is different, and then there's a myRA, which is different from the other two. There's something called the "nonqualified deferred compensation plan." One of the savings vehicles in our tax code is actually called the SIMPLE IRA, but of course it's not simple at all; the SIMPLE IRA requires two different IRS forms (Form 5304 and Form 5305) and a ten-page book of instructions (Publication 4334). Each different tax-free savings plan has its own rules about who can use it, how much you can put in, how much you can take out, when you can take it out, what you can use the money for, and how much tax you'll owe. To deal with this expanding labyrinth of regulations, a billion-dollar advisory industry has sprung up just to help Americans figure out how to put money in a savings account.

Many other countries also use the tax code to encourage savings, but no place has made it as convoluted as the U.S. mess. In Canada, for example, the tax-free savings account is called, sensibly, a "Tax-Free Savings Account." Anybody can use it; you can put the money into any bank or investment account; you can deposit and withdraw at any time, for any reason. The interest and dividends are always tax-free. The plan is so clear-cut and so popular that savings have skyrocketed. It is a vastly simpler way to achieve the same goal that our tax writers have turned into an inscrutable muddle.

- The 535 members of the U.S. Congress—the people who write the tax laws—have given themselves various tax breaks and deductions that other Americans don't get. This is probably a natural tendency among people who write the law. As it happens, though, some countries have found ways to combat this predictable effort by legislators to reduce their own tax bills. Slovakia, for example, has a rule that members of the national legislature and the prime minister's cabinet always have to pay 5% more in tax than any other Slovakian with the same income.

SHOULD WE DOUBLE THE TAX on sugared soda pop as a way to combat obesity? Should we impose a tax of 0.0001% on every Wall Street transaction? Should we tax commuters for driving to work when traffic is terrible? Should we give companies a tax break for raising wages? Should we tax gasoline at $4 per gallon? Should we triple the cigarette tax? In each case, other countries have given these ideas a test run.

This is not to suggest that tax systems in other nations are all simple, efficient, and rational. Because the tax code in any democracy is a political animal, there are strange anomalies of taxation everywhere.

Most countries, for example, tax income at a graduated rate; that is, the more income you have, the higher rate of tax you have to pay. But Great Britain, for reasons that evidently made sense to Parliament, has imposed a tax rate of 60% on incomes of $160,000 per year but 45% on incomes of $230,000 or more.[1] Similarly, there's a strange quirk in the tax structure in the Netherlands. The sales tax (actually, value-added tax) on dog food is 19%, but the tax on rabbit food is 12%. Dutch bunny lovers apparently have more lobbying clout than puppy owners.

IT USED TO BE that other countries around the world studied our tax code. In the 1980s, the United States was a recognized policy leader on tax issues. When our 1986 tax reform produced a huge drop in income tax rates, virtually every other developed democracy followed our example with major rate reductions.

Today, though, the United States is well behind the curve on tax innovation. Indeed, we've completely missed the boat on the most important taxing invention of the last half century—that is, the value-added tax (VAT), a new form of the familiar retail sales tax. Economists love this tax because it doesn't punish people for working hard and making money; it taxes spending, not earning or saving. Governments love the VAT because it is easy to collect and hard to evade. This innovation is so useful, fair, and simple that some 175 countries have adopted it in recent decades, often using revenues from the VAT to cut income tax rates. The only places that don't use a VAT are a handful of poor countries and the world's richest country, the United States. We've missed out on a powerful new technology. When it comes to taxation, Americans are still pounding out letters on typewriters and dropping them in the mailbox, while the rest of the world has moved on to e-mail and texting.

I looked at the VAT, and variations on the VAT, in several countries. New Zealand, for example, has a broad form of this tax called the GST— the goods and services tax. Graham Scott, the Finance Ministry bureaucrat who designed the New Zealand system, told me that the tax has to be paid on anything that is purchased—from a manufacturing plant buying basic commodities to a consumer buying the finished product in a department store. "The GST applies to all the services, too," Scott told me. "Lawyers, dentists, plumbers, architects—they're all taxed." New Zealand is one of several countries that have recently legalized the sex trade. So I asked if a prostitute working in a brothel is expected to collect sales tax from the customers. "Why, yes, of course," he said, as if the answer were the most obvious thing in the world. "We haven't figured out whether it's a good or a service, but we know it's taxable."

Taxation experts constantly predict that the United States will establish a value-added tax, which would make it possible to reduce income tax rates for every individual and corporation. "The VAT

makes so much economic sense that even the U.S. Congress will
eventually recognize its value," says the UCLA Law School professor
Eric Zolt, who has helped design tax codes for about forty countries.
"Mark my words," Zolt says forcefully, "the United States will have a
VAT within five years. Of course," the professor concedes, "I've been
saying that for the last twenty years."

THESE DAYS, WHEN CONGRESS takes up tax reform, the "reform" generally makes things worse. A Congress that produces something like
Section 7803(c)(2)(B)(ii)(IX) in the name of reducing complexity hardly
seems likely to agree on any serious changes that would improve the
system. Even with one party controlling both Congress and the White
House, tax reform would be a stretch in our acidic political atmosphere.
So how could Congress and the White House agree on serious changes
to the tax code when our country is ferociously divided?

The fact is, we've done it before, in a time of severely divided government. In the mid-1980s, a strong conservative in the White House
and a strongly liberal Speaker of the House—that is, Ronald Reagan
and Tip O'Neill—reached agreement on the biggest transformation of
the federal income tax since the tax was created in 1913. The Tax Reform Act of 1986, passed by a divided Congress and signed by a Republican president, was widely admired; it was precisely the kind of change
that almost all tax experts favored. That reform was based on principles that have been adopted by countries around the world. If we go
back to those fundamental principles, the United States could achieve
serious tax reform, even in our current state of political gridlock.

Another benefit of looking at other countries is that comparative
analysis can tell us where Americans stand relative to the rest of the
world when it comes to how much tax we have to pay. During his
campaign for the presidency in 2016, Donald Trump repeatedly said,
"The United States is the highest-taxed country in the world." Was
he right?

2.

"LOW EFFORT, LOW COLLECTION"

The Gallup poll surveys Americans every year about the taxes they pay, and every year a hefty majority says that taxes are too high.[1] Whenever I mentioned this to economists in other countries, they laughed. Nobody in the world's other rich democracies would say that American taxes are too high. Relative to other countries like us, the United States is One Nation, Undertaxed.

This is not a political statement or an editorial opinion. It's a fact: Americans pay significantly less than our counterparts in the world's other advanced, free-market economies. In terms of the overall tax burden, Americans pay less. In terms of specific taxes—income tax, sales tax, gasoline tax, and so on—American rates are almost always lower. (On the other hand, Americans tend to give more than anybody else to charity, because we use private charities to perform some of the tasks funded by taxes elsewhere.) The one clear exception to this pattern is the corporate income tax, where the official tax rate and the "effective" rate (how much corporations actually pay, after the tax lawyers have orchestrated various avoidance mechanisms) are higher in the United States than in almost any other nation.

A standard way to measure national tax burdens is to calculate a country's total tax revenues—national, state, and local—as a percentage of gross domestic product (the sum of all the wealth produced in the country in a year). This statistic, called the **"overall tax burden,"** is measured annually by the Organization for Economic Cooperation and Development (OECD), which is sort of a United Nations but with membership limited only to the richest countries. For many years now, the OECD's calculation of overall tax burden has shown that total tax revenues in the United States are much lower than in most other advanced countries.

For the year 2014, the OECD reports that overall tax burden for all of its thirty-five member countries averaged 34.18% of GDP. Some countries impose taxes at a considerably higher level. In Denmark, taxes amounted to almost half—49.58%—of all the wealth that country produced in 2014; in France and Belgium, the tax take was about 45% of GDP. A few European countries, like Ireland (28.71%) and Switzerland (27.03%), taxed somewhat below the OECD average. Generally, though, the overall tax burden in the democracies of Western Europe was in the neighborhood of 40% of GDP.

In the world's richest country, the United States, taxes were far lower: 25.88% of GDP. Of the thirty-five richest countries, in fact, the United States rated thirty-second in total taxes paid; only in South Korea, Chile, and Mexico did people face a lower tax burden than Americans.

Here's the OECD's chart of total tax revenue as a percentage of GDP, by country, for the year 2014:

Country	Overall tax burden
Denmark	49.58
France	45.49
Belgium	45.00
Finland	43.84
Italy	43.69
Austria	42.82

Country	Overall tax burden
Sweden	42.78
Iceland	38.92
Norway	38.68
Luxembourg	38.37
Hungary	38.23
Netherlands	37.52
Germany	36.57
Slovenia	36.49
Greece	35.77
OECD average	34.18
Portugal	34.17
Spain	33.85
Czech Republic	33.09
New Zealand	32.52
Estonia	32.43
Poland	32.08
United Kingdom	32.07
Japan	32.04
Israel	31.25
Slovakia	31.25
Canada	31.22
Latvia	28.87
Turkey	28.76
Ireland	28.71
Australia	27.85
Switzerland	27.03
United States	**25.88**
South Korea	24.59

Country	Overall tax burden
Chile	19.75
Mexico	15.15

Source: Revenue statistics: Comparative tables,
OECD Tax Statistics

This comparison raises an intriguing question about the impact of high taxes on the overall economy. In America, it is often said that high taxes stifle economic growth. But Denmark and Sweden have a much higher tax burden than the United States, and yet both countries have had higher rates of growth than the United States for most of the last five decades. In those nations, clearly, high taxes did not stifle growth.

Another international institution, the World Bank, makes its own comparison of the tax burden in different countries. The World Bank uses a different formula from the OECD's, but it comes to the same conclusion: the United States is a low-tax nation. To determine this, the bank's economists use three basic measurements:

- **"tax capacity,"** which describes how much revenue a government would take in if it taxed all the income and all the wealth at the average tax rate of all countries;

- **"tax effort,"** which measures how much of that potential revenue the country actually tries to take in through taxes;

- **"tax collection,"** which measures how much of the tax that should be paid under the nation's law is actually collected.

The United States, as the world's richest nation, naturally leads all others in tax capacity. But when it comes to tax effort and tax collection, we rate near the bottom of all the advanced countries. Most of the rich democracies in the world—Australia, Austria, Belgium, Britain, France, Italy, the Netherlands, Norway, and so on—are classified as "high effort" and "high collection" countries. In contrast, the United States (along with Canada, Japan, and South Korea) is rated as both "low effort" and "low collection."[2]

Because Americans pay less than their counterparts in other rich countries in overall taxes, it's not terribly surprising that we pay less, for the most part, for specific types of taxes, such as the income tax, Social Security tax, sales tax, gas tax, tobacco tax, capital gains tax, and taxes on wealth and inheritance.

Taxes on Labor: This means the taxes that are imposed on wages and salaries—essentially, the income tax on earnings plus the taxes that pay for health care, pensions, and so on (in the United States, that would mean the total of a worker's personal income tax, Social Security tax, and the Medicare tax). The average tax on labor in all OECD countries in 2013 was 36%; for Americans, it was 31.3%. Of the thirty-four member countries, the United States ranked twenty-fifth in taxing wages and salaries.

The Top Rate: It's not easy to compare income tax collection from country to country, because each country has its own definition of "income" and its own schedule of exemptions, deductions, and so on. But you can match up the top marginal rate of tax in various countries—that is, the maximum tax rate imposed on the highest level of income. France is the world champion at soaking the rich, although it finally had to cut the 75% top rate it imposed on the biggest earners. In 2013, Denmark taxed top earnings at 60.4%, and several advanced countries (for example, Belgium, Germany, Sweden, and Portugal) had a top rate higher than 50%.

In the United States, the highest rate at the start of 2017 was 39.6%. If you add in the average top rate in state taxes, high-income Americans on average pay 46.3% in tax on their highest earnings. On this score, the United States rates a little below the average; seventeen of the OECD countries have a higher top rate, and sixteen are lower. The lowest rate on the rich is in the flat-tax nation of Hungary, where everybody, rich or not, pays income tax at 15%. But Hungary has to impose the world's highest sales tax to make up the revenues lost due to its minimal income tax rate.

In the United States, however, hardly anybody pays tax at that top rate because you have to be pretty rich before the highest rate kicks in. Americans pay 39.6% only on income higher than $418,400; that rate hits less than 1% of U.S. taxpayers. Other countries start applying the top rate at much lower income levels. In Belgium, the top rate is 53%, and it applies to any income above $56,171; half of all taxpayers are subject to the highest rate. In Sweden, the top rate (56.7%) kicks in at $81,698; that hits about 45% of all taxpayers. In Norway, the top rate is 40%, which is just about equal to America's. But Norwegians have to start paying at that rate at an income of $95,270.[3]

Capital Gains Tax: A capital gain is the profit you make by trading stocks and bonds, or real estate, or commodities like gold. If you sell some shares of stock for $50,000 more than you paid for them, the $50,000 you gained is considered income. But in many countries, this kind of income is taxed differently (and often at a lower rate) than "ordinary income" from wages and salaries. Some countries—for example, New Zealand, the Czech Republic, and South Korea—have zero tax on profits from capital trading. In the United States, the federal tax on capital gains for most people is 15%; for those making more than a quarter of a million dollars per year, it goes up to 23.8%.

Because many states also tax capital gains, the average capital gains tax in the United States is about 19.1%—lower than in most of the other rich democracies (although it's obviously higher than in the countries with no tax on capital gains). Here's a comparison of some nations' tax rates on capital gains in 2012:[4]

Australia: 22.5%

Austria: 25%

Britain: 28%

Czech Republic: 0%

Denmark: 42%

Finland: 32%

Ireland: 30%

Mexico: 0%

South Korea: 0%

Spain: 27%

United States: 19.1%

Sales Tax: Americans usually have to pay a retail sales tax on most things they buy at a store. Generally, there's a state sales tax and often a city or county sales tax on top of that (although four states, Delaware, Montana, New Hampshire, and Oregon, have no sales tax). On average, the sales tax adds about 8% to the price of the item.[5] But the United States, as we've seen, has no national sales tax, or value-added tax. In most other rich countries, in contrast, the sales tax—whether it's called a VAT or a New Zealand–style GST—is about three times as high, in the range of 20% to 25%. The highest VAT in the world is found in Hungary; it was 27% in 2016.[6]

The result is a serious tax break for Americans. A Swede who buys, say, a $2,000 computer will pay an additional $500 in sales tax. A Texan buying the same computer would pay just $160 in tax. And an Oregonian would pay no sales tax.

Gas Tax: Because gasoline is a standard commodity sold around the world, market forces make the price of a gallon roughly the same everywhere—until you figure in the gas tax. Americans pay far less to fill the tank than drivers in any other rich country, because gas taxes here are far below the levels elsewhere. Of the richest thirty-five advanced democracies, the United States has the second-lowest level of fuel taxes; Mexico is lowest, with a gas tax of zero.

In the United States, the federal tax on a gallon of gas—18.4 cents—hasn't changed for two decades. Every state imposes a gas tax on top of the federal levy. In 2014, California's was the highest, at $0.71 per gallon; in most states, it's closer to $0.40 per gallon. On average, Americans pay total taxes of $0.53 per gallon; Californians have to pay $0.89 per gallon.

Overseas, the gas tax is six to eight times higher. Turkey has the stiffest tax on gasoline, at $4.32 per gallon. In western Europe, the tax generally runs over $3.00 per gallon.[7] Here's a breakdown of gasoline taxes—federal, local, and sales tax all included—in some of the rich countries:

Country	Tax per gallon
Turkey	$4.32
Israel	$4.20
Netherlands	$3.79
Norway	$3.67
U.K.	$3.44
Germany	$3.29
OECD average	$2.62
Austria	$2.46
Japan	$2.16
United States	$0.53

Source: OECD

Of course, those taxes come on top of the basic price of the gasoline itself. In the fall of 2016, when Americans were groaning about gasoline that cost about $2.10 per gallon, Europeans were paying $6.00; they considered that normal.

That explains why the rich countries of Europe and East Asia have such well-developed mass transit systems; even the most luxurious bullet train is generally cheaper than driving any significant distance. And why German, Japanese, and South Korean carmakers were so far ahead of Detroit in producing fuel-efficient cars.

Tobacco Tax: Taxing cigarettes is a twofer; it brings in steady revenue, and at the same time it discourages people from taking up an unhealthy habit. Consequently, the tax tends to be steep almost everywhere; in many countries, more than half of the price per pack is tax.

But American smokers get off easier. The U.S. federal tax on cigarettes is $1.01 per pack. States and cities then load on additional levies. Americans, on average, pay about $6.00 for a pack of cigarettes, of which roughly half is tax. The U.S. price is a bargain by European standards, where the same pack of cigarettes would cost about $9.00. In Canada, the same pack would cost about $10.00. The world's highest price for cigarettes is in Australia, where a single pack costs about $16.00—two-thirds of it being tax.[8]

THE ONE AREA WHERE we (almost) lead the pack in tax rates is in the income tax on corporations. At the start of 2017, the U.S. corporate tax, at 35%, was the second highest in the world. Although France's basic tax rate was a tad lower (33.3%), the French added special surtaxes for big corporations that brings the total rate to 38% for major French companies. Since the beginning of this century, almost all the other industrialized nations have cut their corporate tax rates, partly to give their domestic businesses a competitive advantage and partly to lure corporations away from the United States and other high-tax nations. The United States and France have been the only holdouts.

Here's a sampling of federal corporate income tax rates, as of 2016 (note that some countries have a basic corporate rate and then a higher rate for oil companies):

Country	Corporate tax rate
Ireland	12.5%
Ireland (oil companies)	25%
Germany	15.85%
China	25%
Japan	23.9%
Sweden	22%
U.K.	20%
U.K. (oil companies)	30%
Mexico	30%
United States	35%
France	38%

Source: ey.com, *2016 Worldwide Corporate Tax Guide*

Our corporate tax code, of course, is riddled with exemptions and deductions and credits that sharply reduce the amount of tax corporations actually pay. Still, the amount that American corporations actually pay—this is known as the "effective rate"—is generally higher than corporations pay in other countries. Some giant companies have managed to manipulate these tax breaks so skillfully that they pay little or no U.S. income tax. U.S. companies have also devised intricate and ingenious runarounds so that their profits are taxed overseas, at the lower corporate rates due in foreign countries.

Beyond that, the United States is one of a handful of countries that impose corporate tax on income earned anywhere in the world, not just in the home country. In most industrialized countries, a company pays tax to its home country only on profits it has earned at home. The United States, though, imposes tax on an American company's earnings no matter where the income was earned. However—and this is a multitrillion-dollar "however"—the foreign earnings are not taxed until the corporation brings them home to the United States. That is, a company can avoid the tax on its foreign earnings by keeping the profits overseas. And that's precisely what they do. U.S. corporations have a vast accumulation of foreign earnings stashed in banks and securities around the world. Because that money has never been brought home, the companies don't have to pay tax on it.

Yet this is a costly form of tax avoidance. If you can't bring the money to the United States, you can't use it here for salaries or capital investment or for paying dividends to stockholders. It seems possible that American companies have been way too clever about stashing their earnings overseas. There is so much corporate money out there—more than $2 trillion, by many estimates—that stockholders and employees of the companies are demanding that the funds be "repatriated" and distributed at home as salaries or dividends. The companies don't want to pay the U.S. tax on that money, but at the same time they don't particularly want to keep their profits stuck forever in a bank in Bratislava.

The extravagant tax on corporate income, though, doesn't change the basic pattern we saw a few pages back. Overall, the United States is a low-tax country, compared with other rich democracies.

It shouldn't come as a surprise, then, that the United States also rates low, comparatively, when it comes to government spending. You'd never know it from listening to our political debates, but the international organizations that study such things all agree that the U.S. government is a frugal penny-pincher—compared with the other rich countries, at least.

The World Bank each year computes government spending as a percentage of overall wealth (GDP) for all the world's countries. In the poorest countries, where almost nobody has any money, government spending amounts to about 10% of GDP. In the rich countries of western Europe and East Asia, government spends roughly 20% to 26% of GDP (once again, Sweden and Denmark usually have the highest rate of government spending). In the United States, in 2015, governments at all levels spent a total of 15.5% of our GDP, which puts us near the bottom of the list. Among the world's richest countries, only South Korea and Mexico had a lower rate of government spending.

The U.S. government is a huge spender, of course, on some things. We pour more money into national defense than anybody else; our defense budgets, in fact, are bigger than those in the next eleven countries *combined*. But American governments spend much less than other advanced democracies on social support for low-income and retired people.

Americans—individual citizens, that is, not the government—make up for that diminished public spending on social programs by generous private giving to charities, churches, schools, and hospitals. In 2013, American citizens and foundations gave some $335 billion to charity—about 2% of our GDP. Most other rich countries lag far behind us on this score. The French give 0.02% of GDP to charity—that is, one-hundredth of Americans' giving. The British contribute 0.07% of GDP to charity; Canadians, 0.05%.[9] As this pattern shows, the French, Brits, Canadians, and others expect government to bear the burden of social support for the needy; that's why they willingly pay high taxes. Americans choose to make private donations a much bigger share of social spending.

While Americans pay much less in tax than our counterparts overseas, we complain about it much more.

There's no country where people gripe as much as Americans do about taxes in general and the Internal Revenue Service in particular. Hardly anybody in any nation enjoys paying taxes. But in most developed countries, the national tax agency is a respected and admired branch of government. Swedes rate their national tax bureau as the most respected of all government agencies. All over the world, tax bureaucrats proudly wear neckties, jackets, and baseball caps bearing the agency logo. Tax bureaus like Her Majesty's Revenue and Customs in the U.K., the Agenzia delle Entrate in Italy, Spain's Agencia Tributaria, and Nigeria's Federal Inland Revenue Service have their own banners, mascots, songs, and slogans. ("We can't make paying taxes pleasant, but at least we can make it simple.")

Chile's Servicio de Impuestos Internos has adopted a mascot—a furry little chinchilla that serves as the tax bureau's friendly face to the public. Ivo the Chinchilla (his name is a play on IVA, the Spanish equivalent of a VAT) stars in stage plays and movies, telling adults and schoolchildren how important it is that people pay all the tax they owe. "¡Son bacanes, los impuestos!" Ivo says in one film: "They're awesome, those taxes!" Then he gets downright rhapsodic about the blessings of taxation. "When the government builds schools and bridges and hospitals and playgrounds," Ivo says, "it's all thanks to people paying their taxes on time."[10]

One of the most beloved movies in Japan—a runaway winner of the Best Actress, Best Actor, Best Director, and Best Picture Oscars there—was *Marusa no onna,* or "Audit Bureau Woman." (In the English-dubbed version of the movie, the title is *A Taxing Woman.*) It tells the tale of a charming but tenacious tax auditor in the Tokyo Audit Bureau of the National Tax Agency.

Our plucky heroine, played by Miyamoto Nobuko—Japan's Meg Ryan—starts out investigating small local businesses. When she assesses a $2,000 penalty against a mom-and-pop grocery store, the owner responds in a rage: "Why do you go after small fry like us? Why don't you aim at the really big tax cheats?" Chastised, Nobuko asks to be assigned to the account of a wealthy, well-connected gangland kingpin, a man who rides around Tokyo in a chauffeur-driven white Rolls-Royce—but never pays much tax. She spends the rest of the film following the big white Rolls on her little red motor scooter, uncovering a long trail of forged receipts, hidden cash, and fake bank accounts. In the climactic scene, when Nobuko digs through a mountain of paper and finds the telltale document that will send the tax evader to jail, the whole theater bursts into delighted applause. The credits tell us that the film is dedicated to "the steadfast resolve of the incorruptible Japanese Revenue Service."

It's hard to imagine Hollywood casting Meg Ryan, say, or Amy Schumer as a peppy, pretty tax collector in a sympathetic film about the "steadfast resolve" of the Internal Revenue Service. In America, rather, employees of the IRS say they routinely face anger and hostility when they tell people where they work. In 2010, an antigovernment fanatic flew a small plane into the IRS building in Austin, Texas, leaving one employee dead and a dozen injured; the pilot left a suicide note boasting of his attack on "Big Brother IRS man." The agency is a common target of columnists, cartoonists, comedians, and congressmen. Politicians and pundits routinely compare IRS agents to terrorists. One of the regular events on the congressional calendar each year is a hearing where angry senators or representatives line up a group of hapless IRS bureaucrats at the witness table and berate them for a couple of hours because the tax system is so complicated and difficult.

Many members of Congress, of course, are serious, fair-minded public servants, but the institution has always had its share of grandstanders and hypocrites. When I was a congressional correspondent, I always thought the acme of arrogance and phoniness came in those IRS-bashing sessions before one committee or another. This is, after all, a classic case of blaming the messenger. It's Congress that makes our tax code so complicated and difficult. It was Congress, not anybody in the IRS, who wrote Section 7803(c)(2)(B)(ii)(IX) and all the other impenetrable sections of the code. For the members who created this unruly mess to criticize the bureaucrats who have to administer it is like a chef who spills a vat of tomato soup and then complains to the janitor because the floor is dirty. And yet these hearings continue, Congress after Congress, because Americans love complaining about taxes and the agency that collects them.

Nobody likes paying taxes. But we pay them, because taxes are inescapable—nothing is certain, of course, except death and taxes—and because we're convinced that taxes are necessary. But why are taxes necessary? What are they good for, anyway?

TAXES: WHAT ARE THEY
GOOD FOR?

One Saturday afternoon, a great teacher of ethics told his students that their class session would take place at a local temple. The teacher had an important lesson about paying for public programs—in essence, about tax policy.

The teacher and his followers arrived at the synagogue just before the service started and stood in the rear, watching as the worshippers filed in. It was the custom then that the front rows were reserved, for a fee, by wealthy families. The benches at the back were left for the poorest members of the community, those who couldn't pay for a better row. Shortly after the service began, the rabbi called for a collection, to pay for the maintenance of the temple and for its social programs in the neighborhood. When the plate was passed, an imposing man in the first row, beautifully dressed and flanked by a retinue of family and servants, ostentatiously donated 1,000 ducats. A couple rows back, a man with even fancier clothing and even more servants made a great show as he gave 2,000 ducats. Eventually, the plate made its way to the back row, to a poor widow, dressed in rags and carrying a moth-eaten cloth handbag. She dug around in the bag for a while and eventually extracted two coins—two "mites," worth about a penny each—and placed them in the collection plate.

At which point, Jesus Christ told his disciples, "Verily I say unto you, that poor widow gave more than anyone else."

This story is known as "the widow's mite"; it's told in two of the New Testament Gospels.[1] Christ's statement can today be recognized as a central principle of tax policy around the world: The funding of community programs, whether through donations to the synagogue or taxes paid to the government, should be carried out in a way that is proportionate to wealth. If the rich man pays $10,000, but still has a million left in the bank, his tax burden is actually lighter than that of a widow who pays $10 but has no savings to back it up. The crucial point is not how much somebody pays in taxes but rather how much she has left after paying. This biblical lesson has been invoked time and again to justify a tax code that calls on the rich to pay higher rates than the poor.

When taxes work that way, people tend to perceive them as "fair." And that perception is crucial to a successful tax regime: no system of taxes can be successful unless the taxpayers believe that the system is essentially fair. Nobody likes to pay tax, but people will pay if they sense that the regime is treating everyone justly. Opinion polls in every country show that people think the rich are undertaxed and should pay more. You might say that this is evidence of envy or resentment. Or you might conclude that these surveys reflect a basic human sense of fairness, an innate appreciation for the proportionate system of payment that Christ demonstrated so vividly in the temple. The American sage Will Rogers captured this concept precisely. Of course people like low taxes, Rogers said, but there's something even more important: "People want JUST taxes, more than they want lower taxes. They want to know that every man is paying his proportionate share according to his wealth."

This, then, is one of the basic reasons for taxes; they can make a population feel that its government is treating everybody fairly. That, in turn, enhances the political legitimacy of the state; it gives people a stake in good government and makes them better citizens. Some economists have argued, in fact, that this is the main reason to have a proportionate tax system in the first place.[2]

Which is something of a stretch. The main reason for taxes is to pay for the activities of government, for the goods and services we have decided to provide collectively rather than leave every man for himself. Highways, parks, playgrounds, schools, courts, Coast Guard cutters, air traffic control, auto safety, the patent office, the Food and Drug Administration, old-age pensions, seniors' health insurance, student loans, spies, libraries, collecting the trash, clearing the snow, putting out forest fires, printing money, issuing passports, battling ISIS, catching crooks—the list of public functions, even in a nation like the United States that is relatively hostile toward government, could easily fill this whole page. We do these things through government— although the choice is often controversial—after concluding that there are certain areas where a public endeavor is preferable to the private sector.

The fire department, for example, was not always a government function. In the first century B.C., the richest man in Rome was an entrepreneur named Marcus Licinius Crassus, a figure so grandiose and so enamored of ostentatious display that his name became an English adjective. The crass Mr. Crassus had business interests ranging from silver mines to the slave trade, but perhaps his most lucrative operation was his private fire department, the biggest of several commercial firefighting firms in Rome. When a house caught fire, his chariot carrying a big water tank would clatter through the stone streets. At the site, Crassus would start negotiating with the frantic homeowner to set a price for his services, while the hapless customer watched the flames spread. A common result was that Crassus acquired the property, with the former owner obliged to pay him rent for life. The homeowners of Rome began clamoring for a public fire department, to free themselves from capitalists like Crassus.

Crassus, who became the biggest real estate magnate in Rome, began investing his money in carefully selected politicians, lobbying against any Roman senator who proposed to make firefighting a government function. One of his fiscal beneficiaries was a popular general named Julius Caesar. In return, Caesar stood up for Crassus's business interests and gave him various prestigious positions, including the command of an army fighting the treacherous Parthians in what is now Syria. This did not end well for poor Crassus, however. He was defeated at the Battle of Carrhae in 53 B.C. When the Parthians realized they had captured the richest man in Rome, the ancient histories say, they poured molten gold down Crassus's throat, on the theory that his lifelong thirst for gold should be quenched in death.

With Crassus out of the picture, the Romans fairly soon decided that the fire department was a function not well suited to the private sector. Almost all governments everywhere have reached the same conclusion. Around the world, firefighters proudly ride their long red trucks down the street during each city's annual municipal parade. In Japan, city fire departments hold exhibitions on January 6 every year, the national Firefighters' Day, where kids get to try on fireproof suits and sit at the wheel of a huge hook and ladder. When I went to the Tokyo event one chilly January, there was a sign at the entrance: **"Honorable Tokyoites, we respectfully thank you! Your tax payments supplied our equipment."** After all, fire departments aren't free; like the other activities of government, they must be paid for. And that's why the only things certain, as Benjamin Franklin famously observed, are death and taxes. (And some people get hit with both at once, as we'll see when we discuss the inheritance tax.)

This aspect of taxation was crystallized in the famous dictum of the Supreme Court justice Oliver Wendell Holmes Jr.: "Taxes are what we pay for civilized society." That slogan today is engraved over the main door of the Internal Revenue Service on Constitution Avenue in Washington, D.C. Of course, the IRS doesn't choose to remind us that Justice Holmes made that comment in a dissent against a decision of the court majority; it came in an otherwise forgotten legal dispute known as the Philippine Cigar Case.

The case of *Compañía General de Tabacos de Filipinas v. Collector of Internal Revenue*[3] was decided in 1927, but the international maneuvers the tobacco company employed would be familiar today to the corporate finance executives who dream up complex cross-border deals to avoid paying taxes. The Compañía General de Tabacos owned a warehouse in Manila; it needed fire insurance on the building and the cigars stored inside. The Philippine government imposed a tax of 1% on insurance premiums. The company did not want to pay. So the tobacco company in the Philippines arranged for its sister company in Barcelona to buy the insurance policy; the Barcelona office hired a broker in Paris, who bought insurance from one company in France and another in Britain. The Compañía General then argued it didn't have to pay the tax, because the policy wasn't purchased in the Philippines. This dispute wound its way up to the Philippine Supreme Court, which ruled unanimously that the tax had to be paid.

Because it lost its lawsuit in the nation's highest court, you might think the cigar company would just shell out the 1% tax. But in those days, the losing party in a case before the Supreme Court of the Philippines had one more avenue of appeal.

In 1927, the United States was a colonial power; its scattered empire included the Philippine Islands. A legal case decided in the colonies could be appealed to the U.S. Supreme Court. The U.S. chief justice then was William Howard Taft, a former president and a man who never met a tax he didn't hate. So Compañía General de Tabacos took its case to Washington—and won.

Chief Justice Taft's opinion for the court majority is about as convoluted as the mechanism the tobacco company used to buy insurance. After several pages of impenetrable prose—"The collection of this tax involves an exaction upon a company of Spain lawfully doing business in the Philippine Islands effected by reason of a contract made by that company with a company in Paris on merchandise shipped from the Philippine Islands for delivery"—Taft concluded that the

company didn't have to pay the 1% tax. Six other justices concurred,
so the Compañía won by a vote of 7–2.

The two who sided with the Philippine tax authority were Oliver
Wendell Holmes Jr. and Louis Brandeis, a pair of justices who became
known as the Great Dissenters because so many of their dissenting
opinions turned into majority holdings in succeeding decades. In the
Philippine Cigar Case, Holmes quickly brushes aside the tax-avoidance
scheme, concluding that an insurance policy on a warehouse in the
Philippines should be liable for the Philippine insurance tax. He goes
on to explain that nobody likes paying taxes but it's important to look
beyond one company's tax bill and see "its organic connection with
the whole." Seeing the whole picture, according to Holmes, reminds
us that individuals and corporations get a lot of benefit out of the
taxes they pay. "Taxes are what we pay for civilized society," he explains, "including the chance to insure."

Taxes, though, are not the only way to pay for civilized society.
Governments have other ways to get by. At the simplest, most brutal
level, a government that has a police force and an army can simply
commandeer goods and services; countries like China, Venezuela, and
Russia have occasionally decided to "nationalize" oil wells or gold
mines or factories and then sell the output to earn government revenues. The previous owner of the well or factory might bring a lawsuit,
but these actions tend to get snarled in the courts for years or decades.
Even modern democracies like the United States sometimes use this
approach; our government commandeered services from me and millions of others through the military draft during the Vietnam War.
The problem with just seizing stuff, though, is that the citizenry hates
it, so the commandeer approach tends to produce revolutions.

Governments have a convenient monopoly on the printing of currency (or legal currency, at least). In theory, a government that didn't
want to tax its citizens could just print the money it needs to provide
common services. The problem here is inflation, which increases
sharply as more and more money floods into the marketplace, with

severe repercussions. A less damaging way to make money from printing money is the concept of "seigniorage," which is the difference between the face value of a bill and the cost of printing it. The U.S. government spends about six cents for the paper and ink used to make a $10 bill, which means a seigniorage gain of $9.94 when a new $10 bill is put into circulation. The Treasury says it earns something over $100 million each year this way. As long as a government doesn't print so much money that it triggers inflation, seigniorage can be a small but steady contributor to revenues.

Governments can also bring in money by borrowing. When the U.S. government spends more than it takes in—in fiscal 2016, we ran a deficit of $590 billion—it borrows money from banks, investors, and foreign governments to make up the difference. For all the breast-beating in our political debates about "unsustainable deficits," the U.S. government is a relatively conservative borrower compared with other rich countries. Among the thirty-four richest countries, total government debt averaged 111% of GDP in fiscal year 2014; the U.S. debt was actually below average, at 106% of GDP.[4] Countries like Italy (147%), Portugal (141%), and Ireland (133%) had significantly bigger debts, as a share of their total wealth, than the United States. Not surprisingly, Greece ranks near the top of debtor nations, with outstanding loans that total 188% of its GDP. The world champion at borrowing money, though, is the government of Japan, which has been running annual deficits for years greater than 225% of its GDP. This is less of a burden for Japan than it would be for most other countries because Japanese people have traditionally been prodigious savers, and their bank deposits provide most of the money the government needs to borrow. So Japan has huge debts, but it is indebted mainly to itself.

Borrowing money can be less painful than taxes, but here, too, there's a limit. At some point, the interest charges become a significant part of the national budget, which means either reduced government services or higher taxes just to pay the interest. And if a government gets so deep in debt it can't borrow any more—as happened to Greece after the Great Recession of 2008–9—the result can be severe austerity. Dozens of the planet's two hundred or so countries are too poor to get a loan; for many of them, foreign aid from the United States, other rich nations, and UN agencies is an important source of revenue.

Finally, governments can sell goods and services to bring in cash. The U.S. government charges entry fees at national parks and sells timber from the national forests. It collects royalty payments when somebody mines coal or drills for oil on public land. It collects fees from banks to finance the Federal Deposit Insurance Corporation (FDIC) and from pharmaceutical companies to pay for testing new drugs. For a few lucky countries, government sales bring in all the revenue needed; some of the oil kingdoms in the Middle East collect no taxes from their citizens.

In ancient times, the king taxed what he could see. The Romans would measure the crop from a farmer's field, or count the number of cows in the stable, and take 10% in tax; thus the tax collectors, or "publicans," were derisively called tax farmers. In the 1790s, France imposed the "contribution des portes et fenêtres," a tax on doors and windows, on the theory that only well-off people could afford such luxury; naturally, some homeowners bricked in their windows when they suspected the tax collector was coming around. Using the same tax-the-rich logic, European governments in the eighteenth century collected a duty on the elaborate wigs that the gentry wore and the powder they used to keep their wigs white.

As the nation-state concept developed and countries began to have discernible borders, the easiest way to collect taxes was export and import duties. There were only so many ports of entry, so this didn't require a large number of tax offices. And this tax was not easy to evade; after all, it's hard to conceal a clipper ship sailing into harbor with a cargo of tea from India. Custom duties brought in 90% of federal revenues for the newborn United States in its first decades; our government nearly went broke during the War of 1812, when the

British navy blockaded all American ports.[5] In the young United States, the U.S. Customs House was the most imposing building in all port towns; these old structures can be seen today at the edge of Boston and Baltimore harbors. The handsome redbrick Customs House in Salem, Massachusetts, where Nathaniel Hawthorne worked while writing *The Scarlet Letter,* still stands as a reminder of the nation's first revenue service.

Over time, though, as a nation's domestic economy builds up, "internal revenue" becomes more important than taxes at the ports. State and local governments create their own tax systems; the property tax has always been an important source of revenue for local government, because you can't pick up your house or farm and move it to the next state.

In the twenty-first century, the United States and other established countries have come to rely on income and consumption taxes as their main sources of revenue. But newer nations are replicating the history of taxation we saw in the United States. Achilles Amawhe, a senior director in Nigeria's Federal Inland Revenue Service, told me that he has watched his country's tax bureau grow throughout his career. "I was just a boy when Nigeria won her independence," he said. "And as soon as I got out of school, I went to work for the nation, in the tax bureau. I have devoted my life to giving my country an honest, efficient, and respected tax service." Achilles gave me a baseball cap bearing his agency's logo, FIRS, and told me that the whole history of Nigerian tax was in that hat. "We started with custom duties; then we began taxing inland enterprises; then the provinces opened their own tax offices, and we became the 'federal' service. So FIRS—the Federal Inland Revenue Service—captures the development of taxes in our new nation."

But maintaining a civilized society is not the only reason for taxation. Governments use taxes for numerous other purposes beyond the basic task of raising revenue to pay for public programs. "Virtually everything governments attempt to do with direct expenditure programs they also attempt (for better or worse) to do with taxation policy," notes the economist Sven Steinmo. "Indeed, no other public policy issue has been used so widely for so many purposes. . . . Raising revenue, redistributing income, encouraging savings, stimulating growth, penalizing consumption, directing investment, and rewarding certain values while penalizing others are just some of the hundreds of goals that any modern government tries to promote with its tax system."[6] Tax has become a multipurpose government tool that performs many missions.

Encourage Good Behavior

For example, taxes turn out to be a powerful instrument for getting people to do what government would like them to do. The U.S. government wants to encourage you to contribute to charity, to buy an electric car, to get a college degree, to support your dependent children, to buy health insurance, to insulate your attic, to invest in oil wells, to fund a retirement account, and to take out a mortgage to purchase a home; accordingly, all those desirable practices provide a deduction, an exemption, or a credit that will lower your federal income tax bill. Inducing desirable behavior can also help to build "civilized society," although that aspect of taxation does not appear to be what Justice Holmes had in mind. But governments everywhere use the tax code to promote good citizenship.

When the government of South Korea wanted corporations to use more of their profit for wage increases and less of it for dividends, the corporate tax code was amended to reward companies that raised their workers' pay. To encourage people to leave their cars at home, Germany gives a tax break for commuting expenses, but only for those who commute by bus or train. Canada and Australia think it's beneficial for individuals to support political parties and candidates, so they offer a tax credit for political contributions. Unlike the United

States, though, Canada has a strict limit on contributions—nobody can give more than $4,800, total, in one year—so the maximum tax credit is $650.

Discourage Bad Behavior

In the same way, taxes are often an effective tool to discourage people from doing things perceived to undermine the common good. This kind of levy is sometimes called a "sin tax." A sin tax is the exception to the consensus view among economists that taxes should be "neutral"—that is, designed so that people base their decisions on business or personal grounds, not on tax considerations. But taxes imposed on what we don't want people to do are specifically designed to influence our decisions and conduct. The father of modern economics, Adam Smith, strongly endorsed this kind of tax in his famous study *The Wealth of Nations:* "Sugar, rum, and tobacco, are commodities which are nowhere necessaries of life, which are become objects of almost universal consumption, and which are therefore extremely proper subjects of taxation." For Smith, taxes on sugar, rum, and tobacco had a double benefit: they discourage consumption of unhealthy products, thus reducing the cost of health care over time; they also bring in a steady flow of revenues, because those who smoke, drink, and eat candy generally do so even when the national economy is in a slump.

The great success story in the realm of taxing bad behavior is the cigarette tax. In the mid-1960s—the period depicted in the smoke-filled TV serial *Mad Men*—more than 40% of Americans smoked daily; they paid less than thirty cents per pack, including sales tax. After the surgeon general first warned, in 1966, that "smoking may be hazardous to your health," the federal and state governments started taxing tobacco products heavily, to discourage the habit and to help offset the health-care cost governments were facing because of illness due to smoking. The taxes have consistently gone up since then—Americans today pay twenty times the 1965 price for a pack of cigarettes—and the number of smokers has consistently gone down. Today less than 16% of Americans smoke regularly. The experts attribute this partly to improved education efforts but largely to that huge increase in the sin tax on smokers. When cigarette taxes go up, smoking goes down.

Governments also try to prevent the excessive use of beer, wine, and liquor. As the United States proved between 1920 and 1933, outright prohibition doesn't work in a free society. So different countries have tried different approaches; Germany, for example, has an "apple-juice law," requiring that bars and restaurants include nonalcoholic drinks on the menu at a price lower than the cheapest beer or whiskey. Several provinces in Canada set a minimum price for alcoholic beverages so the bartender can't lure people in with free or cheap drinks. But here, too, taxation has proven most effective. When the journal *Addiction* studied changes in alcohol taxes around the world, it concluded that a 10% increase in the tax on a drink reduces alcohol consumption by about 5%, which is enough to avoid tens of thousands of deaths and accidents each year.[7] After British Columbia raised liquor taxes in 2002, deaths attributed to alcohol dropped by 32% over the next six years; the Canadian government attributes this to the higher price of booze.

As obesity has become a bulging health problem in many wealthy countries, the so-called sugar tax has begun to spread as a way to cut the consumption of high-calorie cola, candy, and junk food. Adam Smith would presumably approve. France, Denmark, and Belgium have all imposed various versions of the "fat tax." Mexico, where the problem of obesity is even greater than in the United States, imposed new taxes in 2014 on sugared soda pop and junk foods like potato chips, cookies, and cheese curls. The sugar tax makes a regular Coke cost about 25% more than a Diet Coke; it makes a candy bar significantly more expensive than an apple. To complete the symmetry, the government promised to use some of the money from the sugar tax—initial revenue estimates were $1 billion annually—to improve the purity of the country's water supply, because a lack of clean water is one of the reasons Mexicans consume so much soda pop in the first place.

Some countries, eager to enhance civic participation, charge a tax penalty for people who fail to vote. Mandatory voting is particularly popular in Latin America; among the nations that penalize nonvoters are Argentina, Brazil, Costa Rica, Ecuador, Peru, and Uruguay. The mechanism is pretty simple. You get a certificate at the polling place that says you voted; you attach that to the tax return. If the tax agency doesn't receive proof that you voted, you pay more tax. President Barack Obama proposed a similar penalty for American nonvoters; so far, this idea has gone nowhere.

Taxes designed to curtail certain actions or purchases don't always work. Following the oil shocks of the early 1970s, the U.S. Congress was eager to reduce Americans' consumption of petroleum and thus reduce the nation's dependence on foreign oil. One proposal called for a minimum level of fuel efficiency in all cars, so that it would be illegal to sell or buy a car that used too much gasoline per mile. But that was considered too draconian for the automobile-dependent United States, where the chance to buy a muscle car is considered a basic American birthright. So Congress instead passed the "gas-guzzler" tax in 1978, imposing a hefty tax on any car that gets less than 22.5 miles per gallon. The point was to discourage the purchase of these profligate vehicles. You can still exercise your God-given right to buy a gas-guzzler, but you have to pay extra for the privilege. (Nobody thought of minivans or SUVs back then as family cars, so they weren't included on the taxable roster in 1978.)

There's a two-page addendum to IRS Form 1040—it's Form 6197—that collects the tax for wasteful autos; the top rate is $7,700 for a car that gets less than 12.5 miles per gallon. In 2014, according to the Environmental Protection Agency, no car sold in the United States was that extravagant, but seventy-eight different models from twelve different makers were officially labeled "gas-guzzlers." The thirstiest passenger car sold in the United States was the Bentley Mulsanne, rated at 15.9 miles per gallon; the ten-cylinder Lamborghini Gallardo Spyder was second worst (16.2 miles per gallon), followed closely by the twelve-cylinder Ferrari FF (16.4 miles per gallon). Did the tax discourage anybody from buying one of these notorious fuel gulpers? Sales figures don't show it, which is not surprising. The gas-guzzler tax on that inefficient Bentley Mulsanne is $3,700 (in addition to the normal sales and registration taxes); it doesn't seem likely that somebody who wants to ride around town in a $279,000 Bentley would choose a Ford hybrid instead just to save $3,700 of tax.

There's a libertarian appeal to tax provisions that aim to nudge people to do the right thing. The taxpayer retains the liberty to make personal choices—to smoke cigarettes, to commute by car, to wash down a bag of Chili Cheese Fritos with a pitcher of beer. To pass a law prohibiting such behaviors smacks of the nanny state. It's less intrusive to let people decide for themselves whether to engage in these behaviors. But government imposes a tax penalty to offset the social cost of those personal choices, and that penalty may have the added benefit of steering people away from undesirable choices. Similarly, offering a tax break for insulating a house is less invasive than passing a law requiring that every homeowner install insulation.

Even when they're effective, though, there's a clear downside to all these tax preferences and penalties: they increase the complexity of any country's tax code. Each new tax break or surcharge requires adding one more line to the tax return—or maybe twenty more lines, or maybe a whole new schedule, like Form 6197 for the gas-guzzler tax. Each tax deduction forces taxpayers to gather and keep track of the necessary documentation. Each one forces the taxing agency to perform audits to make sure the taxpayer is really entitled to the deduction she's claiming. In Britain, for example, anytime a taxpayer takes the deduction for a charitable contribution, both the donor and the charity have to provide a notarized piece of paper to substantiate it. An Australian can deduct the cost of uniforms for her job, but first she has to obtain a certificate from the Register of Approved Occupational Clothing.

Beyond that, tax breaks tend to last forever. Every new preference spurs an army of interest groups and lobbyists who will fight to keep it in the code long after the economic rationale for it has expired. And each eternal deduction, exemption, or credit reduces the government's revenue, eternally.

Stimulate Economic Growth

Taxes consume a significant portion of the total national wealth in every wealthy country. So it seems entirely reasonable that a nation's taxes would have a significant effect on the overall economy. Accordingly, politicians constantly try to design tax regimes that promote investment and job creation and thus prompt greater economic growth.

But different politicians have different theories about what kind of tax change will stimulate the economy. These differences were particularly sharp as the developed world responded to the Great Recession that spread around the globe beginning in 2008. In the United States, the initial idea was to cut taxes so that people and companies would have more money to spend; then consumer spending and business investment would haul us out of the economic swamp. The United States issued an income tax rebate and cut the employee's share of Social Security by 2%, providing ready cash and increased take-home pay for all working Americans. Most of Europe went in the other direction, raising the VAT to offset government deficits. Britain, where the tax rate had been 17.5%, cut it for one year and then reversed course, raising it to 20%. Hungary, which already taxed purchases at 25%, raised it to 27%, giving it the distinction of charging the highest sales taxes on the planet; Ireland's VAT went up in stages from 21% to 23%, Spain's from 16% to 21%, Italy's from 20% to

22%. This was a sort of stealth tax hike; most consumers who have to pay the VAT don't realize that it has been increased.

At first glance, it would appear that America's program of stimulus through tax cuts worked better than Europe's austerity through tax hikes. The United States came out of the Great Recession much sooner than Europe, and American growth rates since then have been higher than those in most European countries. But it's not clear that America's economic growth was due to lower taxes. In fact, most of the post-Recession growth in the United States happened after taxes were raised. That 2% cut in the Social Security tax was repealed after two years, lowering every worker's take-home pay. Congress and the president cut a deal to increase taxes on top-bracket earners in 2013. Yet the U.S. economy continued to grow at a moderate pace with the higher taxes; the unemployment rate fell from 8% at the time those tax increases took effect to 5% three years later.

Despite this ambiguity, politicians have no hesitation about claiming that any tax policy they champion will be a major stimulus. They say that when they raise taxes; they say that when they cut taxes. When Britain hiked the VAT rate to 20%, the chancellor of the exchequer explained that this tax increase would let government reduce its borrowing, which would increase private-sector capital and spark a major economic boom. When President George W. Bush proposed across-the-board tax cuts in 2003, the White House predicted that this tax reduction would create 2.1 million new jobs and spark a major economic boom. (In the event, both the British and the American predictions proved wrong.) In the United States, Republicans frequently predict that tax cuts will "pay for themselves," because the resulting economic growth will lead to higher tax revenues. This something-for-nothing theory, first proposed by Arthur Laffer, sounds enticing in a campaign speech. Sadly, it has never worked in practice.

Economists, for the most part, are considerably less confident than politicians about the economic effects of raising or lowering taxes. Two experts at the University of Michigan, Joel Slemrod and Jon Bakija, surveyed the data and the academic literature on this point. "The first thing to note about recessions and recoveries is that they generally occur for reasons that have little or nothing to do with taxes," they report. Does a tax cut increase job creation, as the Bush White House asserted? "In a word (okay, two words), not much. . . . [C]laims about the effects of tax cuts on the number of jobs are suspect," Slemrod and Bakija conclude. Can a tax cut really increase revenues? "A reduction in tax rates does not cause the economy to expand enough to recoup the revenues . . . at least in recent U.S. history," Slemrod and Bakija explain. Do lower taxes stimulate economic growth? The two economists point out that over the last half century several countries with much higher tax burdens than the United States have had better growth rates, and here at home "the strongest growth period was when the top tax rates were highest."[8]

Nonetheless, in all the developed democracies, right-of-center parties (they're called "Conservatives" or "Christian Democrats" or "Republicans") consistently push for tax cuts as a way to improve economic growth. All the Republican candidates in the 2016 U.S. presidential race promoted this idea. "We've got to lower the tax burden," candidate Jeb Bush said on the stump, "to get this economy moving again." Meanwhile, the left-of-center parties ("Social Democrats" or "Labour" or "Liberals" or "Democrats") often take the opposite stance, pushing for tax increases—on the rich, that is. That brings us to the next major mission of the tax code.

Offset Inequality

The president of the United States declared in 2013 that economic inequality has become "the defining challenge of our time," one that poses "a fundamental threat to the American dream, our way of life, and what we stand for." Barack Obama was referring to statistics showing a large and growing gap in wealth and income between the richest Americans—the so-called 1%—and the rest of us. The phenomenon that the president was talking about is not limited to the United States; income inequality has been increasing sharply in almost every industrialized democracy.

"Redistribution of wealth" has become a controversial concept in the United States in recent years. Obama got himself in hot water during his 2008 presidential campaign when he told a voter named Joe Wurzelbacher (aka "Joe the Plumber") that "when you spread the wealth around, it's good for everybody." The political press declared this sound bite a blunder, and Republicans made it a key campaign issue for weeks. "This sounds a lot like European socialism," said the GOP candidate, John McCain. In fact, though, the idea of spreading the wealth around through taxes is hardly limited to Europe. Tax codes almost everywhere have been designed to achieve this goal. "If income redistribution is considered a desirable social goal, then taxation is clearly an important means to this end—and moreover one that every country in fact utilizes," notes the tax economist Richard M. Bird.[9] Even countries experimenting with a single-rate flat tax have preserved some element of redistribution by exempting low-income workers from paying the tax.

The mechanics of redistribution are fairly simple: you raise taxes on the richest citizens and use the added revenue to provide education, health care, jobs, or straightforward cash payments to the poor. To do that, a country needs a tax structure that works the way Christ recommended to his disciples on the day they went to the temple—a system that taxes people in proportion to their ability to pay.

In America's current political discourse, it is the conservatives who complain about progressive taxes that place the greatest burden on the rich. Traditionally, though, economic conservatives were strong defenders of this principle. None other than Adam Smith said that "it is not very unreasonable that the rich should contribute to the public expense, not only in proportion to their revenue, but something more than in proportion." F. A. Hayek, the Austrian economist who has become an idol for many American conservatives, made the same point in his classic work *The Constitution of Liberty*. The rich should be expected to pay more, Hayek reasoned, because "a person who commands more of the resources of society will also gain proportionally more from what the government has contributed."[10]

Edwin R. A. Seligman, a professor at Columbia who helped lead the charge in the United States for a progressive income tax at the start of the twentieth century, maintained that the course of history was moving all modern countries inexorably toward a tax code based on ability to pay—or "tax justice," as he called it. In his 1914 text, *The Income Tax: A Study of the History, Theory, and Practice of Income Taxation at Home and Abroad,* Seligman set forth his argument in majestic prose:

> Amid the clashing of divergent interests and the endeavor of each social class to roll off the burden of taxation on some other class, we discern the slow and laborious growth of standards of justice in taxation, and the attempt on the part of the community as a whole to realize this justice. The history of finance, in other words, shows the evolution of the principle of faculty or ability to pay— the principle that each individual should be held to help the state in proportion to his ability to help himself. . . . Even where actual fiscal institutions represent more or less thinly disguised efforts of the dominant economic class to roll the burdens on the shoulders of the weak,—even here it is rare to find a cynical disregard of all considerations of equity.[11]

Those considerations lay at the heart of the first tax law ever written in the United States. In 1634, the elders of the Massachusetts Bay Colony decreed that each man was to be assessed "according to his estate and with consideration of all other his abilityes whatsoever."[12] But that principle was forgotten in nineteenth-century America, where "the dominant economic class" successfully fought back efforts to institute progressive taxation. When Congress enacted a graduated income tax in 1894, the Supreme Court quickly voided the statute. The justices were almost apoplectic at the idea of asking the rich to pay more. "If the Court sanctions the power of discriminating taxation," Justice Stephen J. Field wrote for the majority, ". . . it will mark the hour when the sure decadence of our government will commence."[13]

The hour of sure decadence commenced sooner than Justice Field probably expected. By 1913, the United States had changed the Constitution (via the Sixteenth Amendment) to get around the Supreme Court, and the income tax became law. From its first day, the whole point of the U.S. income tax was to redistribute the tax burden from farmers and small landowners to the new class of tycoons and robber barons who had sprung up during the Gilded Age. The first income tax had a progressive rate scale, with the top rate at 7%. It was so carefully aimed at the richest Americans that less than 4% of households had to pay at all.[14] Recently, there has been considerable public concern about the fact that 47% of Americans pay no income tax; the presidential candidate Mitt Romney opined that these are people "who are dependent upon government, who believe that they are victims, who believe the government has a responsibility to care for them. . . . These are people who pay no income tax." In fact, though, the U.S. income tax was initially designed to apply only to those in the top income brackets; its primary purpose from the start was to offset inequality.

Enhance the Legitimacy of Government

It may be difficult for Americans to understand that a tax system can be an important tool for building citizenship. A regime of taxes considered fair and reasonable, and an honest, efficient agency to collect them, can give people confidence in their own government. Because taxes hit just about every citizen in one way or another, everybody has a stake in effective taxation. This is particularly true in young nations or in countries where corrupt government has traditionally been a fact of life. Achilles Amawhe, the man who gave me that baseball cap from Nigeria's revenue service, is acutely aware of this tax function. "When we won our independence, we had to prove to ourselves, and to the world, that we could carry out self-government," he told me. "I always knew that an honest tax agency would be a symbol of that."

In fact, a promise of rigorous universal tax collection can be a winning political strategy. When Alexis Tsipras and his Syriza Party challenged the longtime incumbent government of Greece in 2015, he ran on a pledge to "fight the oligarchy that is evading taxes," and he won, in a country where ducking the tax man had long been considered standard operating procedure. As prime minister, Tsipras appointed an "anticorruption czar" with a mission to make all Greeks, rich or poor, pay the taxes they owed. The czar himself, Panagiotis Nikoloudis, saw his role as something considerably bigger than just bringing in revenues. Rather, it was his duty to convince the people of Greece that government can work. "If people see that I'm clean, and the prime minister is clean," Mr. Nikoloudis said, "and that those who are not clean will eventually go to jail, I like to hope it will inspire a change in Greek society."[15]

The theory that good taxes make good citizens (who then demand good government) has spawned a considerable academic literature in the field of political science. In a 2014 study, Lucy Martin of Yale University set up experiments to test the proposition that people insist on better government—and get it—if they have to pay for it through taxes. In a series of field tests in Uganda, Martin set forth a situation where both taxpaying and untaxed citizens were told that a public official was corrupt. Those paying taxes proved to be far more indignant about this and were more inclined to punish a guilty leader. In poor countries that depend primarily on foreign aid for their revenues, Martin found, citizens tend to tolerate poor government and official corruption. But that attitude changes when taxes become due. "Taxation generates a significant increase in the level of accountability citizens demand from leaders," she concluded.[16]

In modern society, taxes go far beyond the basic mission of paying for government programs. This may be one reason why the U.S. tax code has become so ridiculously complicated; for each new mission, there's a new privilege or penalty or preference written into the law. This complexity is exacerbated by the enormous impact of money on American politics. Each year, hundreds of different contributors, each with his own pet cause, manage to persuade Congress to insert a particular loophole or exclusion into the Internal Revenue Code. America's tax system is like an old inner tube that has been patched a dozen times—and still leaks.

And this is exactly the wrong way to design a tax system. It violates the most important rule of good taxation—a principle the economists call "BBLR."

4.

BBLR

The modern world has tens of thousands of international organizations, ranging from the Fédération Aéronautique Internationale (based in Lausanne, Switzerland) to the World Association of Zoos and Aquariums (based in Gland, Switzerland). Some are more than a hundred years old. The first wave of internationalization occurred in the late nineteenth century, when amazing innovations like electricity, telegraphy, steamships, and railroads created a need for global agreements on time zones, power grids, weights and measures, and so on. The drive for standardization came from Europe, which is why we still measure time and longitude based on a meridian running through Greenwich, England, and why the global standards for the meter and the kilogram are stored in a vault in Sèvres, France. In the twentieth century the United Nations, the World Health Organization, Interpol, the International Olympic Committee, the International Committee of the Red Cross, NATO, and the like were created.

In recent decades, the Internet and the smartphone, Facebook and Snapchat, have sparked a new rush of international organization creation. There's an international Video Electronics Standards Association and an International Programmers Guild. There are global fan groups for dozens of video games you've probably never heard of. There are hundreds of global associations for specific industries, ranging from the International Federation of Beekeepers' Associations to the International Society of Sugar Cane Technologists to the International Association of Wood Anatomists.

Inevitably, there's also an international organization of international organizations: the Union des Associations Internationales, based in Brussels. In 2015, its annual directory (published in English, Spanish, German, and Esperanto) listed 68,029 global groups.[1] Several of the international associations listed in that huge directory focus on issues of national finance and taxation. There are world federations of accountants and investment advisers, of tax law professors and import duty collectors. There's the World Trade Organization, which struggles to get countries to agree on rules of cross-border commerce.

But the heavyweight players in this field, the three organizations that have the most clout in the realm of budgets and tax policy, are the World Bank, the International Monetary Fund, and the Organization for Economic Cooperation and Development.

These three institutions often work together on the same international problems (although they don't always agree on the solutions). So it's easy to confuse them. Even John Maynard Keynes, the British economist who was a central player in creating all three, said he always thought of the World Bank as a "fund" and the International Monetary Fund as a "bank." In fact, though, their basic functions are somewhat different:

- The World Bank, formally known as the International Bank for Reconstruction and Development, was set up in 1944 to finance the rebuilding of nations shattered by World War II. After a decade or so, with reconstruction and development moving along well in Europe, the bank turned its focus toward the planet's poor countries, now generally called "developing countries." It finances programs and projects to enhance economic growth and provides advice on spending, borrowing, and tax policy to the countries it supports.

• The International Monetary Fund, or IMF, works with countries rich and poor to maintain what it calls an "orderly monetary system" for the world, a system in which all nations agree to follow common rules for currency exchange, cross-border taxation, and the like. It, too, provides advice on fiscal issues. The fund can also step in with loans to offset a financial crisis, as it did when several countries faced economic collapse in the Great Recession of 2008–9 and when Greece defaulted on its debts in 2015.

• The Organization for Economic Cooperation and Development, or OECD, is a sort of exclusive club of countries, with membership restricted to the world's richest nations. It currently has thirty-five members, ranging from the United States, the world's leader in total wealth, to Chile and Mexico, the least wealthy of the wealthy. The OECD aims to get these successful nations to work together on common concerns like the environment, tax evasion, and financial fraud. It constantly issues reports and recommendations on financial and governance issues facing its member governments.

These international financial watchdogs all compile comparative data on national and international financial matters; when you see a listing, say, of the world's richest countries, the source is probably one of these three. Such studies are invaluable to the harmless drudges (like me) who write comparative policy books on health care, taxation, and similar topics. The book you're reading now probably couldn't exist without the mountain of charts, tables, and rankings churned out every year by the World Bank and the OECD.

In addition, all three institutions provide advice to nations—big and small, "developed" and "developing," democracies and dictatorships—on everything related to government finance. Which means they pour out a steady stream of reports and recommendations on tax policy. Their economists and accountants know what makes for an efficient and successful tax system and what makes for a bad one. While these organizations sometimes differ from each other on their economic nostrums—there was considerable argument in 2008–9 as to whether "austerity" or "stimulus" was the best medicine for recovery—all of them agree on the core framework that should underlie any national tax regime. When it comes to designing a country's tax system, the World Bank, the IMF, and the OECD all preach the same sermon, relying on the same fundamental principle. This rule is not particularly complicated; it is easy to understand, although not always easy to implement. In fact, it's so simple that the economists generally reduce the essential formula for good taxation to a four-letter word: "BBLR."

That stands for "broad base, low rates."

BBLR means that if the tax *base*—that is, the total amount of income, or sales, or property that can be taxed—is kept as large as possible, then the tax *rate*—that is, the percentage that people have to give to the government—can be kept low. Virtually all economists and tax experts agree that this is the best way to run a tax regime.

A broad-based income tax is one in which just about every penny a citizen earns during the year is taxable, without a bundle of exemptions, deductions, credits, allowances, and so on that reduce the taxable income. A broad-based sales tax is one in which sales tax has to be paid on every purchase, without exemptions for food, medical supplies, and so forth. A broad-based property tax is one that taxes the full assessed value of a home or building or piece of land.

To demonstrate, let's imagine two citizens; we'll call them Bill and Helen. Their economic circumstances are nearly identical, but they live in different states with different income tax rules.

—Bill Broad lives in a state that has adopted a broad-based definition of income. He works for Galactic Airlines, earning $75,000 per year, plus assorted benefits: the company pays $1,000 per month for his health insurance; the company contributes $200 per month to his 401(k) retirement plan; the company pays for his parking fees at the airport where he works, which is valuable because parking would cost $20 per day if he had to pay for it. Bill owns a house in town, with mortgage interest payments of $2,000 per month. He sends his kids to private school, at a cost of $9,000 per year. He donates $50 per month to his church, and $500 each year to the United Fund campaign. The property tax on his house comes to $4,500.

Under the broad-based tax regime in his state, everything Bill receives from his employer is counted as income; that's $75,000 in wages, plus $12,000 in health insurance premiums, plus $2,400 in retirement contributions, plus the value of the company-paid parking, which comes to $5,000 per year. Add it all up, and Bill's gross income is $94,400. That's also his taxable income, because his state doesn't give any deductions for mortgage payments, property tax, charitable contributions, or education expenses. The state income tax rate is 10%, so Bill pays $9,440 in taxes.

—Helen High lives in a state that offers a generous assortment of income tax exemptions, credits, and deductions and makes up for them by imposing high tax rates. She, too, works for Galactic Airlines. She earns the same annual salary as Bill ($75,000); she gets the same $1,000-per-month insurance policy, paid for by the company. She gets the same $200 retirement contribution each month, and the company provides her free parking at the airport. Helen, too, has a mortgage on her house, with $2,000 of interest payments monthly. She, too, has kids in private school, at a cost of $9,000 per year. Just like Bill Broad, she donates a total of $1,100 each year to church and charities. And she, too, pays property tax of $4,500 per year.

Under the narrow-based tax rules where Helen lives, her salary counts as income, but her employer's contributions to her health insurance and 401(k) plan do not. She is not taxed on the value of the free parking her company provides. She gets a deduction for the interest on her mortgage payment and additional deductions for her tax payments and charitable contributions. She gets a credit for her children's educational expenses. So when Helen reaches the "taxable income" line on her tax return, the total, after all those exemptions and deductions, is $52,500. In order to get the same amount of revenue that Bill Broad paid—$9,440—the state will have to tax Helen High's income at a rate of 17.98%. In other words, the tax rate has to be set nearly 80% higher to offset all the tax preferences that slashed Helen's "taxable income."

Because both taxpayers end up providing the same amount of revenue, what's the difference? Why does it matter whether somebody is taxed at 10% or 17.98%, as long as government gets the revenue it needs?

First, nearly all economists believe that tax should be a "neutral" factor when people and corporations are making business decisions. An economy works best if financial decisions are based on sound business principles; if tax considerations influence the decision, they distort the economics. If International Widgets decides to buy a $20 million industrial robot, it should do so because that acquisition makes business sense—that is, this new tool will increase our profit—and not because there's a big tax break for investing in robots. If some millionaire is looking for a bank to hold her life savings, she should look for the most trustworthy bank, rather than depositing her money in the Cayman Islands in order to hide it from the IRS. If a big U.S. tractor company decides to move the headquarters of its spare-parts business to Switzerland, that should happen only if Switzerland is an important hub of the parts business, not because Switzerland has rock-bottom corporate tax rates.

This is where low rates come in. If the rate is low, it's less likely to influence personal and financial decisions; that is, the tax will be "neutral." If the tax you owe is only 10% of your income, it's probably not worth your while to pay a lawyer to design some complex tax haven scheme, or to move a whole branch of your company to a low-tax country. But if the tax man is going to take 17.9% or 35% or (in France) 75% of your income, then the lawyer's complex scheme can save you serious money. The economist John Maynard Keynes was a famous advocate of progressive taxes, but he warned that higher rates run the risk of "making skillful evasions too much worthwhile."[2] High tax rates prompt people to spend money on the tax lawyers and finance wizards who design those skillful evasions. For the lawyers and the finance guys, this is a boon. But for the overall economy, it's a significant loss. The money these taxpayers spent on legal fees and complicated financial constructions could have been invested in ways that would grow the national economy or solve social problems.

BEYOND THAT, A TAX SYSTEM studded with preferences—exclusions, exemptions, accelerated depreciation, intangible drilling credits, and so on—is a complicated tax system. Getting rid of all those loopholes so that all income is treated the same way makes the whole business of taxation easier for both the taxpayer and the tax collector. If dividends you received from a "Subchapter S" partnership (whatever that means) were taxed the same as all other income, you wouldn't have to dig through the verbal jungle of IRS Form 1065 to figure out how much of the dividend is an "unrecaptured section 1250 gain" (whatever that means). If there's no deduction for contributions, charities don't have to produce a certified receipt for each donation, and the contributor doesn't have to track down the nine-digit Tax ID Number of each charity she wants to support.

Getting rid of the complications also makes it easier for the tax agency to check a tax return or to perform an audit. And a broader tax base makes the system feel fairer. If deductions, credits, and such are strictly limited, the average wage earner won't have that sneaking suspicion that rich people have their own special escape clauses to cut their tax burden.

The principle of BBLR applies to other types of taxes as well. Consider a state sales tax. Let's say the total of retail sales in a certain state is $1 billion per year. If the state's sales tax applies to every purchase, without any exemptions, the sales tax base will be the entire $1 billion. With a sales tax of 9%, the state will take in $90 million in sales tax revenue. But if the sales tax exempts food, medicine, children's clothing, and newspapers—these are the common exceptions—the sales tax base is only $500 million. To bring in the same $90 million of revenue, the state would have to double its sales tax rate to 18%. And all those exemptions make the process difficult for retailers, who have to figure out on every sale which items are tax exempt and which are not.

For all these reasons, there is broad consensus among economists and tax experts that a broad tax base, making it possible to lower the rates, is the gold standard for the design of any revenue system. When President George W. Bush appointed a blue-ribbon commission in 2005 to write a new, improved tax code—the President's Advisory Panel on Federal Tax Reform—the advisers' main suggestion was a BBLR approach. In response, each of the predictable interest groups complained loudly about the proposed elimination of its favorite credits and deductions; the plan went nowhere. When President Barack Obama appointed a blue-ribbon commission to find ways to cut the deficit—it was officially the National Commission on Fiscal Responsibility and Reform, but everybody called it "Simpson-Bowles"—that group, too, recommended a BBLR tax reform. In response, each of the predictable interest groups complained loudly about the proposed elimination of its favorite credits and deductions; the plan prompted extensive debate but never got to a vote in Congress.

Because economists are usually not unanimous about anything, it's downright strange to see the virtually universal endorsement of the BBLR principle by academics, tax-reform advocates, think tanks around the world, and the three big international financial organizations. Yet there are a few dissenters. One is Professor James R. Hines, an economist at the University of Michigan. He acknowledges the benefits of a simplified tax system with low rates. But he says it's fairer if the law gives special breaks to taxpayers in special circumstances, like parents or the chronically ill or corporations that have to make large capital investments. Yes, this makes taxes more complicated, the professor concedes, but "good policy is messy." Professor Hines also argues, tongue in cheek, that it's probably better if Congress fritters away a lot of time writing tax loopholes. If all exemptions and preferences were eliminated, he says, "the only tax policy role of Congress would be to choose tax rates. Should we worry about what Congress might do with all the extra time?"[3]

THE OECD PUBLISHES A broad variety of reports and proposals on financial topics, but one of its perennial bestsellers is a 160-page guidebook called *Choosing a Broad Base–Low Rate Approach to Taxation.*

"In general," the guide says, "tax reforms that broaden tax bases and lower rates should reduce the extent to which tax systems distort work, consumption, and investment decisions, increasing output and enabling improvements in social welfare." Governments may think they have good reason to create provisions giving tax breaks to particular groups, but the OECD economists beg to differ. "Whatever the reason, tax provisions entail a loss of government revenues, which necessarily means that other taxes have to be higher than otherwise. . . . These higher rates may create additional efficiency losses, adverse effects on income distribution, and administrative and compliance costs."[4]

Many countries, rich and poor, have moved in the direction of BBLR. Among them are Canada, Great Britain, and Germany, which have eliminated exemptions and credits at various times to broaden the tax base and lower rates. As we'll see shortly, the United States took a big leap toward BBLR some thirty years ago. But then the lobbyists pushed (successfully) to get their preferred exemptions back into the U.S. tax code; this narrowed the tax base, so rates had to go up to bring in the same amount of revenue.

When I asked the economists at the World Bank, the IMF, and the OECD which countries have the best tax system, they agreed on a prime candidate. New Zealand, they all told me, is Exhibit A for demonstrating the merits of the broad-based, low-rate approach. The academic literature supports this conclusion. "The New Zealand tax system stands out in comparative perspective," concluded a 2012 study in the *Journal of Public Policy*. "Over the last three decades, New Zealand arguably moved further than any other advanced economy in neo-liberal tax reform, i.e. in the direction of low rates, broad bases, and neutral taxation. . . . The top rates on labor income in New Zealand are extraordinarily low by international standards. . . . The [sales tax] rate also remained relatively low by international standards."[5]

It's not really surprising that New Zealand followed the economists' advice. This island nation has been a policy leader for decades among the world's rich democracies. The *Economist* magazine noted that "New Zealanders have a right to be smug" at international meetings, because so many of their governmental innovations have been copied around the world.

New Zealand was the first nation on the planet to let women vote (in 1893). It has given new meaning to the term "paying with plastic"; the nation's currency is printed on waterproof, tear-resistant plastic, with transparent windows in the middle of the bill. The money doesn't wear out, it's almost impossible to counterfeit, and it floats if you drop it in a river. As a result, the Kiwis have sold this monetary innovation to dozens of countries. (Kate Sheppard, the proto-feminist who led the world's first successful campaign for women's suffrage, is on New Zealand's plastic $10 bill.) While other nations ponder the idea of privatizing the post office, New Zealand already has competing public and private postal services, with mailboxes of different colors side by side on the street. (I tried both systems and found the government delivery a little cheaper and just as fast.)

The nation has also been a leader in dealing with the indigenous population. As early as 1840, when white colonial settlers around the world—including the U.S. Cavalry—were waging war on the aboriginal residents of their new lands, the British pioneers who came to New Zealand signed a treaty recognizing members of the Maori tribe as equal citizens. (American Indians didn't become U.S. citizens until 1924.) The Maori language has been an official language since the birth of the nation. All government agencies print their documents in English and Maori. The Inland Revenue Department—also known by its Maori name, Te Tari Taake—provides both English and Maori versions of Form IR3, the local equivalent of Form 1040.

A GREEN MOUNTAINOUS ISLAND NATION with almost no manufacturing, New Zealand might seem to be an unlikely candidate for membership in the OECD, an organization limited to the world's richest industrialized democracies. But the Kiwis have built an advanced, prosperous, industrialized democracy—without heavy industry. They've done it by promoting a vigorous business of "adventure tourism" that lures rock climbers, windsurfers, snowboarders, bungee jumpers, and the like from all over the world, and by exporting the fruits of their farms and forests—primarily dairy products, timber, wool, and wine. To compete with much larger agricultural nations, New Zealand promotes its products as "100% pure," containing nothing artificial or genetically modified. The point is made emphatically on the label of a beer called Steinlager Pure, a delicious brew and a successful export found all over Asia. "You are holding in your hand one of the purest beers anyone can make," the label declares. "No additives. No preservatives. Sourced from the purest place on earth, New Zealand."

The focus on purity has been so successful that New Zealand ranks among the richest countries in the world. It was one of the earliest members of the OECD. When it joined that international group in 1973, New Zealand had a tax code that looked like the tax structure in other rich countries. It relied primarily for revenue on a personal income tax, and the tax was riddled with exemptions, credits, and giveaways for particular groups and companies. In short, it was the opposite of BBLR. All those preferences made for a fairly narrow tax base, which meant that tax rates had to be high to raise the required revenue. By the early 1980s, the country's top marginal income tax rate was 66%. "We had an income tax that was like a swiss cheese, it had so many exemptions," a veteran Kiwi bureaucrat, Graham Scott, told me. "And with all those holes in it, the rates had to be kept high to bring in the money we needed."

Graham Scott told me that "in the '70s a wine expert—an enologist, he's called—came to visit from the University of California. Well, this bloke noticed that our Marlborough region [basically, the northeast corner of the South Island] had a geography and a climate that looked like Napa Valley. Well, a few entrepreneurs drove out the sheep and started planting the grapes that you grow in California. And this has turned into a huge export industry. The sauvignon blanc from Marlborough is world famous now; we export more sauvignon blanc to the United States than France does! But at first, nobody had ever heard of a Marlborough wine. So we gave the winemakers all sorts of tax benefits in the beginning. Hell, that's what we always did; in those days, we were giving every industry tax breaks, left and right. That's one of the reasons we had all those holes in the income tax."

In the 1980s, Graham Scott became the policy chief in New Zealand's Finance Ministry, which meant that fixing that swiss-cheese tax code was his job. (He did the job so well that the queen knighted him for his work; he is now Sir Graham Scott, although he seemed embarrassed when I called him that.) When Scott took over the policy shop, the Labour Party—roughly like the U.S. Democratic Party—had just won a national election. The Labour finance minister, Roger Douglas, Scott recalls, wanted to "clean up" the tax code.

"We said, 'Roger, what do you mean, "Clean up"?' And he said, 'Let's cut out all the special business allowances. Let's cut out all the agriculture subsidies.' Frankly, the politics of it were favorable, because Labour didn't have farm support anyway, didn't have business support. So we could get rid of all the special allowances and rebates and deductions. In those days, we had tax incentives for timber companies; for tourist companies; for insurance companies; hell, you could deduct the premiums for your life insurance policy. If a company built a factory for $10 million, we would let them depreciate the whole $10 million in the first five years, even though the building would last for fifty. Well, we killed all of those write-offs. We didn't allow individuals to take the two big deductions that your U.S. has, for mortgage interest and contributions to a church."

THIS WAS BASE BROADENING on steroids, but even so, the bureaucrats did not satisfy Douglas, the finance minister. He wanted to cut the top income tax rate in half. But even with virtually all preferences eliminated from the tax code, the government couldn't get enough revenue with such low rates. To solve that problem, Scott and his fellow bureaucrats proposed a national sales tax—they called it the goods and services tax—and used the same broad-based approach for that levy. Unlike other countries', New Zealand's GST applied to virtually any product or service you could buy (including the prostitutes in the legal brothels). With that addition, the income tax rates could be cut in half for every taxpayer in the nation—with no loss of revenue to the government.

In essence, New Zealand's government said to its citizens, "If you want to make a contribution to charity, that's fine. But you don't get a tax break for it. If you want to take out a mortgage to buy a house, that's good. But you don't get a tax deduction for the interest you pay. You want to put a solar array on your roof? Great idea, but don't expect a tax write-off. If you buy a life insurance policy to protect your family, more power to you. But we're not going to let you deduct the annual premium."

Inevitably, taxpayers and businesses that lost a cherished deduction complained angrily. "But we said to them, if you want to keep that deduction, we'll have to raise the rates for everybody," Scott recalls. "And people understood the trade-off; you lose a deduction, but you get a simpler tax code and much lower rates." From the left, there were complaints that the big cut in income tax rates was a gift to the richest Kiwis. "But we said to them, the tax is still progressive," Scott says. "The more income you have, the higher your tax rate. But a progressive tax doesn't necessarily have to soak the rich." Tax lawyers and accounting firms also complained, Scott told me, "because after all we were putting a lot of them out of business when we took away all the loopholes they used to manipulate."

In the end, the sweeping reform was widely accepted—by individuals, businesses, and both major political parties. "It was a success. Even the conservatives eventually had to accept that this was extremely popular," said Maurice McTigue, who was a member of Parliament at the time from the National Party, the conservative opposition. "A key reason was that we did it big. They changed almost everything at once. And that's an important lesson: if you're going to do tax reform, you'd better make it a large reform. That way, for every change a taxpayer doesn't like, there's something else in the package that he wants."

Despite the predictable efforts of various industry and interest groups to wedge their favorite tax preferences back into the tax code, New Zealand clung fairly tightly to the BBLR principle over the next two decades. Over time, though, some deductions and credits were permitted—including that accelerated depreciation write-off that Graham Scott thought he had killed. All this narrowed the tax base and forced the government to raise income tax rates; the top income tax rate had risen from 30% in 1986 to 39% by 2010. Taxpayers were not happy. And so New Zealand did tax reform again; in 2010, deductions and credits were cut, and that accelerated depreciation scheme was killed (for the second time). Income tax rates could be cut yet again, with no loss of revenue.

The result is a tax code that imposes the lowest rates on average workers of any developed nation. The comparison with the United States is instructive. An American couple bringing in the median family income—about $55,000 per year—and taking the standard deduction will pay about 15% of their annual earnings in personal income tax, another 6.5% in Social Security tax, another 2.9% for the Medicare tax, and roughly 5% in state income tax. In addition, an average American family will pay 5% to 10% of income for health insurance. Add it all up, and the median earner in the United States is paying about 35% of earnings for taxes and health care. (A self-employed American would pay even more, because Social Security taxes and health-care premiums are higher for the self-employed.)

In New Zealand, in contrast, the median wage earner pays about 17.5% in income tax. But that one payment also covers his old-age pension (there's no separate tax for Social Security), plus free health care for life (there's no separate tax for health care), plus free education through college graduation (there's no separate tax for schools). So the average New Zealander's wages are taxed at less than half the rate of the average American's. And yet New Zealand provides more government services than the United States—with half the tax rate. That's the beauty of BBLR.

NEW ZEALAND'S EXPERIENCE IS INSTRUCTIVE, but what does it have to do with the United States? It's an island country, closer to Antarctica than to the equator, with four million people and about as many sheep. It has a unicameral legislature and a government tradition in which elected politicians defer to professional bureaucrats—like Sir Graham Scott—on all the important policy questions. In a country like that, a major change of the national tax code must be easier to achieve than in a sprawling, contentious place like the United States, where nearly all public policy issues are heavily politicized and corporate money flows freely through the halls of Congress. With our fractious politics and our sharply polarized electorate, surely the United States could never bring about a tax reform as sweeping and as successful as New Zealand's swing to BBLR.

But, in fact, we did.

In the mid-1980s, the American political landscape was as fractious as it is today. The Republican president had won a substantial electoral college victory, but the country was polarized. The government then was divided, with a conservative president from California battling a liberal House of Representatives led by a Democrat from Massachusetts. With leaders of both parties constantly maneuvering for political gain, Washington was gridlocked on the major issues. There wasn't much hope for significant progress in any policy area and certainly not on tax reform.

The election in 1980 of President Ronald Reagan, an unabashed tax hater, launched a flurry of tax laws that pushed rates down, up, down again, and up again with no clear pattern. In Reagan's first months in office, he successfully pressured Congress to pass the Economic Recovery Tax Act of 1981—known inside the Beltway as ERTA—giving big tax cuts to every individual and corporate taxpayer. (ERTA was so laden with breaks and credits for various industries that it was called, accurately, "a frenzied craze of tax giveaways."[6]) The economic rationale for this huge tax reduction was the so-called "supply-side" argument that lower taxes would stimulate business activity and bring in more revenue. Sadly, as we've seen, this something-for-nothing theory has never worked in practice. ERTA led to such a big jump in the government's deficit that Reagan and Congress quickly reversed course, increasing taxes the next year in the Tax Equity and Fiscal Responsibility Act—known as TEFRA. That was followed by tax cuts in 1983, and yet another tax increase in the Tax Reform Act of 1984 a year later.

By the time Reagan won reelection in 1984, the U.S. tax code was, as the economist Henry Aaron put it, "a swamp of unfairness, complexity, and inefficiency . . . that represents no consistent policy." Each new exemption or credit spawned many more. Oil drillers had traditionally enjoyed a tax break called a depletion allowance, based on the theory that the amount of oil in the well must be depleting over time. Seeing that, other industries clamored for their own depletion allowances, and Congress responded. By the mid-1980s, the tax code allowed depletion or depreciation allowances that cut taxes for cement companies, Christmas tree farms, apple orchards, gravel pits, railroad cars, rubber importers, cattle growers, and many, many more. There was even a depreciation allowance for human beings; professional sports teams were allowed to write off their players as "depreciable assets" as they slowed down with age.

Nobody defended this mess, but hardly anybody expected things to get better. When the Treasury Department began testing various reform plans in 1984–85, the respected political scientist John Witte wrote that "there is nothing, absolutely nothing . . . that indicates that any of these schemes have the slightest hope of being enacted in the forms proposed."[7]

And yet there were two men in official Washington who still believed that liberals in Congress and the conservative in the White House could agree on significant tax reform. These two were strange bedfellows indeed. One of them, a conservative Republican, was a Wall Street tycoon; the other, a liberal Democrat, was a basketball star.

THE WALL STREETER WAS Donald Regan, who left his post as chairman of the nation's largest stockbrokerage, Merrill Lynch, to become secretary of the Treasury in Reagan's cabinet. Despite his position at the top of the financial community, Regan had a populist, anti-establishment streak. Like everybody else, Regan considered the U.S. tax code an unruly beast that badly needed taming. But unlike most of his predecessors, the new cabinet secretary began talking regularly to tax policy experts deep in the Treasury bureaucracy. He encouraged the bureaucrats to think boldly; among much else, he dispatched a pair of economists to New Zealand to study the bold changes the Kiwis were making under the guidance of Sir Graham Scott. By the end of 1984, Regan and his policy team had put together a sweeping tax-reform plan—it became known as Treasury I—that incorporated the basic principle of "broadening the base to lower the rates." When James Baker replaced Regan as Treasury secretary, he, too, became an advocate for the BBLR approach to tax reform.

This was a concept that the other key reformer, Bill Bradley, had championed even before Treasury I was issued. An all-American at Princeton and a Rhodes scholar, Bradley came home from Oxford to join the New York Knickerbockers of the National Basketball Association. He became the team's biggest star, and the best paid as well; he was given the nickname Dollar Bill. Fellow players steered Bradley to the usual army of tax lawyers and accountants, who showed him all the legal tax-avoidance mechanisms available to the richest of taxpayers. Bradley said he found it appalling. He was even more disturbed when the Knicks' finance chief mentioned that the team could label its star forward a "depreciable asset," and thus cut its taxes. Bradley later recalled that he really got interested in the U.S. tax code when he learned that "I had been a loophole for the New York Knicks."

Bradley was elected to the U.S. Senate in 1978, and he brought to this new position the same determination and diligence that had made him a standout in school and in sports. I was a reporter covering the U.S. Senate on January 15, 1979, when the new Congress convened and the newly elected senators were sworn in, with great hoopla. Right after that formal ceremony, all the members left the Senate floor to attend celebratory parties—all of them, that is, except Senator Bradley. On his first day in the Senate, he spent some three hours at his desk going over the Senate rules with the parliamentarian.

With a seat on the tax-writing Finance Committee, Bradley immersed himself in the policy and politics of tax reform. He made an important discovery: in taxation, the policy issues and the political considerations neatly overlapped. Lowering the rates was something Republicans wanted. Broadening the base—cutting out special interest preferences—was something Democrats wanted. So combining a broad base with low rates should win support from both parties and

thus get a real reform bill through Congress. Bradley used this combination approach in a tax bill he introduced, the Fair Tax Act, which
proposed to cut the top marginal rate by half, to 30%.

"The trade-off between loophole elimination and a lower top rate
became obvious," Bradley wrote later; "the lower the rate, the more
loopholes had to be closed to pay for it."[8] Bradley stuck to the mantra
of "broad base, low rates" for years, telling anybody who would listen
that a significant cut in tax rates would win the votes needed to
broaden the base. "The key to reform was to focus on the attractive-
ness of low rates, not on the pain of limiting deductions."

The enticement of low rates also helped land a crucially important
supporter for tax reform: Ronald Reagan himself. As a major Hollywood star, Reagan had been a member of the financial 1% in the
1950s, when the top marginal income tax rate was 90%. The sting of
the annual tax return, Reagan used to say, was one of the factors that
converted him from a liberal labor union leader to a conservative
champion of business. He saw himself as a defender of the hard-
pressed average taxpayer. On the stump, he loved to tell an old joke:
"The taxpayer—that's the only person who works for the federal government without passing the Civil Service exam."

When Regan, Baker, and Bradley approached the president with a
promise to cut the top rate to 30% or lower, accordingly, Reagan
signed on. In 1984, the popular president announced that far-reaching
tax reform was his top domestic issue—a declaration that made it
harder for his fellow Republicans in Congress to oppose the reform
when the plan came to a final vote in 1986.

And yet the path to passage, as set forth in the definitive history of
the 1986 act, *Showdown at Gucci Gulch,* was hardly smooth. Every
time a reform plan seemed to be getting somewhere in either the
House or the Senate, corporate lobbyists would swarm in to protect
their favored tax break—and each tax break that was approved meant
the rates had to go higher. For most of 1984 and 1985, the efforts to
overhaul the income tax looked like all the other so-called reform

plans of recent years; they made the tax code more complicated and more littered with preferences for the powerful.

At the end of 1985, the House of Representatives, controlled by liberal Democrats, passed a bill that moved in the direction of reform, although it left the top marginal rate at 38%. But when the Senate Finance Committee, controlled by Republicans, took up the issue, the members seemed far more interested in creating new benefits for various corporate groups than in broadening the base or cutting rates. The vaunted effort to reform our tax code turned into the kind of bill that senators called a "Christmas tree"—there were goodies for everybody.

By the spring of 1986, the senators were being denounced, in both national and home-state media, for selling out to special interests. Among those taking the heat was the Finance Committee chairman, Robert Packwood of Oregon, a moderate Republican who was up for reelection that year. The Oregon press was bashing him as a corporate stooge, as the man who killed tax reform. They gave him a brutal nickname: Senator Hackwood.

Having tried everything else, the senators finally turned back to Bill Bradley and his simple formula: broaden the base to lower the rates. At a Finance Committee meeting in mid-April, Chairman Packwood put aside the Christmas tree bill and handed out copies of the Fair Tax Act that Bradley had introduced years earlier. Just as Bradley had predicted, the lure of sharply lower rates proved stronger than the senators' attachment to their special interest tax breaks. With Ronald Reagan and the liberal Democrats pushing together, the drive for genuine tax reform gathered so much momentum that the BBLR bill— the Tax Reform Act of 1986—swept through both the Senate and the House and was signed into law by a beaming president in October.

That 1986 law, generally recognized as "the most significant reform in the history of the income tax,"[9] reduced the top marginal rate for individual taxpayers from 50% to 28%—the biggest reduction of any tax bill before or since. It did that by eliminating a broad range of "tax shelter" breaks available only to the rich. It cut back the deduction for mortgage interest and completely eliminated the deduction for interest on consumer loans, like auto loans and credit cards. It eliminated the deduction for state and local sales taxes. It limited deductions for charitable contributions, IRA deposits, medical bills, and other personal expenses. It set the tax rate on capital gains—that is, profit on stocks, real estate deals, and so on—at the same level as the top income tax rate, so that financiers could no longer cut their tax bill by defining all their pay as capital gains. In fact, the reform changed so many aspects of the tax code that the official name of the basic law of U.S. income tax was updated for the first time in thirty-two years. What had been the Internal Revenue Code of 1954 became the Internal Revenue Code of 1986, which it still is today.

The new law produced significant tax cuts for low-income and median-income Americans and provided tax savings for the rich as well. But somebody had to pay for all that lost revenue, and the burden was shifted largely to corporations. Although the bill cut the basic corporate tax rate, from 48% to 34%, it took away so many of industry's cherished credits, deductions, and depletion allowances that corporate taxes increased by some $120 billion over five years.

In short, Congress and the president achieved a fundamental change in the income tax by heeding two lessons from the New Zealand reform: they broadened the tax base to make low rates possible, and they made a large, sweeping reform all at once so that every change the taxpayers didn't like was offset by changes that they wanted badly.

This stunning and unexpected tax reform, particularly coming out of a politically polarized Washington, D.C., drew attention, and prompted action, around the world. When little New Zealand transformed its tax code, the other wealthy nations found it interesting; when the mighty United States did the same thing, the rest of the world found it imperative, on political and fiscal grounds, to do the same. In short order, Britain, Ireland, Canada, the Netherlands, and other democracies dramatically lowered their tax rates by broadening the tax base. The OECD called this wave of tax reduction a "global revolution," and the United States lit the spark.

But soon the lobbyists and political contributors started leaning on Congress to restore many of the credits, exemptions, allowances, and shelters. Many industries got their depreciation or depletion allowances fully restored. Families got new tax credits for child-care expenses and student loan interest. Under pressure from Wall Street, the tax rate on capital gains was sharply cut; this was a windfall for the wealthiest taxpayers, and one that gave the finance community new incentives for complicated schemes to make salaries look like dividends. All these giveaways narrowed the tax base, which meant tax rates had to be increased to bring in the same amount of revenue. After three increases in the 1990s, the top marginal rate of income tax was back up to 39.6%, where it sat in early 2017. After proudly patting itself on the back because of the 1986 reform, Congress in the next three decades made more than thirty thousand changes to the 1986 code. Most of them ran counter to the ethos of BBLR. Virtually all of them made the tax code more complicated—including that bizarre "anti-complexity clause," Section 7803(c)(2)(B)(ii)(IX).

Three decades after the passage of the 1986 reforms, the U.S. tax code is a mockery of the BBLR principle. It is stuffed to the roof with loopholes that narrow the tax base and thus force tax rates higher. If we are to fix our complicated and inequitable tax code again, Americans will have to agree—as we did three decades ago—to purge many of those deductions, including some of the write-offs that are most popular.

But which ones?

5.

SCOOPING WATER WITH A SIEVE

O n a crisp, clear January night, the president of the United States travels to Capitol Hill to deliver the State of the Union address. After declaring that "the state of our union is strong"—they always say that—the president runs quickly through half a dozen minor policy proposals, pauses dramatically, and then sets forth the administration's major new initiative for the year. "I will send legislation to Congress," the president intones proudly, "that directs the Treasury Department to send a check for $7,500 to anybody who buys a $100,000 sports car. This will provide a generous handout to the wealthiest Americans and a major boon to automakers, including those in Germany and Japan. The average wage earner will get no benefit from this new program. By the way, it will increase the deficit by $700 million each year."

Of course, that's a fantasy. No president would make such a proposal. Welfare for the rich? Subsidies to foreign car companies? A serious increase in the deficit, with minimal benefit for average Americans? We would never establish a federal giveaway like that.

Except we already have.

In the Energy Improvement and Extension Act of 2008, Congress created a lucrative tax break—it's Section 30(D) of the Internal Revenue Code—for people who can afford to buy electric or plug-in hybrid cars. It's formally known as the "new qualified plug-in electric drive motor vehicle credit." It says anybody buying a qualified plug-in electric car—the list of approved vehicles includes sleek, sporty cars like the $105,000 Tesla Model S P85D and the $138,000 BMW i8—can subtract up to $7,500 from the income tax he or she owes Uncle Sam. There are some less exotic cars that qualify—and get a smaller tax credit—but even those models, for the most part, are priced well beyond the reach of an American family making the median income.

In 2016, the IRS estimates, this tax credit reduced government revenues by about $740 million—money that would have come to the Treasury if the credit didn't exist. That $740 million could have been used to treat wounded veterans or tighten border controls or reduce the deficit, if we hadn't chosen to use it to subsidize upper-bracket auto buyers.

No president or member of Congress would dare suggest a spending bill that paid the rich for buying sports cars. But in Congress, Section 30(D) is not considered "spending"; it's a tax credit. In the simplistic formula of congressional politics, spending is bad, and a tax break is good—even when they amount to the same thing. For the government, the impact is identical; the tax credit costs the same hundreds of millions as a spending bill. Because the language is different, though, Congress readily goes along with giveaways like this one.

Indeed, there are hundreds of credits, subsidies, deductions, and allowances scattered through the Internal Revenue Code that would never be authorized if proposed in a spending bill. "If tested in direct expenditure terms," wrote Stanley Surrey, a renowned tax scholar at Harvard Law School, "many tax incentives will be seen as either inequitable—often to the point of being so grossly unfair as to be ludicrous—or ineffective."[1] Ludicrous or not, once these loopholes get into the code, they generally don't go away. The individuals and corporations that benefit from these fiscal gifts fight fiercely to protect them against any efforts at repeal.

That's why it's so hard to achieve tax reform through the mechanism of broad base, low rates. Everybody agrees that BBLR should be the driving principle behind the design of a tax system. But big, expensive giveaways like the credit for fancy sports cars keep working their way into the tax code. It happens in every country.

The easy part of BBLR is the low rates. Everybody likes lower tax rates. Economists tell us that low rates make the tax system "neutral." If the tax burden is small, economic decisions will be based on business and personal considerations, not on tax implications. Governments like low rates because they make a tax system simpler to administer, and they increase voluntary compliance; there's less motivation to evade taxes if the tax takes only a small part of your income. And taxpayers like a low rate because it makes taxation feel less like robbery.

SOME OF THESE TAX INCENTIVES serve a useful purpose, encouraging good behavior and discouraging bad. Supporters of the "new qualified plug-in electric drive motor vehicle credit" would say it encourages people to buy environmentally friendly cars that don't increase our need for foreign oil. But if that's a legitimate purpose of the tax code, why would there also be a deduction for people who buy recreational vehicles, which are notorious gas-guzzlers?[2] Congress doesn't always act logically when handing out tax breaks.

If a government giveaway is justified by social benefits, its backers should make their case and ask Congress to appropriate the money. If a handout to a specific business or group can't be justified as a direct government subsidy, it can't be justified as a tax break, either.

The members of Congress who sponsor these loopholes know that many or most of them could not survive public scrutiny. In fact, the sponsors are so embarrassed to admit what they're up to that they routinely conceal the real impact of a tax break behind obscure clouds of language that nobody can decipher (except the taxpayer getting the benefit).

Section 512(b)(15) of the Internal Revenue Code, for example, pro-vided a tax exemption for any for-profit enterprise started on May 27, 1959, and owned by a religious organization. Its sponsor, Senator Rus-sell Long of Louisiana, never mentioned that the only enterprise in the whole country that met these requirements was a commercial radio station in his state, WWL, a profitable business that was run by Loyola University. There's another section of the code, pushed by the Michi-gan delegation, that gives special preference to "an automobile manu-facturer incorporated in Delaware on October 13, 1916." That would be General Motors, although the name of the firm does not appear.

This kind of loophole is known as a "rifle shot" tax provision, be-cause it is sharply targeted at just a few specific taxpayers. Rich indi-viduals and corporations are willing to pay for these favors—in the form of campaign contributions to the sponsors. That's one of the rea-sons members of Congress are always eager to win a spot on the Ways and Means Committee—the tax-writing committee of the House of Representatives—or its Senate counterpart, the Finance Committee. Appointment to either of those committees opens the spigot for con-tributions to flow freely into a member's reelection fund from donors hoping for a rifle shot of their own.

After loud complaints from journalists and tax-reform activists about deliberately murky legislative language—critics called it "taxa-tion without comprehension"—Congress took aim at rifle shot taxa-tion in 2007. Since then, the rules of each house urge—but do not require—the chairs of the tax-writing committees to identify the re-cipients of any tax break that benefits ten or fewer taxpayers. Because it is in the chairs' discretion whether or not to make this information public, we don't know whether Congress is still larding the tax code each year with giveaways for specific constituents. What do you think?

Among economists, there's a term of art for this form of backdoor government spending. The various exemptions, exclusions, credits, al-lowances, deductions, and such are known as "tax expenditures."

This label was coined by the aforementioned professor Stanley Surrey. In the 1960s, Surrey took a leave from Harvard when his friend John F. Kennedy appointed him to the top policy position at the Treasury Department. This gave him access to all sorts of previously unpublished IRS data on giveaways in the tax code and their cost in lost revenue. When Surrey added them up, he was stunned to find how much revenue the government gave up, or "spent," through tax breaks. Surrey's office at the Treasury issued a report on this form of "expenditure" in 1968. It hit like a bombshell.

Until Surrey's report, nobody knew how much revenue the government lost because of the various credits and exemptions. The 1968 report revealed the totals and made the comparison to the normal kind of government spending. It showed that the sum of the various giveaways was greater than the budget of any federal agency or program, including the Pentagon and Social Security. (It still is today.) Once Congress realized how much it was spending through the tax code, the concept of "tax expenditures" became a central element of tax policy. Today, Treasury is required by law to make public detailed listings each year on the amount lost through tax expenditures for both the individual and the corporate income tax.

Back in his classes at Harvard, Surrey attacked tax expenditures with great zeal. He loved to propose nutty hypothetical spending bills. When he taught his students about the deduction for home mortgage interest, he made it sound ridiculous. He laid it out something like this:

The federal government wants to help some Americans pay their mortgage. Here's how it works: For a couple with $200,000 of income, and a mortgage interest payment of $1000 per month, the government will pay the bank $700 and the homeowners will have to pay only $300. For a couple with $20,000 of income and a mortgage interest payment of $1000 per month, the government will pay $190, leaving the couple to pay $810. For a couple making less than $10,000, the government will pay zero—so the low-income couple has to pay the full $1000 of mortgage interest.

Surrey would then point out that such a proposal—giving a big payment to the rich, a smaller payment to the middle class, and nothing to the poor—wouldn't stand a chance in Congress as a direct appropriation. But, in fact, this system already exists—in the tax code. The mortgage interest deduction—or any deduction, for that matter—saves far more for taxpayers in the top bracket than for the average family or the poor. Surrey's hypothetical was based on tax rates in effect at the time, when the top marginal rate was 70%. But even today, with a top rate of 39.6%, the mortgage interest deduction has the same reverse Robin Hood impact. It saves a rich family $396 for every $1,000 of mortgage interest due—but saves zero for low-income homeowners. Those who least need help get a subsidy, while those who most need it get nothing. This is a common pattern for tax expenditures. "The unfairness of the deduction," Surrey wrote, "in its favoritism for upper bracket taxpayers is . . . evident."

Tax expenditures take several different forms, and the structure of each tax break determines how it affects different groups of taxpayers. As Surrey taught, a deduction or an exemption from income gives a larger tax benefit to the rich, which he considered unfair favoritism. A tax credit, in contrast, gives the same benefit to all taxpayers.

If a tax preference is an "exemption" or an "exclusion" from income, then it reduces the amount of income you have to report. A "deduction" works the same way; a certain amount is deducted from the taxpayer's actual income, to make his taxable income smaller. The tax rate is then applied to the taxable income; the higher the rate you have to pay, the more you save with each deduction. The result: a high-bracket family, paying 39.6% of taxable income, will get a larger write-off than a low-income family paying at the 10% rate. This benefits the rich more than the poor. The low-income taxpayers who need a tax cut the most actually get the least.

In contrast, a tax preference that is structured as a "credit" gives the average earner and the upper-bracket earner the same amount of tax savings. A credit is subtracted from the tax that is due after all the deductions and exemptions have been applied. Thus a tax credit of $100 will cut the taxes of the richest families by $100 and cut the average family's tax bill by the same amount, $100.

STANLEY SURREY'S NOTION OF tax breaks as "expenditures" caught on as well with the economists at the World Bank and the OECD. Those organizations quickly endorsed this American innovation and urged their member countries to tally tax expenditures annually in order to "clarify the trade-off between tax and spending programs in budget decisions." Today more than two dozen of the world's richest countries issue public reports each year on their tax expenditures. (South Korea compiles the same information but does not make it public.)[3]

Despite its prestigious academic pedigree and its broad international acceptance, the very concept of "tax expenditures" remains controversial, in the United States and in many other countries. The basic idea grates on people. If big government allows me to keep some of my own money in my wallet through a tax exemption, how can you call that "spending" by the government? It was never the government's money to spend! Professor Surrey's idea has been ridiculed from both right and left, by conservative Republicans and by Jon Stewart on *The Daily Show*. The British parliamentarian Stafford Northcote offered a famous denunciation of the concept: "The right honorable gentleman, if he *took* £5 out of the pocket of a man with £100, would put the case as if he *gave* the man £95."

In the United States, the chairman of the Senate Finance Committee, the generally mild-mannered senator Orrin Hatch of Utah, was moved to uncharacteristic heat on this topic in a speech on the Senate floor. "The federal government cannot 'spend' money that it never touched and never possessed," the senator complained. "What tax expenditures do is let people keep more of their own money." Hatch argued that the whole idea of a "tax expenditure" was just a gimmick used by liberals to justify tax increases. "When tax hike proponents say 'We are giving businesses and individuals all this money in tax expenditures,' they are incorrectly assuming that the government has the money to give in the first place, when in fact it does not."[4]

Whatever the nomenclature, the annual reports from the Treasury Department and from finance ministries around the world make it clear that some of the rich democracies forgo large sums of potential revenue through tax preferences. On the personal income tax, a broad range of exemptions, deductions, credits, and so on reduce Great Britain's tax revenues by 50% from what they would be without all those preferences. Italy's revenues are 40.6% lower than they would be if all the credits and such were eliminated; in Spain, 34.6% lower; in Austria, 30% lower. In the United States, revenue is 37% lower than it would be without all the tax breaks. That means Congress could cut everybody's tax rate by 37% and take in the same amount of revenue if we didn't have all those tax expenditures.

For sheer creativity, the Italian income tax code is the world champion at inventing new credits. Like the United States and many other countries, Italy gives a tax deduction for paying the mortgage on your home. But the Italians also get a tax break for buying a home, renting a home, or renting an apartment for a child away at college. There is an income tax credit in Italy for "the annual subscription of children between 5 and 18 years old to gyms, swimming pools, and sporting clubs." Any Italian who gets a salary or a pension from the Vatican is exempt from income tax. Italy gives a tax credit for life insurance premiums.[5]

BUT THIS LEVEL OF tax expenditure is not a natural or a necessary aspect of a tax regime. Many developed countries—those that have broadened the base by eliminating tax expenditures—have minimal revenue losses. New Zealand's income tax revenues are just 2% less than what they would be without any preferences. Denmark, Norway, France, and Germany are other countries that have a small revenue loss due to giveaways in the tax code. When these governments feel a need to provide subsidies to a particular group of people or businesses, the parliament passes a bill for a new spending program. That makes the whole process more transparent, it simplifies the tax code, and it means tax rates can be lower than they would be with a plethora of loopholes.

In the United States, the cost of tax expenditures is greater today than when Stanley Surrey's blockbuster report came out in 1968. In fiscal year 2014, the total of tax preferences in the personal and corporate income tax came to $1.17 trillion, far more than any single government program. The breakdown looks like this:

Federal spending by program, 2014	
Social Security	$845 billion
Medicare and Medicaid	$807 billion
Defense (including Afghanistan)	$696 billion
Civilian departments and agencies	$582 billion
Tax expenditures	$1,169 billion

Source: Office of Management and Budget, Budget of the United States, Fiscal Year 2014, Historical Tables 8.5

The United States offers tax breaks for contributing to charity, taking a night-school course, paying local property tax, growing sugarcane, moving to a new city for a job, replanting a forest, insulating the attic, paying off a mortgage, destroying old farm equipment, employing Native Americans, commuting to work by bicycle (but only for a bike that is "regularly used for a substantial portion of travel," whatever that means),[6] or buying a plug-in hybrid sports car. Congress's Joint Committee on Taxation counts more than two hundred separate tax expenditures.

Because many of these giveaways replicate the kinds of benefits provided by governments in left-leaning European countries, tax expenditures have been called America's "hidden welfare state." That is, we give people welfare through the tax code even when we aren't willing to provide the same kind of support by sending a welfare check.

When our family lived in Great Britain, we received a check each month from the government for something called "child benefit." We still had two kids under eighteen then, and we got about $100 per month for each of them. They pay you just to have children! That sure seemed like the European welfare state to me; can you imagine the U.S. government sending welfare checks to an upper-bracket family like ours just for having kids? In fact, we do—through the tax code. An American taxpayer gets a tax exemption for each dependent child under eighteen (plus any child over nineteen who is still a student); in 2016, it was $4,050 per child. For me, the tax saving I got in the United States from the exemption was just about the same amount as those "child benefit" checks I got in Europe. (Beyond that exemption, there's also a "child credit" provision that cuts the tax bill by $1,000 per child for many American families.)

Following Stanley Surrey's example, the Treasury Department reports each year on how much revenue is lost due to each specific tax break. This annual report is a long and nearly impenetrable document that seems designed to make the information as opaque as possible. In its 2015 report, Treasury listed 169 specific tax breaks, including "Exclusion of interest on life insurance savings" ($17.1 billion), "multi-period timber growing costs" ($360 million), and the "Indian Employment Credit" ($30 million). But the report does not bother to show the total cost of all these giveaways; the department's explanation is that the law requires a "list" of tax expenditures but not a "total." (As noted above, if you add them all up, they total about $1.17 trillion.) To complicate things further, the congressional Joint Committee on Taxation issues its own yearly report on tax expenditures, with figures that are different from the Treasury's in many cases.

Every year, the number one exemption is the rule that says the premium your employer pays for health insurance is not counted as taxable income; for 2016, the Treasury Department said, this would cost the government $216 billion. The economists say this makes no sense; paying an employee's insurance premium is the same thing as paying an employee's wages and should be taxed the same way. Other countries that have private health insurance companies generally do not allow this tax exclusion. In any case, health insurance is so much cheaper in the other developed countries that exclusion would amount to a fairly small revenue loss. It's only the United States that adds $200 billion to its deficit every year through this tax break.

After that huge one, the major tax expenditures in the Internal Revenue Code involve deductions for homeowners, tax breaks for retirement savings, the decision not to tax corporate profits that are held overseas, and the deduction for charitable contributions.

To BROADEN THE BASE and lower the rates, we have to get rid of these costly expenditures. It should be easy to go after hard-to-defend tax breaks like the credit for buying a $105,000 sports car or for destroying an obsolete tractor. There are dozens of these loopholes in the code that could not be justified if they were proposed as outright spending programs. Unfortunately, most of the obviously stupid tax expenditures involve a relatively small loss of revenue. If we're going to make any serious headway against the avalanche of giveaways in our tax code—so that the rates can be cut—we will have to get rid of some of the biggest and best-liked tax deductions as well.

Probably the most popular tax break in the Internal Revenue Code is the deduction for charitable contributions. Everybody likes the idea of rewarding people for being generous. You give money to a charity; you deduct that amount from your income; you end up paying less tax. The charity gets money it needs for good causes; the taxpayer saves some money on April 15. The downside is that government takes in $50 billion less revenue every year. (It's possible, though, that the charitable contribution might also save the government some money, by funding a public purpose that would otherwise be left to government.)

This deduction probably matters more to Americans than anybody else because we give more to charity than the citizens of any other country. And the United States has more officially recognized charities—that is, organizations that earn a tax deduction for their contributors—than any other country. The *Chronicle of Philanthropy* says the number of different organizations eligible to receive tax-deductible contributions is over one million; in other countries, the number tends to be a few dozen.

At first blush, the notion of encouraging people through the tax code to give to charity seems as pure and sweet as mother's milk. But the whole idea turns sour when you look at it closely; that's why more and more developed countries have sharply limited this deduction or dropped it altogether.

One major sore point is that the charitable deduction is a deduction and thus saves far more for upper-bracket taxpayers than for the average worker. If a woman so rich that she is taxed at the top rate (39.6%) gives $100 to her church, that gift will reduce her tax bill by $39.60. A woman at the medium income, paying tax at a rate of 15%, will save only $15 for the same $100 contribution. This is the problem Professor Surrey used to illuminate for his students: "The unfairness of the deduction in its favoritism for upper bracket taxpayers is . . . evident."

But that's not the only problem with the deduction for charitable donations:

—Most people who give to charity get no deduction for it. To take advantage of the charitable deduction, you have to fill out the IRS form for "itemized deductions." But only about one-third of all taxpayers use this form. The majority of taxpayers just take the standard deduction, which gives you the same deduction whether or not you give money to charity. Therefore, most people get no tax benefit for giving to charity. The millionaire who gives enough to get her name on a dorm at her alma mater gets a big tax break, while the median-income mom who gives $50 to the local PTA gets none.

—The most common forms of charity don't qualify. In a nation of churchgoers, putting cash in the collection plate at weekly services is probably the most common way people give money, along with giving a homeless panhandler a dollar or dropping $5 into the pot to help fund the school baseball team. But these familiar acts of charity will not get you a tax deduction. Cash contributions don't count.

—It's widely abused. If you write a check for $100 to the Boy Scouts, or give an old car to the public radio station, these contributions are easy to value. But the richest taxpayers often make charitable donations with a cash value that is hard to determine—land or buildings or works of art. The most common problem here comes in gifts of paintings or sculpture to museums. To determine the value of the contribution, the donor or the museum often turns to an "independent" appraiser. The appraiser's fees are paid by the donor or the museum. And the appraiser knows, of course, that those who pay her fee want to claim the highest plausible value; that way, the donor gets the largest possible tax deduction, and the museum can boast about its fabulously expensive new acquisition.

This situation is abused so frequently that tax collection agencies around the world have had to set up their own appraisal offices; in the United States, the IRS has the Office of Art Appraisal Services and the Art Advisory Panel. In about two-thirds of the cases it reviews, the IRS finds that the donated work of art is worth significantly less than the donor's appraisal. That finding, in turn, often leads to an extended and expensive battle in court.[7]

In addition to excessive valuations, donors of artworks have devised various stratagems that let them take the deduction without actually giving up the art. One gambit is called fractional giving. This means that you give the painting to a museum for a fraction of the year (maybe for three months, while you're at your summer home in the South of France), take a tax deduction for this contribution, and then put the painting back in your living room. Congress cracked down somewhat on this scheme in 2008. That reform prompted rich donors to create a different dodge: the "private museum." This means you build a museum next to your house, sometimes way out in the country, with no sign on the door. You give your art to this "private museum" and take a tax deduction—for giving art to yourself. The Glenstone museum, for example, has provided its founder with major tax deductions since it was created in 2006. It is situated on the estate of its owner in Potomac, Maryland, with a gate and a guardhouse to protect the privacy of the collection.[8]

—It's not easy to define a "charity." When Congress wrote the law setting forth which organizations qualify as charities, it threw in everything but the kitchen sink. If any group's activities are "religious, educational, charitable, scientific, literary, testing for public safety, to foster national or international amateur sports competition or prevention of cruelty to animals," it qualifies. Some of the outfits to which contributions are tax deductible are one-room soup kitchens run by volunteers in the church basement; others are huge and highly prosperous organizations. Your gift to Harvard University, for example, is treated as a deductible contribution to "charity," even though Harvard is sitting on an endowment of $37 billion and earns more than $1 billion each year in the securities markets.

The IRS rules list twenty-eight different forms of "exempt organizations." Some are eligible for tax-deductible contributions; some are not. If you send money to the Heritage Foundation, a Washington,

D.C., think tank that advocates conservative policies, that's deductible, but if you send money to Heritage Action for America, an organization that has the same address and campaigns for the same conservative policies, that's not deductible. Keeping track of which organizations are really charities, and which ones are actually business or political operations masquerading as "social welfare" operations, is a full-time job for several hundred IRS staffers. The designations change so often that the IRS finally had to stop printing its list of authorized charities and switch instead to an online document so that it could be updated daily.[9] Because Congress, as usual, failed to make clear distinctions in the laws it wrote, the task of distinguishing charities from non-charities falls to IRS bureaucrats. This became the subject of angry political uproar in 2013 when it was charged that IRS staffers were singling out Tea Party groups for extra scrutiny when they applied for tax-exempt status. To avoid future controversies, the IRS today grants "exempt" status to 95% of all the groups that apply for it.[10]

ALL THOSE ISSUES SHOULD be enough to demonstrate that the deduction for charitable contributions is costly, unfair, and easy to abuse. But there's actually a more fundamental problem with this particular deduction: It doesn't work. Although it costs governments a lot of money in the form of reduced revenues, it doesn't do what it is supposed to do.

The purpose of this deduction is to encourage people to give more and thus increase the money available for charity. But there's no evidence—no studies, no data—that shows people contribute more because of the tax deduction. In the United States, the last few decades seem to show the opposite. When tax rates go up—which makes the deduction more valuable to the giver—contributions stay about the same. When tax rates go down—so that each contribution is less valuable on Tax Day—contributions stay about the same. With the big 1986 tax cut, the top rate fell from 50% to 28%. This made a contribution far less valuable in tax terms, and many charitable groups predicted a disastrous drop in donations. In fact, the effect was minimal. Contributions dropped slightly for a couple of years after the 1986 rate cut and then started going up again.

Still, the politics of eliminating the charitable deduction can be difficult. Here, too, we can learn from other nations. Most developed democracies that used to allow a full deduction for gifts to charity have sharply curtailed or eliminated this problematic tax break.

One common approach is to put a limit on how much any taxpayer can write off for charitable gifts in a single year. The United States has such a limit; generally, people can deduct no more than 50% of their income for contributions. Other countries have made the limit stricter. In much of Europe, the total of deductible contributions can't exceed 20% of income, which means a much lower loss of revenue; in the Netherlands, the limit is 10%. To deal with Professor Surrey's "unfairness" problem—giving the rich a bigger write-off than average earners who contribute the same amount—some countries (for example, Canada and France) give a tax credit, rather than a deduction, for contributions. Most developed countries have a much tighter definition of what constitutes a "charity" that is eligible for deductible contributions. The U.S. roster, more than a million approved charities, runs for scores of pages on the Internet; Japan's entire list of eligible charities fits on one side of one sheet of paper. Japan also gives a tax deduction for contributions to government agencies, but that list is also fairly short.

The best way, though, to avoid the unfairness, the abuses, and the revenue loss from the charitable deduction is to get rid of this deduction altogether. Austria, Finland, Ireland, Italy, Sweden, and Switzerland all have flourishing charity sectors, even after they took away the tax break for contributions; New Zealand, of course, got rid of it in that first base-broadening exercise in the 1980s. None of these countries saw any significant drop in charitable contributions. All over the world, people contribute mainly because of a belief in a particular

cause or because of a basic human desire to help others. Getting a tax
break is, at most, a minor motivation. The tax deduction for charitable contributions cheapens the charitable impulse by implying that
you and I wouldn't give a dime to charity unless we got a little financial gain on the side.

AN EVEN LARGER DRAIN on tax revenues comes from the several
provisions in the tax code that benefit homeowners. Most countries
provide some tax relief for homeowners; the United States is the most
generous of all in this area. Just like the charity deduction, the homeowner provisions are extremely popular. Economically, though, they
don't make much sense. Like the charity deduction, the benefits for
home ownership are strongly skewed to the richest taxpayers. Millions of homeowners—those who don't itemize deductions—get little
or no benefit from the homeowner deductions. Like the charity deduction, they cost a lot in lost revenue; the Treasury Department estimates about $200 billion in 2016. And like the charity deduction,
these tax breaks are unnecessary. They are supposed to encourage
home ownership, but countries that don't allow these deductions have
ownership rates as high as ours.

The economists say that the tax code benefits homeowners in
four ways.

1. The most obscure is something called "imputed rent." If you live
   in the home you own, but don't pay rent to the owner (yourself),
   economic theory holds that you are earning "income" in the form
   of free rent. Some countries—for example, Belgium, the Netherlands, Norway, and Sweden—actually compute how much this
   free rent is worth and tax it as income. In the United States, the
   Treasury Department lists the non-taxation of imputed rent on its
   official list of tax expenditures. The United States has never taxed

imputed rent, though, and surely never will, because homeowners would explode if any government ever tried it.

2. As a general rule, the prices of homes tend to rise over time. When a house is sold, therefore, the homeowner usually gets more than he paid for the house in the first place. This is considered a "capital gain"—a profit on a financial investment. But most people think of their home as a different kind of "investment" from stocks and bonds. And even if a family made a big profit selling their house, most of that money would be needed to pay for the house they had to buy to replace the one they just sold. Accordingly, the tax code reflects that general belief that this is not a typical kind of capital gain. As of 2016, a family paid capital gains on the sale of a residence only if the profit was more than $500,000, so most Americans were exempt from this tax. The Treasury says this cost $39.6 billion in lost revenue in 2016.

3. Homeowners who itemize deductions are allowed to deduct the amount they paid on state and local property taxes on the home. Homeowners love this deduction, of course, but most serious proposals for tax reform—including the Bush plan of 2005 and the Obama plan of 2010—have called for it to be eliminated. After all, it gives a significant tax break to homeowners but nothing to renters making the same income. It gives the owner of a million-dollar house, who may not need tax relief, a much bigger tax deduction than it gives to a less wealthy family living in a simpler house. And it encourages states and cities to increase their property tax levels; people who live in high-tax states get a better deduction than those where property taxes are lower. The deduction for property taxes will cost the Treasury some $36 billion in lost revenue in 2016.

4. The big gorilla of homeowner tax breaks is the deduction for mortgage interest, which reduces income tax revenues by about $100 bil-

lion each year. That is, this one tax deduction costs more than the budgets of the departments of Agriculture, Commerce, Energy, the Interior, and the Treasury combined. Like other deductions, it is a particular boon to those in the upper brackets; about three-quarters of all the deductions for home mortgage interest go to taxpayers making more than $100,000 per year. About half of American homeowners take the standard deduction, which means they get no tax break for paying their mortgage.

While this deduction is promoted by realtors and mortgage bankers as a boon to home buyers, it is just as likely to make a home purchase more difficult. All studies (except those funded by the real estate industry) find that a mortgage interest deduction raises the price of a house. When the OECD investigated the impact of the mortgage interest deduction in wealthy countries where it is still in place, it concluded that "new purchasers . . . are not necessarily the beneficiaries of these tax provisions," because the interest deduction forces them to pay an increased price. Whatever benefit a buyer might get from the tax break is just about completely offset by the higher price of the house.[11] So the deduction doesn't do what it is supposed to do—make it easier for people to buy a home.

Because of the large cost of this tax break and the small impact, Congress has repeatedly tried to take it away. This always fails, because of effective lobbying from realtors and bankers. But Congress has managed to put limits, sort of, on this write-off. It applies only to mortgages up to $1 million, and you get a write-off for the mortgage on only two of your houses, but no more than that. Clearly, these are not limits that touch any average homeowner. Other countries have imposed similar restrictions. Some have made the preference for mortgage interest a credit rather than a deduction, which means everybody gets the same tax break.

But Australia, Canada, Germany, Great Britain, Israel, Japan, the Netherlands, and New Zealand, for example, have no deduction for mortgage interest at all. Yet eliminating the deduction seems to have no impact on home ownership. In all the industrialized democracies, the rate of home ownership is just about the same. Roughly 65% of families own their home in countries that have the mortgage interest deduction, and about 65% of families own their home in countries that do not.

Just like the charitable deduction, though, the write-off for mortgage interest is hard to get rid of. It has been part of the tax code for so long (more than a hundred years) that people see it as a basic right. Beyond that, eliminating the deduction would probably reduce the price a buyer will pay—at least in the short run—and reducing the price of houses would depress the value of what is most Americans' largest investment. There are ways to make the change gradually, so as to protect the investment of current homeowners. Still, anybody who tries to get rid of this tax break faces a severe political challenge.

Some twenty years ago, however, Great Britain figured out a politically palatable way. Until the 1980s, Brits could write off mortgage interest of just about any amount on any number of houses; just as in the United States, this created a boon to the wealthy and a significant revenue loss for the government. And then, gradually, the Inland Revenue began snipping away at this deduction. At first, the size of the mortgage was limited so that it applied only to mortgages of about $75,000 or less; you could take a deduction for interest up to a loan of that amount but no more. This change cut the deduction for the richest homeowners, but it had only a moderate impact on most British taxpayers. So it was fairly easy to enact. In 1988, the deduction was limited to a mortgage on only one house per family; this, too, had minimal impact on average earners, and it, too, was fairly easy to enact. Beginning in 1992, the government ruled that the deduction could not reduce the tax due by more than 25%. That meant upper-bracket taxpayers got less of a deduction than they had before, but average earners did not. Over the next eight years, the deduction was reduced to 20%, then 15%, then 10%, then 5%. Each change caused a protest, but the bottom-line difference each time was so small for most taxpayers that complaints were muted. Finally, in 2000, the deduction was reduced from 5% to zero. One of the most popular of all tax breaks was completely eliminated.

Because this change occurred during a decade when home prices were rising in most of Britain, few homeowners saw the value of their investment decline. Indeed, the Labour Party government that presided over the demise of the mortgage interest deduction easily won the next two national elections. And of course, tax policy experts advocating the BBLR principle were thrilled. Paul Johnson, the director of the Institute for Fiscal Studies, a prestigious London think tank, related the whole story to me with a tone of sheer delight. "This was a triumph of tax policy!" he declared. "The fact that it proved possible . . . gradually to phase it out is good evidence that reform really is possible even when the tax break being abolished is popular and many losers are created."

THE ELIMINATION OF ANY "tax expenditure" will of course create some losers. The beneficiaries, of course, will always make the best case for their particular tax credit, no matter how "ludicrous" it may look to others. One man's "loophole" is another man's "essential provision to provide jobs and growth."

As a general rule, those who advocate the BBLR approach want to reduce tax rates for everybody. But some economists and political figures favor a different reform: they want to reduce rates, but only for taxpayers in the upper brackets. This concept is called a flat tax, and it has its champions in the United States. During the 2016 presidential primaries, five of the Republican candidates proposed a flat-tax regime. But would it work?

6.

FLAT BROKE

Good King Wenceslas looked out, as the great Christmas carol tells us, on the Feast of Stephen, when the snow lay round about, deep and crisp and even. To this extent, at least, the legend of King Wenceslas rings true. The Feast of Stephen—that is, St. Stephen's Day in the Roman Catholic Church—is celebrated on December 26. At that time of year, the province of Bohemia—that is, the western section of the nation we now call the Czech Republic, where Wenceslas ruled early in the tenth century—is normally blanketed in snow. And the carol's story of how the good king trudged through the snowbanks, "though the frost was cruel," to carry food and fuel to a starving peasant rings true as well, because Wenceslas is remembered as a wise and benevolent sovereign, a saint of the church, and one of the great figures in Czech history.

Today Good King Wenceslas looks out over a bustling boulevard in the center of Prague known as Václavské náměstí, or Wenceslas Square. As befits a beloved national champion, Wenceslas is honored with a larger-than-life statue at the top of the square that depicts the good king mounted on an imposing stallion. Along the boulevard beneath the stallion's feet, throngs of people are strolling and shopping and chomping away at the local delicacy, a huge sausage named for the good king: the Wenceslasworst.

But the Czechs have a mischievous sense of humor, which extends even to the point of making fun of their national hero. There's a pizza joint on Wenceslas Square, catering to tourists, that features a menu item called the Good King Wenceslas Christmas Eve Pizza. The description: "Deep pan, crisp and even." A few blocks from that big equestrian statue, there's a rather different image of the good king. This one is a statue of a horse suspended upside down from the ceiling— with Wenceslas mounted precariously on its belly, just about to fall off.

"That horse hanging there, that tells you of course something about the Czech sense of a joke," said my friend Radim Boháček, an economist who learned almost perfect English while a grad student at the University of Chicago. "Like, they take their greatest king and hang him from the roof downside up."

FOR THE CZECHS AND their neighbors in more than a dozen eastern European countries, the whole world turned downside up in 1991, when the Soviet Union fell apart. A cluster of former Soviet republics and Soviet satellite nations suddenly became free and independent countries. The end of the cold war was so quick and unexpected—the experts at the CIA utterly failed to see it coming—that people and politicians on both sides of the former Iron Curtain were left up in the air about its meaning. For one man, that metaphor was literally true: the Soviet cosmonaut Sergei Krikalev, who blasted into earth's orbit in 1991. While poor Krikalev was orbiting the earth aboard the U.S.S.R. space station, the U.S.S.R. ceased to exist. Suddenly he was a spaceman without a country. When he returned to earth in early 1992, the landing zone that had been the Soviet Union's space center was in a newly independent nation, Kazakhstan.

All along the route of the fallen Iron Curtain—from Estonia on the Baltic to Slovenia on the Adriatic—newly installed leaders set about the task of creating democratic governments and capitalist economies. Determined to erase the residue of their dreary Communist decades, they happily accepted all the money and advice they could get from the wealthy members of the European Union to their west. They revamped their banking systems and eagerly sought investors who could create private corporations within their borders.

In the process, they turned tax policy downside up as well. Over a decade beginning in 1994, most of the newly independent nations of eastern Europe adopted a radical new approach to taxation—a much-debated but little-tested concept known as the flat tax.

THE FLAT TAX WAS a new idea that had many parents. Some heavy-duty economists armed with computer simulations promoted this approach, on both sides of the Atlantic. They were joined by politicians, mainly on the right, who sought a tax-reform plan that would appeal to the wealthiest donors and yet sound fair to everybody. In the 2012 presidential campaign, three of the top Republican candidates strongly supported a flat tax; the eventual GOP nominee that year, Mitt Romney, gave it a characteristically Romneyesque endorsement. "The flat tax is an important idea that we will have to consider," he said, thereby managing to sound positive without committing to anything. Republicans embraced the idea again in the 2016 campaign; the presidential hopefuls Rand Paul, Carly Fiorina, Ben Carson, Ted Cruz, and Rick Perry all came out for a flat rate of income tax for everybody. They didn't agree on what the flat rate should be—their proposals ranged from 10% to 19%—but they all argued that it would provide a huge boost to the U.S. economy.

For all this support, though, there is something less than complete agreement about what a flat tax would look like. In turns out that this seemingly simple idea comes in many different flavors.

At the purest level, a flat tax means everybody pays the same flat amount of tax, regardless of income or circumstances. At first blush, this might sound fair. Everybody pays exactly the same—what could be more equal than that? In practice, however, all countries have concluded that it is inequitable to ask a hotel maid earning $20,000 per year to pay just as much in tax as a hotel owner taking in $2 million annually. One advanced democracy, Great Britain, actually tried this pure form of flat taxation in 1990, when Prime Minister Margaret Thatcher instituted her "Community Charge." This system, generally known as the "poll tax," required that everybody in a given community pay the same amount annually for local government services. A tenant in a tiny studio apartment with a bathroom down the hall was expected to pay £250 per year to the city government, and a plutocrat living in a twenty-five-room mansion paid the same £250. Naturally, this system was a big hit with mansion dwellers, but lower-bracket taxpayers responded with outrage. They refused to pay; they threw bricks through the windows of the tax office; they rioted in the streets. Facing this furious backlash, Thatcher's flat-tax plan was quickly abolished, and the Iron Lady herself lost her job as head of government after a mutiny by members of her own party.

More commonly, however, the notion of a flat tax means not a flat *amount* of tax paid but a flat *rate* of tax; that is, everybody pays the same percentage of his income to the government. In its most ambitious form, the flat tax is a plan that sets the same flat rate for several different forms of tax. A good example was the vaunted "9-9-9" plan set forth in the 2012 Republican presidential primaries by a short-lived candidate named Herman Cain. Cain's tax proposal called for a personal income tax with a single rate of 9%, a corporate tax rate of 9%, and a federal sales tax of 9%. Cain himself offered no detail on how much money the "9-9-9" tax might raise; the few analysts who studied the plan concluded it would drastically cut revenues and thus drastically increase the federal deficit. With minimal support from GOP voters, Cain ended his presidential campaign six months after it began, and the "9-9-9" plan was not heard from again.

The most comprehensive and sophisticated blueprint for a flat tax was designed by two respected academics, Robert Hall and Alvin Rabushka of the Hoover Institution, a think tank based at Stanford

University. Their plan combines a tax on corporate earnings with an individual income tax on wages in which everybody pays the same rate of tax (in the latest version of their idea, they set the rate at 19%); it also limits or eliminates some of the most popular deductions and exemptions in our current tax system. The Hall-Rabushka proposal is intricately designed and so complicated that you practically need a graduate degree in economics to understand how it works.[1] Accordingly, it has never gained much popular support.

The form of flat tax that most backers of the idea have in mind is something much simpler. It's an income tax with a single rate that applies to every taxpayer. The income tax in most countries has a graduated, or "progressive," rate structure so that high-income people pay a higher percentage of their income in tax than poor people do. In the United States, there are seven different income brackets, with a different tax rate applied in each case. The rates run from 10% for a married couple with a taxable income of $17,850 to 39.6% for a couple when their income exceeds $464,850. That means the rich couple is paying considerably more in tax, but the rich also have much more left over after the tax is paid. A couple who pay 10% on a taxable income of $17,850 will have just $16,065 remaining for all their expenses during the year; the $465,000 couple, even though they will pay tax at a much higher rate, will still have more than $300,000 left to spend after the tax bill is paid.

The single-rate tax would do away with the seven graduated tax brackets and their seven different rates. It calls on the millionaire and her maid to pay the same percentage of their income in tax. Flat-tax backers say this is eminently fair; after all, everybody pays the same rate.

Advocates also argue that the single rate makes taxpaying simpler; you avoid the pesky business of figuring out which bracket you fall into and which rate you have to pay. But this argument for simplicity is something of a red herring. For taxpayers, figuring out what rate to pay is a tiny part of the complexity of filing a tax return. The hard part—the job that takes days or weeks of digging through W-2s and

1099-Bs and multiplying by 0.159, unless line 16 is greater than line 42(q)—is figuring out what your taxable income is. Once you get that number and enter it on line 43 of Form 1040, the task of determining your tax rate, and how much tax you have to pay, is a cinch. For most people, a computer makes the calculation in the blink of an eye.

Generally, the advocates of the flat tax focus so tightly on "fairness" and "simplicity" that they fail to mention the most important impact of a flat-rate income tax: it would amount to a major tax break for the richest people in the country and a corresponding tax hike for many average workers. While a progressive income tax tends to reduce the gap between rich and poor, a flat-tax regime would serve to increase economic inequality. Even the self-proclaimed multibillionaire Donald Trump acknowledged this in his 2000 book, *The America We Deserve*. "Only the wealthy," Trump conceded, "would reap a windfall, because a flat-rate tax would shift the tax burden from the richest taxpayers to those in the lower brackets."

To see how this shift would work, consider the case of a corporate CEO and her spouse with a taxable income, after exemptions, of $500,000 (a fairly conservative figure for corporate chieftains these days). Under the 2016 U.S. tax code, with graduated rates, they would have to pay $145,646* in federal income tax. If the United States shifted to a flat tax at a rate of 19%, the couple would pay $95,000 in tax; that is, the flat tax would cut this CEO's tax bill by more than $50,000. In contrast, a secretary at the same firm with taxable income of $50,000, after exemptions, would pay $6,611 under the 2016 tax code.† At a flat rate of 19%, however, the secretary would have to pay $9,500; her tax bill would go up by about 50%. In a flat-tax regime,

---

*See the "Tax Computation Worksheet" on p. 89 of the IRS publication 1040 Instructions 2015. Readers who are quick at math will realize that this tax bill, $145,646, is not 39.6% of the couple's $500,000 income. That's because the top rate only applies to earnings over $450,000; most of the couple's income is taxed at lower rates.

†See the 2015 Tax Tables on pp. 77–89 of the IRS publication 1040 Instructions 2015.

the system would shift the burden to the $50,000 taxpayers; they would have to pay more to make up for the big tax cut given to the $500,000 family.

For this reason, flat-tax plans have generally been promoted by high-income taxpayers, by the think tanks and political candidates they fund, and by their supporters in Congress. Of all the advocates, the most visible and exuberant has been Steve Forbes, an extremely high-income taxpayer who inherited a family business (*Forbes* magazine) and a family fortune from his father, Malcolm Forbes. Steve Forbes ran twice, on a flat-tax platform, for the Republican nomination for president. He made the covers of *Time* and *Newsweek*—in the same week!—promoting the idea. He wrote a book about his plan, titled *Flat Tax Revolution;* it came with a blurb on the cover from (who else?) Donald Trump and a gushing preface written by (who else?) Newt Gingrich.

I know and admire Steve Forbes; he is a kind, friendly guy, a good father, and a successful corporate leader. But I was surprised when he ran for president. Unlike his flamboyant father—Malcolm Forbes flew his own blimps and dated Elizabeth Taylor—Steve is a rather shy and understated gentleman, much happier in an arcane policy debate than in the turmoil of a hand-shaking, baby-kissing political campaign. (For this reason, perhaps, his two campaigns flopped.) When I saw him on the stump, though, I realized why he was running: the presidential campaign was an irresistible opportunity to make his pitch for the flat tax.

"We're going to abolish the IRS!" Steve would shout happily to any voters who would come to his speeches. "Your tax return will be the size of a postcard! You'll file your taxes in five minutes! We'll tear up thousands of pages of IRS regulations! We're finally going to have an income tax that is simple and fair to everybody!"

In his book on the flat tax,[2] Forbes called for a flat rate of 17% on all earned income—that is, salaries and wages paid by an employer. He proposed eliminating many of the taxes that plague wealthy investors, like the capital gains tax and the inheritance tax. He also

proposed to eliminate almost all deductions and exemptions that reduce taxable income, including the popular deductions for mortgage
interest and charitable contributions. Removing all these complicated
exemptions and deductions, he said, would reduce an individual's
tax return to seven lines, which would fit on a postcard. As an added
benefit, he argued, this simplicity would sharply cut government
corruption.

For all the fervid support of Steve Forbes and other influential flat
taxers, the idea never really caught on in the United States or other
wealthy countries. That was due to two basic problems with the
proposal.

First, there's the issue Donald Trump identified: "A flat-rate tax
would shift the tax burden from the richest taxpayers to those in the
lower brackets."

Second, simple mathematics tells us that a flat tax would generate
significantly less government revenue than the current progressive
rate structure. If the rate were set at 17% to 20%, the range proposed
by many flat-tax backers, most Americans would pay less tax, and as
we just saw, the richest Americans would pay vastly less than they do
now. For some people, of course, this reduction in government revenues would be a feature, not a bug. In the abstract, just about everybody likes lower taxes and less government. In practice, though, the
government programs and benefits supported by tax revenues are
highly popular, and just about nobody likes killing them.

Even Steve Forbes and other conservatives who back the flat tax
agree that cutting government revenues would be a problem. So they
have come up with an argument that says cutting taxes wouldn't reduce the revenues that fund government programs. "A flat tax which
combines stark simplicity with a tax cut would generate more, not
less, government revenue," Forbes maintained in his book. This would
occur, the advocates say, because lower taxes would have a dynamic
impact on the economy, prompting people to work more, to start new
companies, to do more business. With this flat-tax boom, people's

incomes would grow so much that they would end up paying more in taxes, even at sharply lower rates. By the same reasoning, a tax increase would lead people to work less and thus shrink the economy.

This argument is referred to as dynamic scoring. Another term for it, offered by the first President Bush, is "voodoo economics." The problem with it is that recent experience doesn't support the purported dynamic result. Tax increases, under the dynamic scoring theory, should stifle economic growth. But it's hard to square that theory with actual experience from the 1990s. At the beginning of that decade, two presidents (George H. W. Bush and Bill Clinton) raised taxes on the upper brackets. The American economy then had its strongest decade in half a century. Similarly, tax cuts don't always have the predicted dynamic effect. At the beginning of the twenty-first century, President George W. Bush pushed through the two biggest tax cuts in American history. This was followed, a few years later, by the nation's worst recession in seventy-five years.

Would a flat tax, then, be a boon to the national economy? It's never been tried in the United States; the federal income tax has had a progressive rate structure since the very beginning. But we do have laboratory experiments on the concept—thanks to those newly minted nations in eastern Europe, where the world turned downside up in the early 1990s.

IN THEIR FIRST HEADY DAYS of independence from Communist rule, of democracy and free markets, the formerly Soviet nations to the west of Russia raced to adopt the prominent features of capitalism. Almost overnight, there were stock markets and chambers of commerce, real estate agents, fast-food chains, and TV ads ("Operators are standing by!"). When I toured several of these new democracies a few years after the fall of the wall, the cities were still largely gray, run-down collections of Soviet-era factories and housing blocks. But there were also some stylish boutiques and multistory department stores offering a wide range of Western goods; there were billboards advertising headache remedies and local brands of vodka.

Independence was a stunning development for all the new nations, but nowhere more so than in the Baltic nation of Estonia. Estonia was one of those European nations that enjoyed its finest hour in the late Middle Ages, when the port city of Tallinn was a bustling center of shipping for a trade union of northern nations known as the Hanseatic League. Over the centuries since then, Estonia had been ruled by Sweden, Poland, Denmark, Russia, Germany, and the U.S.S.R.; one of the tourist attractions today in the capital city is the Museum of Occupations, with a swastika over one door and a red star over the other. For all those conquering powers, the minuscule Baltic state was a minor holding, not worth any attention or expenditure. Being ignored for all those centuries paid off, in a way; with little development in the central city, much of Tallinn survives unscathed from the days of the Hanseatic League. Today the center of Tallinn is one of the world's great repositories of medieval architecture, with a looming old castle and towering church steeples protected by a massive fortress wall around the city.

But Estonia, like the other former Soviet republics, faced major obstacles in the effort to build a capitalist economy. The new nation had virtually no private industry and minimal investment capital to build businesses. Estonia desperately needed to attract private capital and promote business development. In these straits, the national legislature turned to a youthful historian, Mart Laar, to head the government. Laar had become active as a student in Estonia's main center-right political party; the party elders quickly realized that this young volunteer had the intelligence and the personal charm to go far in politics. And he did; he was elected prime minister in 1992, at the age of thirty-two, the youngest head of state in Estonian history. When I met him, two decades later, Laar had ascended to the position of elder statesman; he was the head of Estonia's central bank. But he still had an abundance of charm and a lively sense of humor.

As the nation's new prime minister, Laar turned his attention to the dismal local economy. Having studied capitalist economies in the West, Laar quickly eliminated government price controls and Soviet-style regulation of business. He created legal protections for private property so that landowners would be willing to fund development. He set two important national goals: Estonia would join the European Union and adopt the euro as its currency; both goals were met, early in the twenty-first century. And he changed the nation's complicated tax structure to a single-rate income tax—the flat tax.

As Mart Laar told the story years later, he knew nothing about economics or taxation.

"I had read only one book on economics," he said. "It was Milton Friedman's *Free to Choose.*" (This assertion probably wouldn't stand up to close examination, because Laar had recently earned a Ph.D. in history from the University of Tartu, Estonia's version of Harvard.) In that 1980 volume, a seminal text for a whole generation of free-market economists, Friedman argues for a flat-rate tax on everybody, with minimal exemptions and deductions. Friedman suggests that an income tax at a flat rate of 23.5% would bring in enough revenue to fund all legitimate government operations. But then, Milton Friedman had a rather strict view of what government could legitimately do; he opposed national parks, Social Security, the Food and Drug Administration, public housing, mortgage subsidies, agriculture supports, and so on.[3]

When Laar started talking about a single-rate tax system, internal and external advisers forcefully urged him to drop the idea, he recalled later. "Experts advised against it and said it was a very stupid idea. My finance minister said, 'Don't do it.' The IMF said, 'Don't do it.' But it's not very easy to convince a young person that he is wrong. And I was that kind of young person. So I did it."[4]

In 1994, the Laar government dropped Estonia's three-bracket progressive income tax structure and replaced it with a single 26% tax rate that applied to both personal income and corporate profits. This "radical change," as Laar described it, was electrifying news for proponents of the flat tax in the West; it immediately made an obscure place called Estonia stand out from all the other former Soviet states. "At the stroke of a pen," the *Economist* reported, "this tiny Baltic nation transformed itself from backwater to bellwether, emulated by its neighbors and envied by conservatives in America who long to flatten their own country's taxes."[5]

"The flat tax came to be sort of our national trademark," Professor Viktor Forsberg, an economist at the University of Tartu, told me one frigid January afternoon as we toured the four-hundred-year-old campus. "And it made some economic sense in a country where almost nobody was rich. We all had roughly equal incomes, so we didn't need the equalizing effect you'd get with a progressive tax structure. So why not get some attention with a flat-rate tax?

"For a small, little-noticed country," the professor continued, "it was useful to have a trademark. The problem is that now we're stuck with it. The flat tax eventually outlived its benefit, but it's our trademark, so we can't fix it."

In the first years of Mart Laar's flat tax, the Estonian economy soared. By 1997, the country's GDP growth rate was 11%, making it one of the fastest-growing economies on earth. Growth rates above 7% continued into the first years of the twenty-first century. (Of course, growth rates tend to look large when a country starts from a minuscule base, as Estonia did.) And government revenues went up. "After decrease of the level of taxation, budget revenues did not fall but increased significantly," Mart Laar wrote some years later in his English-language blog. "Introduction of flat-rate proportional income tax helped to boost economic activity and create new working places."[6]

But nobody can measure how much of the post-independence boom in Estonia was due to the experiment with the flat tax. There were a lot of other things going on. In the 1990s, all the eastern

European nations saw significant economic growth with the development of free markets and private property rights. They benefited from the so-called enlargement effect; that is, they all got major financial support from the European Union, which wanted to enlarge its membership by taking in the former Soviet states. They all offered much lower labor costs than the western European nations.

Beyond that, Estonia was the closest of the new nations to Scandinavia, and thus cashed in on investment and tourism—Tallinn opened several lavish Vegas-style casinos—from wealthy countries like Finland and Sweden. Estonia cleverly set its liquor taxes far below Scandinavian rates; as a result, the fast ferries crossing the Baltic a dozen times per day were—and still are today—jammed with Finns, Swedes, and Danes who brought movers' dollies and kids' wagons on the ship to cart home massive quantities of cheap Estonian vodka. With an excellent higher education system, the nation also had a talent for high-tech advances. There wasn't a word in the language for innovation, so the Estonians created one: *innovatsiooni*. They might not have had a word for it, but they knew how to do it. Estonia built up a mini Silicon Valley in the suburbs of Tallinn; among other successes, the Internet phone service called Skype is a product of Estonian *innovatsiooni*. The former dusty backwater is today a global leader in computerizing government functions. You can renew your driver's license, cast a vote, close on a real estate transaction, borrow from the library, or renew a prescription from a computer screen at home. Of course, Estonia has an e-tax system for paperless filing of tax returns; the national tax office says the average time it takes to file a tax return is seven minutes. (When I tried it, with help from a kind Estonian accountant, Jüri Kalda, my fictional return took just under ten minutes, start to finish.)

"It's hard to say, as an economist, that our boom in the '90s was due to any single factor," Professor Forsberg said. "Yes, the flat tax may have helped. But we might have had the same economic result with a more traditional graduated income tax."

To other eastern European nations—Estonia's economic competitors—the flat-tax idea looked to be a winner. Fearful of losing out
on a wave of investment, Estonia's closest neighbors, Lithuania and
Latvia, moved quickly to flat-rate systems—33% in Lithuania and 25%
in Latvia. Russia adopted a flat-rate income tax in 2001, at the bargain-
basement rate of 13%. But then Russia, where tax avoidance was a
national pastime and government revenues drew much more from energy exports, had never relied heavily on the income tax in any case.
Gradually, the idea spread south to Romania, Bulgaria, and Serbia.
And at the dawn of the twenty-first century, the flat tax found an ar-
dent champion in the person of Ivan Mikloš, a young economist in
Slovakia, the eastern half of what had been Czechoslovakia.

The nation of Czechoslovakia, created after World War I, was always something of a shotgun marriage; the Czechs and Slovaks spoke
roughly similar languages but were never really comfortable about
sharing a country. After the Soviet Empire collapsed, the two halves
were free to part company; in 1993, they did, under an arrangement
known as the Velvet Divorce. At the beginning, the Czechs were
significantly more prosperous than their Slovakian cousins to the east.
For most of the 1990s, per capita income in the Czech Republic was
40% higher than in Slovakia. Prague, the Czech capital, is one of Europe's greatest cities, and it did a booming business drawing tourists
from Germany and other western European countries; Slovakia's capital, Bratislava, a smaller, dustier town, attracted few foreign visitors.
In its first decade of independence, Slovakia tried—in vain—to generate economic activity with infrastructure projects and Soviet-style
central planning.

Looking back on those dark days, a Slovakian banker, Vladimir
Vano, told me that the country "made a nice case study in how government spending does not create growth. We built dams and highways and public buildings, but we did not try to build a corporate
sector. And we were just not keeping up economically with our neighbors in central and eastern Europe." The U.S. secretary of state at the

time, Madeleine Albright, called Slovakia "the black hole of Europe." She said that in 1997, and it clearly stung. Some seventeen years later, just about everybody I met in Slovakia reminded me of that insult.

After a severe economic downturn at the end of the 1990s— unemployment reached 20%—Slovakian voters threw out their left- leaning government and installed a center-right party. The new government hired Ivan Mikloš, a smart, no-nonsense economist, to be finance minister, with a mission to revamp the nation's tax system. By the time I met him, Mikloš's party had lost an election, and the former finance minister had been relegated to a minute closet of an office in an annex building of the parliament. Still, he glowed with pride as he described the taxing revolution he brought about in 2004.

"We had then five income tax brackets, with the top rate at 38%," Mikloš told me. "And I was told to be radical, so I began looking at the countries that had gone really radical—gone to the flat tax. I liked it; I liked it a lot, because it seemed simple and it had worked, we thought, in Estonia. We did not have a big polarity of income, so we didn't need stiffly progressive rates to offset inequality, like some countries have. But there was a fiscal dilemma: it just wouldn't bring in enough reve- nue. So I had several no-sleep nights. Finally, I decided to give it a try."

As in New Zealand, Slovakia's tax reform was driven forward by a finance minister who wanted major change and a chief bureaucrat in the ministry who knew how to bring it about. Mikloš, the finance minister, turned to the ministry's chief economist, Ludovit Ódor. "Mr. Mikloš had the general idea, and we designed a system that sig- nificantly simplified our tax regime," Ódor said. "And we did have trouble at first with lower revenues. But the flat tax became a strong marketing tool. We needed to market ourselves as a country that wanted investment. And we got it; Audi, Samsung, Hyundai—lots of companies built factories here."

To enhance the marketing aspect of their new tax system, the Slo- vaks decided on a fairly unusual system, sometimes called a unified tax code. They set the same rate of tax—it was 19%—for the individual income tax, the corporate income tax, and the national sales tax. Herman Cain would have called it the "19-19-19 plan." With this change, the largely forgotten nation of Slovakia became a darling of American conservatives. Both Steve Forbes and George W. Bush made the trek to Bratislava to congratulate Ivan Mikloš. In his flat-tax book, Forbes called Slovakia "the poster child for economic reform."

After the Mikloš reform, Slovakia's statistics were impressive. As foreign manufacturing companies rushed to invest in Slovakia, GDP shot upward, unemployment fell dramatically, and government revenues gradually began to rise. Sleepy Slovakia was suddenly on the world's economic map; it was dubbed the "Tatra Tiger," a name that evokes the nation's largest mountain range. As in Estonia, though, it is not clear how much of this economic growth was due to the tax reform. Slovakia formally joined the European Union in 2004, the same year the 19-19-19 system took effect. The pension system was changed; some industrial regulations were loosened. Even Ludovit Ódor, the Finance Ministry economist who designed the flat tax, agreed that "it is hard to disentangle one factor to say why our economy improved. We did sort of a big bang of reform all at once. So you can't tell which part of performance is due to which part of reform."

The leaders of the Czech Republic were paying close attention to the Slovakian reforms. With a population twice as large as Slovakia's and an established industrial base, the Czechs didn't worry much about economic competition from their eastern neighbor for the first decade after the countries parted ways. Once the Tatra Tiger began to roar, though, a movement developed in Prague calling for the Czech Republic, too, to give up its graduated income tax—it had five rates, ranging from 12% to 42%—and shift to a flat tax.

One of the leaders of this campaign was my friend Radim Boháček, an economist at the premier Czech college, Charles University, and a member of the Czech Academy of Sciences—though he looks more like a heartthrob in some teen romance movie, with a square, bronzed face topped by a sweeping wave of brown hair. Professor Boháček studied economics at the University of Chicago—Milton Friedman's school—and came home to Prague with a Ph.D., nearly perfect English, and a firm belief in the social and economic benefits of low taxes.

"What I learned at Chicago is a basic truth about taxes: rich people will try to of course avoid paying," Boháček told me. "The more you raise the rates, the more incentive rich people have to hire accountants and strategize. Then they can duck just out. What you want is a broad-based tax without exemptions or loopholes—because once you have special exemptions or deductions, people who can afford lawyers will take of course advantage of them."

But Boháček and others who agreed with him gained little headway in left-leaning Czechoslovakia—until the Slovakian experiment and its 19-19-19 tax code began to be noticed in Prague. "All the central and eastern European countries were competing for investment," explained Petr Guth, a tax accountant in Prague. "And we saw that foreign investment heading into Slovakia. Of course you couldn't say it was all due to the 19-19-19 flat-rate system. But the idea just grew here that in order to compete with the rest of eastern Europe, we had to do it, too."

In 2008, the Czechs finally paid heed to the low-tax advocates like Radim Boháček, setting the income tax at a single rate of 15%, at the low end of the range of tax rates in eastern Europe.

By 2008, then, the "Flat Tax Revolution"—as the *Wall Street Journal* described it—had swept nearly all of eastern Europe (Poland was the notable exception). A grid of flat-rate tax regimes among the former Soviet republics and satellites looked like this:

Country	Date begun	Rate
Estonia	1994	26%
Lithuania	1995	33%
Latvia	1995	25%
Russia	2001	13%
Ukraine	2003	13%

Country	Date begun	Rate
Serbia	2003	14%
Slovakia	2004	19%
Georgia	2005	12%
Romania	2005	16%
Czech Republic	2008	15%
Bulgaria	2008	10%

There was some adjustment of the single rate, up or down; Estonia gradually cut its income tax rate from the initial 26% to 21%. Some countries used the switch to a flat tax as a reason to eliminate some well-entrenched deductions and exemptions; some kept these loopholes in place. None of the flat-rate tax countries relied on the income tax alone for revenue; in most of them, the VAT and Social Security taxes levied against payrolls were just as important for raising government revenue as the flat-rate income tax and corporate tax. The flat-tax countries allowed the lowest-income people to escape the income tax entirely, because the tax didn't apply to the first few thousand dollars of annual income. This kept some element of progressivity in a flat-tax regime.

As long as the local and global economies were growing, or at least fairly stable, the flat-tax nations of eastern Europe were doing well. Many were attracting investment; the combination of a low, flat-rate tax system, cheap labor rates, and minimal government regulation drew in large sums of foreign money.

But in the wake of America's Great Recession, the flat tax no longer seemed so sweet. The problem was a predictable one: the flat tax just did not bring in enough money. Financial aid from the European Union, which had been substantial for all of eastern Europe in the first post-Soviet years, began to dry up. The rich nations of western Europe, watching the low-tax countries to their east luring away wealth and investment, were no longer willing to finance nations they came to see as economic competitors.

The flat-tax countries scrambled to offset the reduced revenue. Primarily, they did it by raising other taxes. They raised the VAT rate, which increased consumer prices; nearly all the eastern European countries have sales taxes in the range of 20%. Hungary imposed the world's highest rate of sales tax, 27%, to make up for the revenue shortfall of its flat-rate income tax. Most of the flat-tax countries jacked up their Social Security taxes. In the United States, the Social Security tax on wages is 15%, with half paid by the worker and half paid by the employer.* By comparison, Estonia had to raise its Social Security tax to 34%, all of it paid by the employer. The payroll tax for Social Security in Slovakia went to 47.6%, paid mostly by the employer; in the Czech Republic, the tax was 45.5%, with the worker paying 11.5% and the employer paying 34%. Russia, in a throwback to its Communist days, chose to soak rich investors. The Russians doubled the tax on dividend and investment income to 30% so that people who made their money in the stock market paid significantly more in tax than people working in a factory or on a farm.

Even champions of the flat tax began to despair. "The point we had always worried about," said Ludovit Ódor, the architect of Slovakia's 19-19-19 plan, "was finding the correct rate for a flat-rate tax. And after the crisis, we were not really able to do that. In practice, you can't find a single tax rate that is high enough to raise the revenues you need but low enough for average working people to afford." As a fiscal matter, governments needed the higher revenues that would come from imposing higher taxes on the upper brackets. As a political matter, there was also a question of fairness. The boom years at the start of the twenty-first century had created a class of "oligarchs"— that is, newly rich investors and industrialists—in many of the former Soviet countries. This created political demands to go after the wealthy and make them pay more.

Countries in eastern Europe began to rethink the idea of the flat

---

*Note: the employee also pays the Medicare tax.

tax. The pattern was similar in several countries. After the global recession of 2008–9, they largely adopted tough austerity measures, including wage and benefit cuts, at the direction of the European Union and the International Monetary Fund. As national economies began to revive, in 2011 and 2012, voters lashed out at the austerity regime and began electing left-leaning governments that promised to raise taxes on the rich to fund more government programs.

In Slovakia, the leftist party leader, Robert Fico, became prime minister in the 2012 election after promising to return to a progressive income tax. Fico made the classic argument for graduated rates: it is fair, he said, that the richest, who benefit from many government services, should pay a little more for the common good. When Fico's party came to power, his finance minister, Peter Kažimír, kept the 19% tax rate for most people but added a second bracket, at 25%, for those earning more than $53,000 a year—a princely sum in Slovakia.

When I met Peter Kažimír, at a café on Bratislava's medieval central square, I thought at first that this friendly young man must be a driver or an aide to the finance minister. With an easy smile, a good grasp of the millennial generation's English idiom, and an untamed bush of brown hair, he seemed more like an earnest grad student than a senior member of the national government. In fact, he turned out to be an iron-willed politician who came to office determined to do away with the flat-rate tax no matter who raised hell about it.

"We had campaigned on a promise of progressive taxation, and we had won with it," Kažimír recalled later. "So I thought at first it would be easy to add an additional bracket for the highest incomes. But there was a backlash—furious!—from the business community and the conservative parties. Well, we were going to add another bracket; that was settled. So I had to come up with a way to deal with all the opposition."

To cool public anger over scrapping the flat tax, Kažimír devised a policy that I have not found in any other country: a special surtax on the people who write and administer the tax laws. Thus, in addition to creating a new tax bracket for the wealthiest Slovakians, the 2012 tax-reform act stipulated that members of the national parliament and the prime minister's cabinet would pay 5% higher rates than anybody else in the country. "We did it as a gesture of solidarity," Kažimír said. "The message was, okay, if the parliament is going to raise taxes, we'll see to it that members of parliament pay more than anybody else.

"It's the same kind of political bullshit you probably have in your Congress," Kažimír told me. "We needed the extra revenue. And if the way to get it passed was to stick members of parliament with a higher rate—well, I was like, let's do it."

The next domino to fall was the Czech Republic, which had been the last of the eastern nations to adopt a flat tax. Just as in Slovakia, a left-leaning party emerged on top in a national election, in the fall of 2013, on a promise to dump the flat-rate tax. In 2014, the Czechs introduced a second, higher bracket for the largest incomes—a tax rate of 22% for people earning more than $61,000 per year (which is to say, the 1% of the Czech population). The new government referred to this 7% additional rate for the rich as a "solidarity tax." The implication was that rich people could demonstrate a sense of solidarity, a sense of community, by paying more to fund programs that helped everyone.

Efforts from the left to scrap the flat-rate tax have grown stronger in several other flat-tax countries as well, leading some observers to suggest that the experiment will not last much longer. "All the countries need more revenue," said Andreas Peichl of the German think tank IZA. "And there is a feeling that the economic crisis hurt the poor but spared the rich, and therefore the rich should pay more. But it's not easy to do that if you only have one tax rate."[7]

Back in Estonia, where this particular revolution began, the government has so far stuck with the flat tax. But even there, the policy has sparked a furious controversy.

"I don't think there's a single serious economist in this country who would advocate keeping the flat-rate tax," said Viktor Forsberg, the professor who took me on a tour of the University of Tartu. "You have to look at what we pay for it. To make up for the lost revenue, we had to raise the VAT tax to 20%. That discourages people from buying. To make up for the lost revenue, we have to charge employers 34% of any worker's wages to fund our social and health-care programs. No wonder we have an unemployment problem! Anybody who wants to hire you has to pay not only your salary but an additional 34% to the government.

"What we don't need is a single rate of tax for everybody," the professor continued, his voice rising. "What we do need is to reduce the Social Security taxes, to make it cheaper to hire and get people back to work! What we do need is a lower sales tax, to get people to spend! And the way you pay for all that is the way every wealthy country in the world does it—with progressive taxes!"

DOES THE FLAT TAX WORK? Yes, a flat-rate income tax regime can work, under certain conditions. The flat tax works in a country that is a former Communist state, with no investment capital and low wage rates, which needs to build a capitalist economy from a base of approximately zero. The flat tax works if people are willing to pay a 20% sales tax on everything they buy, to make up for lower revenue. The flat tax works if employers are willing to pay 34%, or more, in Social Security taxes for every employee they hire. The flat tax works in a country where almost everyone has the same amount of wealth so there's no need for the distributive effect of graduated rates. And if all these conditions are met, the flat-rate tax will probably work as long as the economy is on a path of steady growth.

For countries that don't meet these requirements, it probably makes more sense—in terms of fiscal health as well as fairness—to adopt progressive rates, in which the wealthy pay a higher percentage of their income in tax than middle- or low-income people pay. But what happens if a country turns that proposition into a policy of soaking the rich?

7.

THE DEFINING PROBLEM; THE TAXING SOLUTION

I n the spring of 2014, the marketing staff at Harvard University Press began to sense that they had a blockbuster bestseller on their hands. This was not a frequent occurrence at the press, a prestigious academic publisher that churns out scores of learned volumes each year in fields like microbial ecology, medieval philosophy, and molecular physiology. But in those early months of 2014, there was enormous prepublication buzz about a forthcoming Harvard book. It was an unlikely blockbuster, to be sure: a 699-page treatise on economics written by a scholar who was hardly a household name even in his own neighborhood in Paris. But Professor Thomas Piketty's tome *Capital in the Twenty-First Century,* thick as a brick and somewhat heavier, rocketed to the top of the bestseller lists as soon as it hit America's bookstores. A *New York Times* story on the Frenchman's U.S. book tour was headlined "Economist Receives Rock Star Treatment."

The reason that an unknown French economist suddenly achieved rock-star stature in the United States was that Piketty's book focused squarely on an increasingly worrisome issue in the American zeitgeist: the inequality of wealth and income.

———————

SINCE THE START OF the Great Recession in 2008, Americans have struggled with a nagging new concern: a nation where everybody is supposed to be created equal was, in fact, increasingly unequal, with a widening chasm between a small cohort of extremely rich Americans and everybody else. In 2016, the richest 1% of Americans owned more of the nation's total wealth than the bottom 90% combined. And only the rich were getting richer. Census data showed that median income for the average American family actually fell by 8.6% in the first fourteen years of the twenty-first century, while a lucky few at the very top were taking in staggering amounts of money.[1]

Economists had been tracking the imbalance of wealth in the United States and other advanced democracies for several years; indeed, Thomas Piketty was one of the pioneers of this line of research. Inequality as a political issue caught the public's attention in the summer of 2011, when a ragtag group of protesters in New York City set up tents in a small park not far from the financial district and declared themselves the "Occupy Wall Street" movement. "We Are the 99%," their banner read; the protesters loudly declared that 99% of Americans were getting the shaft because of the economic and political clout of the richest 1%. Almost overnight, similar encampments with similar banners sprang up in city parks around the country and overseas; by mid-October, the *Washington Post* tallied more than nine hundred Occupy gatherings in eighty different nations. The protesters generally agreed on what they were complaining about: big business got large government bailouts after the global recession, while ordinary citizens lost their jobs, their homes, and their savings. But the various groups never settled on what they wanted to do about it. There were few if any specific demands for action from the Occupiers. As the urban campers began to leave their muddy tent cities in the cold of winter, it was hard to identify any policy change spurred by this occupation.

And yet the Occupy movement did make a lasting contribution to American political discourse. The notion stuck that the country was divided between a filthy rich 1% and everybody else. Politicians from left to right—from the Democratic senator Elizabeth Warren to the Republican presidential candidate Donald Trump—declared that the American economic system is "rigged" to benefit the rich at the expense of the rest. In the 2012 election, Democrats never missed a chance to remind the voters that the Republican presidential nominee, Mitt Romney, was a certified 1-percenter, with bank accounts in Switzerland and the Cayman Islands. Even some of the superrich deplored the increasingly lopsided distribution of wealth. "Too much of the GDP of the country has gone to too few of the people," warned Lloyd Blankfein, the CEO of Goldman Sachs, whose net worth, about $450 million, put him in the top one-tenth of the 1%. "If you grow the pie, but too few people enjoy the benefits of it, the fruit, then you'll have an unstable society."[2]

In December 2013, the president of the United States addressed the issue and declared it the most pressing problem facing the nation, "a fundamental threat to the American Dream."

"I believe this is the defining challenge of our time," Barack Obama said. "We face . . . a dangerous and growing inequality and lack of upward mobility that has jeopardized middle-class America's basic bargain—that if you work hard, you have a chance to get ahead." In recent decades, the president went on, that "basic bargain" had begun to fray.

As a trickle-down ideology became more prominent, taxes were slashed for the wealthiest, while investments in things that make us all richer, like schools and infrastructure, were allowed to wither. And the result is an economy that's become profoundly unequal, and families that are more insecure.

In fact, this trend towards growing inequality is not unique to America's market economy. Across the developed world, inequality has increased. But this increasing inequality is most pronounced in our country, and it challenges the very essence of who we are as a people. Understand, we've never begrudged success in America. . . . In fact, we've often accepted more income inequality than many other nations for one big reason—because we were convinced that America is a place where even if you're born with nothing, with a little hard work you can improve your own situation over time and build something better to leave your kids.

The problem is that, alongside increased inequality, we've seen diminished levels of upward mobility in recent years. A child born in the top 20 percent has about a 2-in-3 chance of staying at or near the top. A child born into the bottom 20 percent has a less than 1-in-20 shot at making it to the top. The idea that so many children are born into poverty in the wealthiest nation on Earth is heartbreaking enough. But the idea that a child may never be able to escape that poverty because she lacks a decent education or health care, or a community that views her future as their own, that should offend all of us and it should compel us to action.[3]

Obama's concern was echoed by repeated pronouncements from the most respected man in the world, Pope Francis. In his 2013 apostolic exhortation, *Evangelii gaudium,* for example, the pontiff argued passionately that tolerating the inequality of income and wealth was both unholy and dangerous.

"Just as the commandment 'Thou shalt not kill' sets a clear limit in order to safeguard the value of human life, today we also have to say 'thou shalt not' to an economy of exclusion and inequality," the pope wrote. "How can it be that it is not a news item when an elderly homeless person dies of exposure, but it is news when the stock market loses two points? This is a case of exclusion. Can we continue to stand by when food is thrown away while people are starving? This is a case of inequality."

There are people, of course, who disagree with the president and the pope, arguing that inequality is a boon to society at large. "The great growth of fortunes in recent decades is not a sinister development," wrote the business historian John Steele Gordon in the *Wall Street Journal*. "All our lives have been enriched and enhanced" by the products we buy from billionaires. In the *Times* of London, the Conservative Party parliamentarian Matt Ridley called on his colleagues to "start spreading the good news on inequality." The good news, he said, is that everybody is getting better off; it just happens at different rates. "Any increase in wealth inequality or pre-tax income inequality in Britain or America is caused by the rich getting disproportionately richer, not by the poor getting poorer."[4]

With all the talk of inequality, some of the 1% began moaning out loud about the focus on their wealth, giving birth to a curious new American species: the whining billionaire. "From the Occupy movement to the demonization of the rich . . . I perceive a rising tide of hatred of the successful one percent," the Silicon Valley magnate Tom Perkins wrote in an open letter. "I would call attention to the parallels of fascist Nazi Germany in its war on its 'one percent,' namely its Jews, to the progressive war on the American one percent, namely the 'rich.'"[5] The Nazi parallel was taken up by the investment banker Stephen Schwarzman, who was unhappy with proposals to reduce inequality by ending a lucrative tax break for his industry. "It's a war," Schwarzman was quoted as saying. "It's like when Hitler invaded Poland in 1939."[6]

There have always been differences between the rich and the poor. But today, the most striking gap is between the very rich and everybody else. In the United States, the median household income has been about the same—about $55,000—since the start of the century. But the top earners have seen big increases in income since 2000; as of 2015, the top 1% of American families had income of $405,000. To make the top one-tenth of 1% took income of $1.9 million.

Using the standard international measure of inequality, President Obama was basically correct when he said that among the advanced democracies the imbalance is "most pronounced" in the United States. The customary gauge of economic inequality is called the Gini coefficient, named for the Italian economist who thought it up. In the Gini rankings, a nation where everybody had the same amount of wealth and the same income would get a Gini score of 0; a country where one person took in all the income, and nobody else earned a cent, would get a score of 1. That is, the lower the Gini number, the smaller the gap between that nation's rich and poor. Generally, the world's poor countries—where a few families control the wealth, and tens of millions live in squalor—have high Gini coefficients. Nations like Lesotho, Botswana, Honduras, and Haiti have Gini numbers near 0.6, making them the least economically equal societies on the planet. Among the rich countries, the democracies of western Europe tend to score around 0.3; the world champions at economic equality include Sweden, Denmark, and Norway, where high wages for working people and high taxes on the rich bring the Gini index down to about 0.25.

The United States had a Gini coefficient in 2014 of 0.4—the worst rating among rich countries. Among the thirty-four members of the OECD, the club of industrialized democracies, only Mexico and Chile ranked higher than the United States on the inequality scale.

As these facts became more widely known, inequality emerged as a matter of broad concern among Americans, the stuff of kitchen-table and watercooler conversations all over the country. In New York, Washington, Cambridge, and Palo Alto, every self-respecting think tank—right, left, center, or far out—held erudite seminars on the issue. Magazines did cover stories; cable channels produced special reports. People began describing the United States as a "winner take all" society. A nation that had long cherished the belief that anybody can make it big began to mock that very idea. In 1960, John F. Kennedy had famously said that economic growth would benefit everybody: "A rising tide lifts all boats." Half a century later, the joke was that "a rising tide lifts all yachts," because only those with multimillion-dollar pleasure craft of their own were riding the economic wave.

Widespread concern over this trend was the reason Piketty's heavy economics tome became a number one bestseller in the United States. Still, it was not exactly beach reading. Because you, gentle reader, have been kind enough to read this book, I will repay the favor by providing a summary of the professor's argument, thus saving you the $40 price of the book and the hours required to read it.

Capital in the Twenty-First Century is actually more like three books than one. First, it's a history of the rich/poor divide, based on three centuries of wealth and income data that Piketty and his colleagues gathered from the United States, the U.K., France, and Sweden. Piketty relies heavily on mathematical models and statistical tables, but he thoughtfully spares his readers all that stuff, sticking it in a "technical appendix" on the Internet. In the book, he draws lessons from literature. He studies "the nature of wealth" as described in the nineteenth-century social-climbing novels of Jane Austen and Honoré de Balzac, where the economic classes were essentially set in concrete and the only way to move up in the world was to inherit from Uncle Moneybags or to marry well. This social dynamic explains the famous opening line of Austen's *Pride and Prejudice:* "It is a truth universally acknowledged, that a single man in possession of a good fortune, must be in want of a wife."

The historical data show that inequality of wealth in the United States and Europe grew sharply toward the end of the nineteenth century, the so-called Gilded Age, and into the first two decades of the twentieth. Then, because of policy innovations (like the income tax), the Great Depression, and the leveling effect of world wars, the gap between the rich and ordinary working people grew smaller through much of the twentieth century. By the 1970s, the wealth disparity was the smallest it had been for a hundred years. But inequality began to grow again in the 1980s and has continued to do so into the twenty-first century, particularly in the United States. By 2012, the top 1% of American households took 22.5% of the nation's total income—the highest share since 1928.

Piketty then says the renewed growth of inequality in recent decades is due partly to "the explosion of wage inequality in the United
States (and to a lesser extent Britain and Canada) after 1970." It became the norm for the top brass in American corporations to be paid
annual salaries and bonuses that would have been deemed embarrass-
ing, indeed disgraceful, in the past. In the 1950s, the CEO of an
American industrial or retail company was paid about twenty times as
much as the average worker at the firm, and those CEOs were considered "rich." Today, the boss is routinely paid two hundred, four
hundred, six hundred times as much as her typical employee and is
"superrich." In recent years, the Walmart CEO has earned about $25
million annually; that's a thousand times what an hourly clerk on the
retail floor will make in the same year. The CEO of the Chipotle
restaurant chain, Steve Ells, was paid $13.8 million for 2015, about
seven hundred times as much as a cashier in his stores.

This "explosion" in compensation often has little to do with performance, Piketty notes. For the year 2014, Yahoo's CEO, Marissa
Mayer, was paid more than $42 million, even though the company's
sales and profits fell every year under her leadership. Chipotle's sales
and profits plummeted in 2015 due to food poisoning problems at
several outlets, but its CEO still collected that $14 million.

But developments in the private sector, Piketty says, are not the
only cause of the burgeoning financial imbalance. A key contributor
to inequality, he says, is government policy. When governments decide to bail out big banks while millions lose their homes to fore-
closure action by the same banks, the policy exacerbates the problem
of inequality. Such policies transfer wealth from middle-class homeowners to upper-bracket bankers and their shareholders—not through
private markets, but because of decisions by governments. Similarly,
tax policies that give generous breaks to the wealthiest—like that
$7,500 giveaway to people who can buy a $105,000 car—exacerbate
the trend toward concentration of wealth in a lucky few. When the
national tax code says that money earned from trading securities will

be taxed at a much lower rate than money earned from working at a job, the tax law itself is adding to inequality. This is not surprising, Piketty says, because the government officials who approve corporate bailouts and write the tax laws are often beholden to the financial elites for political contributions.

But the major reason for growing inequality, Piketty argues, is that rich people today make most of their money not from wages but from capital investments—stocks, bonds, commodity trades, real estate, patents, and so on. And earnings from capital (that is, from financial transactions) are growing faster than earnings from labor (that is, from working at a job). That is, you can make some money cooking hamburgers or serving hamburgers, but you won't make as much as a guy who buys and sells the stock in a hamburger chain.

In other words, Piketty says, "the rich get richer" has become a fundamental law of economics, especially in the United States. Because our Supreme Court has defined donating money as a form of political speech, economic clout in the United States turns quickly into political clout. Rich political donors can get the politicians whom they finance to champion tax and regulatory policies that increase the wealth of the wealthy. The "forces of divergence," in Piketty's phrase, are stronger than any influences that might reduce inequality. Piketty maintains that the notion of a nation where all are basically equal is dying; as the book states it, "The egalitarian pioneer ideal has faded into oblivion." And if current patterns of inequality in income and wealth continue for a few decades, "the consequences for the long-term dynamics of the wealth distribution are potentially terrifying."

But Piketty offers a series of solutions. The basic answer, he says, is tax. He proposes significantly heavier taxes on the rich. This would reduce their wealth, and the revenues could be used for education, jobs, or handouts to increase the wealth of everybody else. The income tax burden, he says, should fall more heavily on those who make their money on financial dealing; he says the U.S. system, in which the tax on capital gains is much lower than the tax on wages and salaries, is simply upside-down and thus counterproductive for dealing with the growth of inequality.

Income taxes on the rich, he says—both on their salaries and on their capital gains—should be substantially higher than they are now. How high? "According to our estimates, the optimal top tax rate in the developed countries is probably above 80 percent." That's a tax rate more than double what the highest earners pay today in the United States. If this 80% top marginal rate were applied to earnings over $500,000, Piketty says, the tax regime would help to even out inequality without stunting economic growth.

Beyond the income tax, though, Piketty proposes a tax on wealth. It would work like the property tax that most American homeowners pay already. For the property tax, the county sends around an assessor to appraise the value of your house, and the tax due is some percentage of the appraised value. In a wealth tax regime, the assessor appraises not just your house but all your wealth—your cars, your boat, your jewelry, your bank accounts, your investment portfolio, the art on your walls, your vacation home, and the Persian rug on the floor of your vacation home. If the total wealth exceeds a certain amount, you pay a tax on the whole thing. If the assessor finds that all the money and stuff you own is worth a total of $5 million, and the wealth tax rate is 2%, you'd have to fork over $100,000 in wealth tax. And the assessor will come around next year to bill you again.

One obvious problem with a national wealth tax is that wealthy people can, and do, switch nations to avoid the tax. You can't move your city mansion or your mountain condo to a different state, but a rich person facing a $100,000 tax bill each year might well pack up his art, rugs, and jewelry and move to a country that doesn't tax wealth. Piketty has a solution: make the wealth tax a global tax. That is, all countries should agree to a standard tax on wealth so that a zillionaire can't cut his tax bill by moving across the border. Being a fairly down-to-earth economist, Piketty freely admits that this "global wealth tax" is not a realistic possibility at the moment. He holds out hope, though, that the member nations of the European Union might agree on a continent-wide wealth tax, and maybe the idea would spread from there.

It's hardly surprising that Thomas Piketty would propose taxing the rich as the primary solution to the problem of inequality. Piketty is French, and France is the world champion at soaking the rich through taxes. In the United States and other rich democracies, those who worry about inequality routinely argue for higher tax rates on the upper brackets and other changes designed to reduce the gap between the rich and the rest. In his "defining challenge of our time" speech, Barack Obama called for tax reforms and invoked the concept of BBLR—getting rid of tax breaks for the wealthy in order to broaden the taxable base and thus lower rates. "And by broadening the base," the president said, "we can actually lower rates to encourage more companies to hire here and use some of the money we save to create good jobs rebuilding our roads and our bridges and our airports, and all the infrastructure our businesses need."

The Nobel laureate Joseph Stiglitz—probably the only American economist whose books sell as well as Piketty's—also makes the case for tax increases to counter inequality. Stiglitz would get rid of the reduced tax rate for capital gains. "A fair tax system would tax speculators at at least the same rate as those who work for their income," he argues. "To provide revenues for public investment and other public needs, to help the poor and the middle class, to ensure the existence of opportunity for all segments of the population, we'll have to impose progressive taxes, and, most importantly, do a better job in closing loopholes."[7]

BUT FRANCE HAS GONE further than the other rich democracies when it comes to imposing a variety of taxes on *les riches*. "We have a long tradition in this country of going after the rich," Professor Martin Collet told me at a charming outdoor café near the Place de la Bastille one sunny Paris afternoon in late June. "In a couple of weeks, we will celebrate Bastille Day. It's a national holiday; we remember when the peasants rose up—it was just down the street from here—against the rich and the monarchy, in 1789. Back then, we cut off their heads. Today, we try to cut a hole in their bank accounts."

Dr. Collet, a *professeur des universités* at Université Panthéon-Assas, is one of the country's leading tax economists. He took me through the history of taxation in France, going back to the post-Bastille First Republic. France has always been a high-tax country, even compared with its neighbors in western Europe; today, it ranks second among the world's richest countries in total tax burden, with taxes taking about 45.5% of the nation's total wealth, or GDP. That places it just behind Denmark (49.58%) but far ahead of the United States, where taxes total about 26% of GDP.

The French support this heavy rate of taxation partly because the revenue funds an expansive list of government services, including universal health insurance, generous old-age pensions, free universities, cheap public transit, and free exercise clubs. The World Bank reported that France spent 24% of its GDP on government in 2015—as much as big-government meccas like Sweden (25.9%) and Denmark (26.1%). As we've seen earlier in this book, the United States is downright thrifty by comparison, spending 15.5% of its wealth on all levels of government combined in 2015. (The World Bank reports for government spending don't include transfer payments like Social Security and food stamps.)

In France, though, taxation is not merely a way to provide money for government to spend. It's considered an element of social cohesion, a symbol of fundamental French values. The First Republic, in its zeal for new terminology, replaced the standard word for "tax" (*impôt*) with the French word *contribution,* and to this day French politicians routinely talk about taxes as "social contributions," as a way to maintain the essential French ideal of *égalité.* "For most of the French left, and a chunk of the right, high taxes are a hallmark of a decent society that puts fairness before profit and public service before business," the *Economist* noted. In terms of *égalité,* at least, this tax regime seems to have worked; France has always had a lower Gini coefficient (that is, a more even distribution of wealth) than most of its European neighbors or the United States.

When the Great Recession hit France in 2008, Nicolas Sarkozy, a center-right politician, was president. (Sarkozy supports free higher education, a complete ban on handguns, and unemployment compensation that never ends, but in European terms that makes him "center-right.") Along with other leaders across Europe, Sarkozy opted for a policy of austerity—tax cuts, reduced government spending, limits on labor unions—as the proper course for economic revival. This didn't work. Sarkozy lost his bid for reelection in 2012, and the Socialist candidate, François Hollande, raced to victory by promising to increase public spending and to pay for it with a "supertax" just for the rich: a tax of 75% on income over €1 million ($1.25 million) per year. (This proposal actually made Hollande something of a moderate in the presidential race; the candidate from the Left Front pledged to impose a tax of 100% on incomes over $375,000.) Hollande's supertax on what he called "the arrogant and grasping rich" drew strong support from liberal newspapers and from prominent economists, including Thomas Piketty. Looking across the Atlantic to the demonstrations by "the 99%" in America, Piketty said that "Hollande's 75-percent tax is the right response to the Occupy movement. The irony is that the street movement is happening in the United States, while the political response is coming in France."[8]

Although the supertax actually touched only a minute fraction of French taxpayers, it ran into furious resistance. The Conseil Constitutionnel, a sort of Supreme Court, ruled that a tax rate of 75% amounted to a "confiscation" of wealth, in violation of the French Constitution. Hollande went back to the drawing board and came up with a slightly different implementation of the 75% rate; the Constitutional Council threw that one out as well. Eventually, Hollande was able to impose his supertax by requiring that employers pay the additional tax on incomes over €1 million, rather than directly imposing the top rate on high-earning individuals. Professor Collet argued that this alteration reflected the basic reason for the supertax in the first place. "It was never designed to bring in a great deal of revenue," he told me. "The goal was to convince companies to rein in the compensation of their top officers. It's insane that any CEO would earn more than a million euros in one year, in a country where the average worker makes less than one-twentieth as much."

Regardless of who actually paid, the supertax meant that France would have the highest top income tax rate in the world. As if that weren't enough, *les riches* also face the wealth tax, which Professor Piketty called for in his book. In France, this is formally called "l'impôt de solidarité sur la fortune"—that is, "the tax on fortunes for the good of society"—but it is broadly known as the ISF, the tax on fortunes. If the tax assessor determines that your bank accounts, real estate, stocks, cars, jewelry, and so on have a total value greater than about $1.5 million, you have to pay the ISF. The least rich of the rich are taxed at 0.5%—that is, about $7,500 on a "fortune" of $1.5 million. The tax goes up from there; the top rate, 1.5%, applies to any French family with total wealth around $12 million or more. In total, the ISF is paid by half of 1% of all French families. It raises less than 2% of tax revenues. It could be eliminated with minimal impact on the national budget. "It brings in perhaps €4 billion per year—essentially nothing!" Professor Collet explained. "But if any government were to drop it, you're sure to lose the next election."

This is a Willie Sutton approach. Sutton, a Depression-era crook, was asked why he kept robbing banks and famously answered, "Because that's where the money is." Still, this form of tax has been decidedly out of favor for the last ten years or so. It used to be common for developed countries to have a wealth tax that worked like the French ISF; in 1990, more than half of the members of the rich nations' group, the OECD, had a wealth tax in place, in addition to the normal income, property, corporate, and sales taxes. But most nations repealed the wealth tax around the start of the twenty-first century.

In 2016, only a handful of countries still imposed an annual tax on overall wealth. France, Norway, Switzerland, and India all have permanent wealth tax regimes. In France and Switzerland, the tax only hits millionaires. In contrast, Norway imposes the tax at a fairly low level; anybody with total wealth greater than about $130,000 gets hit with the wealth tax. The widest definition of "wealthy" is in India, where a 1% wealth tax kicks in for anybody whose net worth is more than 3 million rupees, which comes to about $45,000. (In India, that still means a small percentage of the population.)

Responding to the economic strictures of the Great Recession, Iceland and Spain reinstituted the wealth tax in 2008, but both governments called this a "temporary" measure. When Cyprus faced a collapse of its banking system in 2013, the government imposed a onetime wealth tax on bank deposits; it simply seized between 4% and 20% of the savings of anybody who had more than €100,000 (about $130,000 at the time) in a Cypriot bank. (This was unpopular, of course, but less so than it might have been because many of the biggest depositors in the banks of Cyprus were rich Russians trying to evade taxes back home.)

One big problem with a wealth tax is that it is intrusive—much more so than the familiar property tax. A county appraiser trying to gauge the value of your house for property tax purposes can get a decent estimate just from public records—like how much that house down the street sold for last month. But if the government decides to tax everything you own, the appraiser has to probe your bank accounts, investment accounts, safe-deposit box, living room, closet, jewelry drawer, garage, and so on. It's offensive enough to have government snooping around like that for any reason, let alone to increase your tax bill.

That's why another form of wealth tax, different from the ISF, is much more common. This is the inheritance tax. Sometimes it takes the form of a tax on the dead person's "estate"—a legal entity that holds the wealth of the deceased until it is distributed to the heirs.

Sometimes it's a tax the lucky daughters or nephews have to pay after they inherit the money. Any jurisdiction that has an estate or inheritance tax also has to put in place a gift tax at roughly the same tax rate; without that, a rich person on his deathbed would give away all the money in the form of gifts to avoid the inheritance tax.

The United States, naturally, has made this whole process more complicated than any other country by adding yet another variation, the generation-skipping transfer tax, with its own five-page form (Form 709), two worksheets, and nineteen pages of instructions. Whether it's an "estate tax," an "inheritance tax," a "gift tax," or a "transfer tax," the result is the same: the government gets some of the money that was meant for the heirs. This is considered preferable to an ISF-style wealth tax for several reasons. First, it's less intrusive. When somebody dies, a court—in the United States, it's called a probate court—has to determine the precise value of his entire estate. So the appraisal is being done anyway; it's not just for tax purposes. Second, it doesn't penalize people for their hard work. By definition, you pay inheritance tax only on money you didn't work for at all. Third, because almost every country imposes the tax only on wealthy people—in the United States, it only applies to estates of about $11 million or more—the heirs will come out just fine, thank you, even after the estate tax is paid. If some rich American leaves $100 million to his granddaughter, the estate tax could be as high as $41 million. That's a hefty tax bill, but it still leaves the lucky kid $59 million to scratch by on. It's hard to feel sorry for a sudden millionaire because the tax man took a share before she got her windfall.

In the United States, the estate tax is designed so that it affects only a tiny fraction of American families. There's no tax at all on an estate worth less than $5.45 million; if you leave your money to your spouse, the exemption is doubled, which means there's no estate tax due unless you leave behind more than $10.9 million. About 2.6 million Americans die each year, but only 4,700 leave behind a legacy large enough to incur an estate tax; that's about two-tenths of 1% of all the decedents. In the

United States, at the start of 2017, there was a single tax rate (40%) for all estates over $10.9 million, and the same rate applied to all heirs. (In many countries, a sibling or a child inheriting money pays a lower rate of tax than a friend or a distant relative.) With the $10.9 million exclusion, a lucky son inheriting $50 million from his late father would lose $15.64 million to the estate tax, but he'd still have a hefty $34.6 million left to spend. About twenty states and the District of Columbia have an estate tax that has to be paid in addition to the federal levy.

Many other developed countries tax estates. Most of them have a tax that kicks in at a much lower point than the $5.45 million minimum in the United States. The rates vary widely, as this chart shows:

Country	Tax begins at (in U.S. dollars)	Tax rate
France	106,000	5% to 45%
Netherlands	128,620	10% to 40%
Germany	423,782	30%
Japan	247,000	55%
U.K.	488,280	40%
Spain	872,000	34%
Finland	1,009,000	19% to 35%

In the United States, the estate tax has been hotly controversial, even though it touches only one out of every seventy thousand Americans. In the 1990s, a group of wealthy families hired a consultant, Frank Luntz, to wage a political campaign against this form of wealth tax. Luntz is a master of political euphemism; when the George W. Bush administration agreed to let timber companies clear-cut the trees on sizable stretches of federal land, Luntz named the initiative "Healthy Forests." To battle the estate tax, he came up with the label that has stuck: the "death tax." He designed a campaign around the idea that government shouldn't penalize you for dying. (Of course, the tax burden falls on the living heir, not the decedent, but those

who campaign against the "death tax" ignore this nuance.) Supporters of the tax have come up with politically charged labels of their
own; they call the estate tax the "lucky rich kids' tax" or the "Paris
Hilton tax"; in his stump speeches during the 2016 presidential campaign, the Democratic contender Bernie Sanders used to remind his
audiences that "Paris Hilton never built a hotel."

Under George W. Bush, opponents of the "death tax" won a temporary victory. Bush's 2001 tax-reform plan phased out the estate tax
over the following decade so that the rate fell to zero in the year 2010.
For budget reasons, though, the death of the "death tax" was short-
lived; the zero rate lasted only one year. This led to anecdotes (none
proven, so far) about financial advisers' telling their rich clients, "If
you're going to die anyway, it would make fiscal sense to do it in
2010." After Barack Obama's reelection in 2012, the "lucky rich kids'
tax" was made permanent at the current rate of 40%; the minimum
estate that triggers this tax (as noted, it was $5.45 million in 2016)
goes up slightly every year.

The tax on a large inheritance used to be a standard element of
revenue raising in all developed countries. In recent years, though,
several nations—including high-tax venues like Austria, the Czech
Republic, Norway, and Sweden—have eliminated the tax. In general, the reasons for dumping this tax are related to the "death tax"
idea; that is, enough is enough. If some poor guy paid taxes for sixty
years, we ought to give him a break when he's dead. In Canada, the
argument against the inheritance tax was a clever slogan: "No taxation without respiration." (Canada, though, imposes a capital gains
tax and a "probate fee" that heirs have to pay; these increase with the
amount inherited, so the impact is roughly equal to an inheritance
tax for large estates.) After Sweden repealed its inheritance tax in
2005, the economist Henry Ohlsson explained, perhaps tongue in
cheek, that Sweden taxes rich people so heavily in their lifetime that
there was not much revenue to be gained by taxing what little they
had left when they died.[9]

France, of course, had both the inheritance tax and the wealth tax—not to mention the health insurance tax, the Social Security tax, the carbon tax, the income tax, the capital gains tax, and a national sales tax of 20% on almost everything you could buy—when François Hollande finally imposed the 75% top income tax rate in 2013. Although the "supertax" was popular with Frenchmen earning an average income, some of the wealthiest French taxpayers viewed it as the last straw in a relentless effort by the national government to milk them dry. Near the end of 2012, with the new tax due to take effect with the New Year, Hollande came face-to-face with a basic fact about high taxes: at some point, people just refuse to pay. When rates get too high, it's cheaper to hire a lawyer who can design some intricate scheme of tax avoidance than it is to pay the tax. Or, it's cheaper just to flee the tax altogether. For Hollande, this predictable backlash took the form of *l'affaire Depardieu*.

For more than four decades, Gérard Depardieu was a shining light of French cinema, as leading man, national heartthrob, producer, and financial angel. He played in or produced more than 170 films. This made him an extremely rich man, and he became even richer through wise investments in real estate, works of art, vineyards, and so on. Like many self-made millionaires, Depardieu grew more conservative politically as he grew more rich. He supported Sarkozy in that 2012 election and was already complaining about the heavy taxes he had to pay long before Hollande targeted his ilk with the supertax. When the 75% tax rate took effect, Depardieu swore that he would never pay it. To prove that he was serious about this, he left France and took up official residence in Néchin, Belgium, a farm village just north of the French border. In a letter to a Paris newspaper, Depardieu declared himself finished with French taxation. "I have paid €145 million in taxes over 45 years," he said. With the advent of the supertax, he concluded that enough is enough. He would give up his French passport rather than pay another centime to a voracious government determined to penalize hard work and success.

Hollande and his backers fired right back, arguing that Depardieu would be nothing without France and noting that dozens of his films, like many French business ventures, had received financial help from the national government—that is, from French citizens who willingly paid their taxes. Hollande's second-in-command, Prime Minister Jean-Marc Ayrault, pronounced Depardieu a "pathetic" (*minable*) figure. That comment in particular seemed to sting. A few weeks later, Depardieu showed up in Russia and accepted a Russian passport directly from the hand of Vladimir Putin. Russia, the Frenchman announced, "is a great democracy and not a country where the prime minister gets to call one of its citizens 'pathetic.'"[10]

But there was little political profit for the French president in a long-running contretemps with a famous matinee idol. And Gérard Depardieu was not the only prominent figure to gripe about the new levy. Once the 75% tax took effect, in 2013, other prominent representatives of *les riches* began to talk about giving up their passports as well. The Union of Professional Football Clubs, the French equivalent of our National Football League, announced that it would cancel several weekend matches to protest the tax on its top players. In the end, the supertax, which never raised any significant amount of revenue, proved costlier to the politician who imposed it than to the few wealthy citizens who had to pay it. A beleaguered Hollande announced that he would terminate the 75% tax bracket in 2015, just two years after it took effect. The whole experiment seemed to demonstrate clearly that there is a limit to how high any government—even in France—can raise tax rates.

THE UNITED STATES PROBABLY doesn't have to worry about its wealthiest citizens fleeing the country to avoid high taxes, because of a strange quirk of American taxation: the richest generally pay lower rates than those who earn less. As a general rule, the rich pay a higher rate of tax than the poor or the average earner. This is the principle that Jesus

Christ enunciated in the parable of the widow's mite. The United States has adhered to this rule since the first days of the income tax a century ago; at its birth, Teddy Roosevelt declared that the progressive income tax would serve as "a cure for the disease of wealth." Indeed, in those first years the income tax was much more about reducing inequality than raising revenue; for the first decade of its existence, only the richest 4% of Americans had to pay the new federal income tax. Edwin R. A. Seligman called the income tax a manifestation of "tax justice," which he defined as "the principle that each individual should be held to help the state in proportion to his ability to help himself." Even among the wealthiest Americans, Seligman wrote in 1914, "it is rare to find a cynical disregard of all considerations of equity."[11]

But today this basic principle does not apply to the so-called superrich—that is, to the tiny group of taxpayers who report adjusted gross income (Line 37 on Form 1040) of $10 million or more. In 2011—that's the latest year for which we have data on this—an American family at the median annual income (just over $51,000 then) paid about 6% of adjusted gross income in federal income tax. A family earning double the median income paid about 13% in federal income taxes. In the higher brackets, a family with adjusted gross income of about $200,000 had an average income tax bite of 17.9%. And the "rich"—that is, taxpayers making between $500,000 and $10 million per year—paid federal income tax at an average rate of 24.5% of their adjusted gross income.[12]

This fits the pattern of progressive taxation. But the pattern falls apart when we get to the tiny smidgen of the population with an annual income over $10 million—about twelve thousand taxpayers in all. They paid an average of 20.4% of their adjusted gross income in federal income taxes in 2011. That's a lower rate of tax than the so-called rich. An even tinier segment—the four hundred or so taxpayers reporting more than $100 million in income—paid income tax at an average rate of 18%. Many taxpayers in the "superrich" category actually paid a lower rate of tax than people making 1% of their income.

This strange peculiarity of the American tax code has been reduced to a popular bumper sticker: "Warren Buffett paid a lower tax
rate than his secretary" (a statement that Buffett has confirmed). The
explanation takes us back to the distinction that lies at the heart of
Thomas Piketty's bestseller—the difference between the return on
capital investments (stocks, bonds, real estate, derivatives, and so on)
and income from wages.

The superrich get most of their income from capital. Capital income is taxed at a lower rate than "earned income," which comes
from labor. As of 2016, the highest tax rate on capital income was
23.8%; the highest tax rate on labor was almost twice as high: 39.6%.
If you make most of your income from capital, you pay tax at a lower
rate than people who make most of their income from working for
wages. For the superrich, return on capital amounts to half their income; for average families, capital represents less than 2% of their
income. The Tax Policy Center in Washington estimates that 75% of
the savings due to the lower rate on capital gains in 2013 went to
taxpayers with income over $1 million. That's why the wealthiest of
all Americans pay lower rates of tax than many people who get their
income from wages.

Most of the world's industrialized democracies have a lower rate
of tax for capital gains than for labor income, although each country
has its own set of rules on the definition of "capital" and the length
of time the investment must be held to get the lower rate. A few
countries—for example, Belgium, Malaysia, and of course New Zealand, the home of BBLR—don't tax capital gains at all. The argument
for a lower tax rate on capital income—an argument supported by
many economists—runs as follows: (1) economies need capital investment to grow and create new jobs; (2) capital investment by definition is risky (you could lose it all); and (3) therefore, a lower rate of
tax on potential gains is necessary to encourage people to make those
essential, but risky, investments.

Historically, it's not clear that the third part of this argument bears out. In 1986, none other than Ronald Reagan endorsed a new internal revenue code that taxed capital gains at the same rate (28%) as the top rate on labor income. For the next decade or so, investment soared and stock markets went through the roof, even without a reduced capital gains tax. Just after his election to a second term, Barack Obama signed into law tax changes that significantly raised the capital gains rate (from 15% to 23.8% for the wealthiest taxpayers). Again, it would be hard to argue that this increase suppressed capital investment. In the first four years of the higher capital gains rate, all American stock indexes hit new records over and over again. The S&P 500 index rose from 1,438 on December 1, 2012, to 2,191 on the same date four years later.

Whether or not the preferential rate makes sense for investors who risk their capital in the markets, it is much harder to justify the special-case capital gains preference that gives investment bankers, hedge fund managers, and other salaried workers in the financial industry a generous tax break not available to employees in any other field. This giveaway is known as the "carried interest" rule; the name evokes a time when a clipper ship captain held a financial interest in the cargo he carried across the sea. It says that a broker or banker who invests other people's money can count his own salary as "capital gains" and thus pay tax on it at the reduced, capital gains rate. Some of the biggest earners in the nation take advantage of this provision every year to save tens of millions of dollars in federal income tax. That explains why Warren Buffett pays a lower rate than his secretary (and it's legal). The secretary's pay is taxed as "ordinary income." Much of Buffett's pay is taxed as "capital gains"—at about half the rate. And this is a major reason why the superrich end up paying tax at a lower rate than workers making far less.

For decades, economists and politicians from left and right have attacked the carried-interest rule as a distortion of the basic capital gains proposition. "Why should someone who does not put any of their own money at risk pay the lower tax rate that Congress intended to reward those who do win such risky bets?" argues the business professor Peter Cohan, himself a former hedge fund manager. In the 2016 presidential campaign, politicians from Bernie Sanders and Hillary Clinton on the left to Donald Trump and Jeb Bush on the right called for termination of this loophole. "The hedge fund guys didn't build this country," Trump said. "These are guys that shift paper around and they get lucky."[13]

One smart line of investment that the hedge fund guys make every year is their contribution to members of Congress. The politicians, in turn, serve their funders by protecting the carried-interest preference from all challengers. Despite its unpopularity, this particular tax break has proven so hard to eliminate that Barack Obama sought to circumvent it instead: he proposed to keep the carried-interest provision but to add a new requirement—it's been dubbed the Buffett Rule—that says anybody with adjusted gross income over $1 million must pay at least 30% of it in income tax. It was this presidential initiative that prompted the financier Stephen Schwarzman to evoke the Nazis: "It's like when Hitler invaded Poland in 1939." Warren Buffett himself has supported the Buffett Rule, but it has never been enacted. Because Obama knew when he proposed the idea that it had no chance of passage, he was (fairly) criticized for promoting a "rule" that was more political posturing than actual policy.

Generally, we don't get to see the benefits of the carried-interest preference for any specific taxpayer. But that changed, briefly, in 2012, when the Republican presidential nominee, Mitt Romney, was pressured into releasing a couple of his tax returns. In the year 2010, Ann and Mitt Romney reported adjusted gross income of $21.6 million; most of this was deferred salary paid by the investment firm from which Romney had retired twelve years earlier. The couple gave generously to charity—about $7 million—and reported capital losses on various transactions. This reduced their taxable income to $17.1 million. Had this income been reported as salary, they would have paid more than 35% of it in income tax. But under the tax code, almost all of the Romney income was deemed carried interest. Consequently, their tax rate fell to 13.9%—a lower rate than taxpayers earning less than 1% of their income. To add to the candidate's embarrassment, the return showed that Romney held some of his money in the Cayman Islands, a famous haven for people trying to hide money from the tax authorities. Romney conceded that he had accounts in the Cayman Islands but said this was not for tax purposes. To which the attorney Frank Schuchat responded, "To say you put money in the Caymans, but not for tax purposes, is like saying you bought a condom, but not for sex."

The carried-interest tax break is one of those things that make the United States exceptional when it comes to tax policy. "Most other countries would never think of a dodge like 'carried interest,'" notes the tax expert Richard Bird. "It's proof—as if any more proof were needed—that big money gets its way in the U.S. Congress." And this mammoth tax gift to the richest Americans is one of the reasons that the problem of inequality is so much "more pronounced" in the United States than in other developed democracies. As Thomas Piketty's unlikely bestseller said, government principles, including tax policy, contribute in major ways to inequality of income and wealth.

This is why stiffer taxes would be the most powerful antidote to the venom of inequality. But there's clearly a balance to be drawn. As the French Socialists discovered amid the ruin of their "supertax" idea, if personal taxes get too stiff, people find ways not to pay them—or simply flee, *à la l'affaire Depardieu*. And it's not just multimillionaire film stars who cross a border to duck high taxes. Corporations do the same thing, using "convoluted and pernicious strategies."

8.

CONVOLUTED AND
PERNICIOUS STRATEGIES

Caterpillar Inc., the maker of those bright yellow bulldozers, earthmovers, and rock scrapers that have built roads, dams, bridges, and mines all over the planet, is an iconic American manufacturing company, headquartered since 1930 in the quintessential heartland city of Peoria, Illinois. Caterpillar's mighty machines were present at the creation of Boulder Dam and the Golden Gate Bridge, the interstate highway system and the Superdome; they have diverted the Nile for the Aswan project and leveled the tundra for the Trans-Siberian Highway. Unlike many of its American counterparts, Caterpillar has largely resisted the temptation to move planning or production overseas. The design of its construction machinery, power generators, and industrial-strength engines is still largely carried out on the drawing boards of Peoria. Most of its products can still bear the proud notice "Made in U.S.A." In 2014, the company reported global sales of $56 billion and generated $3.7 billion in profit. Caterpillar Inc. ranks among the top fifty manufacturing companies in the world, and its stock has been included for decades in the Dow Jones Industrial Average.

Caterpillar's prices can be hefty. If you're in the market, say, for a medium-sized all-wheel-drive road grader, the Caterpillar 140M2

Motor Grader will set you back some $515,000. Yet these machines sell like mad, because they are rugged enough to work anywhere on earth and they last for decades, even if used every day. In fact, that legendary longevity is the real key to Caterpillar's ongoing financial success. After making a reasonable, but not huge, profit on the initial sale of a machine, the company cashes in big-time by selling spare parts for that same machine for the next twenty, thirty, or forty years. It's the heavy-equipment equivalent of selling the razor cheap and making the big money selling blades. An internal report to the company's board in 2012 said that the sale of spare parts acts like "an annuity continuing long after original equipment sales, and generating . . . profits."[1] Because no construction company wants to see a $500,000 machine sitting idle because of a broken crankshaft, Caterpillar aims to replace any part for any machine anywhere in the world within twenty-four hours.

Accordingly, the spare-parts trade is a crucial element of Caterpillar's overall business and a key contributor to the company's profits. And those profits, of course, are subject to the 35% U.S. corporate income tax rate. Thanks to exemptions, allowances, and credits, Caterpillar has never had to pay income tax at the nominal 35% rate. Still, its actual rate of corporate income tax, the company says, runs about 29%—higher than what its competitors in lower-tax countries have to pay. In return, of course, the Peoria-based firm gets all the benefits of being an American company: the world's richest home market, the patent system and courts to enforce it, the rule of law, a well-educated workforce, extensive transit infrastructure, embassies and consulates in every nation to help it deal with foreign clients, and so on.

As François Hollande learned, though, a heavy rate of tax generally leads to heavy-duty efforts to avoid paying the tax. Sure enough, early in this century, Caterpillar Inc. was searching hard for ways to cut its tax payments. Into the breach stepped PricewaterhouseCoopers (or PwC), the giant accounting and consulting firm that had audited Caterpillar's books for decades. PwC offered major American firms a service it called GTOP, or the Global Tax Optimization Program. The "tax optimization" it had in mind was, in fact, tax reduction; that is, PwC promised to look around the world to find places and ploys that could give a traditionally American firm a much lower rate of tax. For Caterpillar, the auditors quickly decided that the lucrative spare-parts business was the best place to launch a cross-border tax-avoidance scheme.

Until this "tax optimization" program came along, Caterpillar had run its parts business on a fairly simple formula. It designed the parts in Peoria and then contracted with manufacturers—almost all of them in the United States—to build them. Caterpillar bought the parts from the manufacturer, stored them in warehouses (the largest is in Morton, Illinois), and then shipped them to its dealers, around the country and around the world, to sell to the end customer. The profit on those sales accrued to Caterpillar in the United States and was taxed at the U.S. corporate rate.

But PricewaterhouseCoopers, through the GTOP service, designed a different mechanism (different on paper at least). Under PwC's guidance, Caterpillar created a subsidiary in Geneva, Switzerland, called Caterpillar SARL ("SARL" is a Swiss legal term for a corporation). CSARL was then designated—on paper—as the official spare-parts supplier for all Caterpillar customers overseas. The mechanics of design and manufacture didn't change; almost all Caterpillar parts were still designed, built, and warehoused in the United States, and Caterpillar employees in America still dispatched them to the dealers. But now CSARL, the Swiss subsidiary, became—on paper—the official buyer and seller of those parts. When the parts were sold, the profits on these sales were assigned to the Swiss company and taxed by the Swiss government at a top rate of 6%.

It was an aggressive tax-avoidance mechanism—the kind of thing that IRS auditors might question when reviewing the company's corporate tax return. So Caterpillar felt the need to get some legal-sounding imprimatur for its new arrangement. Accordingly, the brass in Peoria decided to ask licensed auditors to judge the legality of the profit-shifting ploy. For this purpose, the company called on its regular auditing firm, PricewaterhouseCoopers—the same firm that had designed the whole Swiss-subsidiary-gets-the-profits scheme in the first place. The PwC auditors concluded, conveniently, that the organizational structure recommended by the PwC tax planners was perfectly legitimate. The auditors also declared, conveniently, that there was no conflict of interest in PwC's auditing PwC's proposals.

This left Caterpillar's spare-parts business with an organization chart wildly out of balance. Responding to questions from a congressional committee, the company said it designed no parts in Switzerland. It manufactured no parts in Switzerland. It stored no parts in Switzerland. Caterpillar had ten warehouses in the United States storing some 1.5 billion spare parts but not a single warehouse in Switzerland. The company had forty-nine hundred employees running the parts business in the United States and sixty-six in Switzerland.

And yet Caterpillar reported to the IRS that 85% of all the profits it made on international sales of spare parts were earned by the Swiss subsidiary and thus not taxable in the United States.

Shifting the parts business (on paper) to Switzerland was not simple and was not cheap. The arrangement consumed months of lawyer time. Caterpillar paid the PricewaterhouseCoopers tax planners $55 million in consulting fees to create the Swiss detour for its spare-parts profit and a few million more for the auditors' determination that there was no conflict in asking PwC to audit a PwC plan. But those millions were small change for Caterpillar, compared with the huge sums the firm was able to keep away from the IRS. The Swiss bypass shifted about $8 billion in profits from the U.S. parts operation in Peoria to CSARL in Geneva in the first fifteen years of the twenty-first century. If its effective corporate income tax rate in the United States was 29%, that meant Caterpillar cut its U.S. tax payments by $2.3 billion.[2]

Not a bad return on a $55 million investment. And that rate of return explains why so many American companies have followed the route plowed by Caterpillar. However high the consultants' fees, and however absurd the resulting organizational chart may look, corporate taxpayers are willing to do what it takes to escape the 35% corporate income tax.

The federal tax on corporate earnings is older than the tax on personal income. The federal corporate income tax was first collected in 1909, four years before the first Form 1040 was sent to a small number of wealthy taxpayers. For some eight decades, the corporate tax rate in the United States was roughly the same as that in other major industrialized countries, so moving to a foreign country would make little difference in the tax a corporation had to pay. Beginning in the 1980s, though, major countries began to cut their corporate income tax rates sharply. The new century brought even lower rates. Between 1997 and 2014, thirty-one of the thirty-four members of the OECD— the club of the world's richest nations—reduced the rate of corporate income tax. The United States did not follow this trend. By 2016, as a result, the base U.S. tax on corporate income was the highest of any major democracy. America's corporate income tax ranges from 15% to 35%, depending on the company's size, but in practice almost all major corporations are in the top bracket, 35%. The French, those nonpareil soakers of the rich, have a slightly lower base rate, but they've added a pair of "temporary" surtaxes that make their corporate rate higher than America's. A few poorer countries, including Argentina and Chad, also tax corporate profits at 35%. But other rich countries, including all of our major economic competitors, have lower corporate rates.

Here's a sample of corporate income tax rates in 2015.[3] The chart on the next page lists the top statutory rate in various countries. Some countries, however, will cut specific deals with individual corporations to give them an even lower rate. That's why Caterpillar's Swiss subsidiary in the spare-parts trade had to pay only 6% in Swiss taxes and why Apple, as we'll see shortly, struck an even better deal with the tax authorities in Ireland.

Country	Rate
Australia	30%
Austria	25%
Belgium	33%
Canada	15%
France	33.3%
Germany	15%
Ireland	12.5%
Israel	26.5%
Japan	23.9%
Mexico	30%
Netherlands	25%
Norway	27%
South Korea	22%
Sweden	22%
Switzerland	8.5%
U.K.	20%
United States	35%

Beyond the high rate, the United States stands apart from most other industrialized democracies in that it imposes the corporate tax rate on a worldwide basis; that is, if a company incorporated in the United States makes a product in Ireland and sells it there, the profit from that sale is subject to the U.S. corporate income tax. The firm won't be taxed at the full 35% rate, because it can subtract the amount it paid in foreign tax from the U.S. tax bill, but some U.S. tax is owed on that foreign-earned income. Other rich countries, for the most part, impose the corporate tax on a "territorial" basis; that means a German company has to pay tax in Germany only on profits earned within Germany's borders. Just a few other major nations—for example, Chile, Greece, Israel, and Mexico—impose a tax on money their firms earn overseas.

But the money an American company earns overseas is not subject to the U.S. corporate tax until it is "repatriated"—that is, until the company takes the money out of a foreign bank or security and transfers it to the United States to pay salaries or dividends or to invest in buildings or machinery. Because of the worldwide basis of American taxation, the money is subject to the corporate income tax when it comes home. The result—rather predictable, if you think about it—is that American corporations routinely choose to leave large amounts of foreign earnings overseas. They deposit the money in a Swiss or Spanish bank; they invest it in German or Japanese corporate bonds; they buy Irish or Italian companies. This practice is so common today that the standard estimates say U.S. companies have more than $2.3 trillion stashed overseas. This huge accumulation of cash outside our borders is a key reason for the recent surge in a tax-dodging process called inversion.

It's important to note that the 35% rate on corporate profits is the "nominal" rate—that is, the figure set forth in the tax law. It's safe to say that no American corporation pays the full 35% in taxes. Any company with a chief financial officer who is not sound asleep all day long can take advantage of the myriad giveaways in the Internal Revenue Code to reduce its tax burden. As a result, the "effective" tax rate paid by U.S. corporations—that is, the percentage of profits that is actually paid in taxes—is well below the nominal 35% level. But estimates differ sharply about just how far below.

The most comprehensive unbiased study of effective tax rates paid by U.S. firms was issued by the Government Accountability Office (GAO)—essentially, the accounting arm of Congress—in 2013.[4] Looking at profits, and taxes paid, in the years 2008–10, the GAO said large U.S. companies actually paid 12.6% of their profits in federal tax. Many companies had to pay state and local income taxes, and some paid income tax to foreign countries on their overseas earnings. But even when all those taxes were added up, the effective rate of tax paid by large U.S. corporations was only 16.9%. The GAO said that companies were able to cut their tax bills far below the statutory rate because of "exemptions, deferrals, tax credits, and other forms of incentives" in the law and because they have successfully transferred much of their profit to foreign countries, as Caterpillar did. Big companies were so successful in the game of tax avoidance that "nearly 55 percent of all large U.S.-controlled corporations reported no federal tax liability in at least one year between 1998 and 2005," the GAO found.

For the business community, which had been fighting for years to reduce the corporate income tax rate, that report from a respected, nonpartisan observer was a serious political blow. While corporate America was complaining about the world's highest corporate tax rate, the GAO study said U.S. companies actually paid tax at about one-third of the nominal rate and at lower rates than big companies pay in many other countries. Critics of the tax preferences for corporations piled on. "Some U.S. multinational corporations like to complain about the U.S. 35% statutory tax rate," said Senator Carl Levin, a Michigan Democrat. "What they don't like to admit is that hardly any of them pay anything close to it . . . due in large part to the unjustified loopholes and gimmicks that riddle our tax code."

In response, corporate America unleashed its own studies, designed to show that the GAO was simply wrong. An analyst at PricewaterhouseCoopers issued a report saying that the total tax burden (including taxes paid to foreign countries) on all U.S. corporations "exceeded 35% for the 2004–2010 period." The Tax Foundation, a respected economic think tank funded by large corporations, disagreed with both the GAO and the PwC studies; its report said U.S. corporations in 2011 paid tax at an effective rate of 29.8%.[5]

Whatever the actual rate paid, it's clear that America's corporate income tax is high enough to motivate corporations to go to enormous lengths to avoid it. "U.S. multinational firms have established themselves as world leaders in global tax avoidance strategies," notes Professor Edward D. Kleinbard, who teaches tax law at the University of Southern California. Indeed, Apple, with the help of tax-law geniuses, managed to shift its profits (on paper) to a legal concoction where it paid no corporate tax at all.

APPLE, OF COURSE, is a famously innovative company, and its lawyers and accountants have been searching for tax reduction stratagems for decades. But the effort picked up significantly in the twenty-first century, as the iPod, the iPad, and, since 2007, the iPhone turned into major generators of profit—profit that would be taxable at the 35% corporate income tax rate. To duck that tax bill, Apple struck deals with the government of Ireland. "Apple, Inc., a U.S. corporation, has used a variety of offshore structures, arrangements, and transactions to shift billions of dollars in profits away from the United States and into Ireland, where Apple has negotiated a special corporate tax rate of less than 2%," a congressional investigation found.[6]

But even a 2% rate was more tax than Apple wanted to pay. So the company bookkeepers set up a subsidiary company, Apple Operations International. This legal entity was incorporated in Ireland but managed and controlled from the company headquarters in Cupertino, California. This "company" had no employees and no address; it had a three-member board of directors, which held its meetings in Cupertino. The home office then created a subsidiary of this Irish subsidiary, Apple Operations Europe, and a separate subsidiary of that subsidiary, Apple Sales International. Those two lower-level subsidiaries of Apple Operations International were also incorporated in Ireland but controlled and managed in Cupertino. Then Apple Inc., the American company, designated its network of Irish subsidiaries to be the official seller of Apple products everywhere outside the United States. These products were developed, designed, and programmed in the United States, and manufactured largely in China, but the right to sell them was transferred (on paper) to the Irish subsidiaries. Sales were excellent; in just four years, from 2009 to 2012, Apple Operations International had income of $74 billion.

The tax bill on this income? Zero. Apple Inc., the sole owner of the Irish subsidiaries, paid no U.S. tax on these earnings. The three companies incorporated in Ireland paid no Irish tax on these earnings. This happy outcome (for the stockholders) was the result of a clever organizational dance around the tax laws of both countries. As the company's tax lawyers had discerned, a company operating in Ireland is subject to Irish tax only if it is "managed and controlled" in Ireland. But under American law, a company is subject to U.S. corporate tax liability only if it is incorporated in the United States. Because those three companies were not managed in Ireland and not incorporated in the United States, they owed no corporate tax to either country. Apple had created $74 billion worth of what the economists call "stateless income." Of course the company still depended on the police, courts, fire departments, roads, infrastructure, educational system, and other government services provided by both the United States and Ireland; it just decided not to pay for those services, at least not on the tens of billions of dollars earned by its Irish subsidiaries.

When confronted about these tactics by angry U.S. senators from both parties—"It is completely outrageous," said John McCain, the Arizona Republican, "that Apple has not only dodged full payment of U.S. taxes, but it has managed to evade paying taxes around the world through its convoluted and pernicious strategies"—Apple executives responded with indignation of their own.

"We pay all the taxes we owe, every single dollar," declared Tim Cook, Apple's CEO, who noted that Apple paid significant sums in U.S. taxes on its sales in the United States—more than $16 million in corporate income tax every day of the year. "We do not depend on tax gimmicks. . . . We do not stash money on some Caribbean island." The problem, Cook said, was that 35% corporate tax rate, which would make it "very expensive" to record those international sales in the United States or to bring home the billions of dollars Apple had assigned to its foreign subsidiaries. The best solution would be for the United States to "eliminate all corporate tax expenditures, lower corporate income tax rates, and implement a reasonable tax on foreign earnings that allows the free flow of capital back to the United States." In short, Tim Cook gave Congress the same message that Gérard Depardieu had given to François Hollande: if you set tax rates high, taxpayers will fall back on "convoluted and pernicious strategies" to avoid them—including taking their money to a different country.

Although Cook did not mention it to the senators, Apple Inc. had actually found a roundabout way to bring home some of the billions it held overseas without paying U.S. tax on the earnings. In 2013, Apple borrowed billions of dollars—that is, it sold corporate bonds—in the United States. It used the interest it earned on the money deposited overseas to pay the interest on the bonds. This maneuver, fully legal, meant that Apple could use the money it held overseas to provide cash at no cost in the United States—without a penny to the tax man.

For all Senator McCain's ire, Apple's subsidiary-of-a-subsidiary-of-a-subsidiary structure—the scheme that placed $74 billion beyond the reach of the tax authorities—was actually not as convoluted as another tax-dodging contraption, the intricate mechanism known as a "Double Irish with a Dutch Sandwich." This one works nicely to shield profits from the tax man for companies that have a good deal of intellectual property, like search engines, software, cancer drugs, or computer operating systems. The "Double Irish" has been used by the likes of Apple and Microsoft, but it's generally agreed, among aficionados of tax avoidance, that the paradigm case of this particular apparatus is Google's international tax shifting, which is complicated to the point of being difficult to pin down precisely.

GOOGLE CREATED A COMPANY called Google Bermuda Unlimited, based in Hamilton, Bermuda. That island nation is famous among tourists for its pink beaches and swaying palms, but it is favored by corporate treasurers for another national asset: a corporate tax rate of 0%. Google's Bermuda subsidiary is the official corporate owner of a separate subsidiary called Google Ireland Holdings. This one is also based in Bermuda, but the name is appropriate because Google Ireland Holdings is the designated corporate owner of yet another Google subsidiary known as Google Ireland Limited, based in Dublin.

Once this corporate structure was established, Google's headquarters in the United States assigned the rights to its intellectual property—its search and advertising technology, the golden goose of Google profits—to the "Ireland Holdings" subsidiary in Bermuda. Then it designated the "Ireland Limited" subsidiary in Dublin as the official seller of all Google advertising in Europe, the Middle East, and Africa. This business brought in huge earnings for "Ireland Limited," the Dublin subsidiary. That would have created large profits for the Dublin subsidiary, which would be taxable in Ireland (at the 12.5% corporate tax rate there). But the Dublin subsidiary paid a "license fee" to the holder of the intellectual property—that is, to the Bermuda subsidiary. The license fees were so large that the Dublin company ended up paying out more than 99% of its earnings to its sister company in zero-tax Bermuda. The result was no taxable income in the United States. Almost no taxable income in Ireland. And lots of corporate income in Bermuda, where there's no tax on corporate income.

It gets worse. There was a problem with the intricate plan outlined in the previous paragraph. The Irish tax code limits how much profit can be transferred out of Ireland to another country; because Google intended to shift virtually all the profits from Ireland to Bermuda, that limit could have stifled the whole complex transfer scheme. But there was an escape route: Ireland has treaties with certain countries (but not Bermuda) that permit such transfers on a tax-free basis. One of those countries is the Netherlands. So the profit earned on Google's advertising in much of the world was collected by Google Ireland Limited, in Dublin, and then transferred to Google Netherlands Holdings BV, a shell company (no employees) in the Netherlands ("BV" is the Dutch equivalent of "Inc."). From there, the money was shifted (on paper) to the Bermuda subsidiary. In essence, the two "Google Ireland" subsidiaries form a sandwich around the Dutch subsidiary. This exercise in three-part harmony means that billions of dollars of earnings built on intellectual property developed in the United States come to Google tax-free. *Bloomberg Businessweek* estimated that the sandwich cut Google's U.S. tax bill by $3.1 billion over a four-year period.[7]

Caterpillar, Apple, and Google are not the only U.S. companies that have devised ornate structures to duck U.S. tax on their international sales. Among others, Microsoft has used a similar stratagem, assigning the profits from its foreign sales to subsidiaries in Singapore and (no surprise) Ireland. But Microsoft took this game one step further; it found a way to duck U.S. taxes on its sales inside the United States. To do that, Microsoft set up a wholly owned subsidiary company in Puerto Rico called MOPR (that is, Microsoft Operations Puerto Rico). Puerto Rico is, of course, a U.S. territory, but the IRS treats it as a foreign country for corporate tax purposes.

Microsoft headquarters in the United States then assigned to the Puerto Rico operation the North American rights to the company's intellectual property in software, operating systems, search engines, and Web-based products. Whenever a Microsoft product that uses this intellectual property (which is to say, all Microsoft products) was sold in the United States, about half of the profit from the sale was attributed (on paper) to the Puerto Rican subsidiary. This meant that a subsidiary with a staff that comprised less than 1% of Microsoft employees was credited with earning half of the company's profit in the United States. Microsoft has negotiated a deal with the cash-starved Puerto Rican government to pay income tax at a rate of about 2% on these profits.

"This structure is not designed to satisfy any specific manufacturing or business need," concluded a congressional study of the Microsoft tax-avoidance mechanism. "Rather, it is designed to minimize tax on sales of products sold in the United States. . . . By routing its manufacturing through a tiny factory in Puerto Rico, Microsoft saved over $4.5 billion in taxes on goods sold in the United States" over a three-year period.[8]

Despite these industrious efforts to escape American taxes, Caterpillar, Apple, Google, and Microsoft still declare themselves to be American corporations. Apple's CEO, Tim Cook, was adamant on this point that day when the senators were grilling him about "stateless income." "I am often asked," Cook said, "if Apple still considers itself an American company. My answer has always been an emphatic 'Yes.' We are proud to be an American company and equally proud of our contribution to the U.S. economy."

But the lure of tax avoidance is so strong that other American companies have been perfectly willing to renounce legal ties to their home country and move overseas (on paper at least) in pursuit of a lower rate of corporate income tax. This is done through a process called an inversion. It's a merger arrangement in which the U.S. enterprise buys (or sometimes is bought by) a foreign company and then moves its legal domicile to the new partner's home country. Because it is no longer an American corporation—even though the management and much of the workforce stay home in the United States—it no longer has to pay that 35% tax on overseas profits. The term "inversion" is used because many of these deals involve a big American company merging with a much smaller foreign firm. The deal inverts the stature of the two, because the smaller foreign company becomes the owner, on paper, of the much larger and richer American "subsidiary."

Since 2010—when a group of lawyers at the Skadden, Arps firm worked out the legalities of this maneuver—dozens of U.S. companies have become former U.S. companies by means of inversion.[9] Burger King, an iconic American burger, fries, and milk shake franchise founded in Florida in the 1950s, is one item on this varied corporate menu. The fast-food giant pulled off a Whopper of an inversion deal in 2014—and became a Canadian company in the process—when it acquired Tim Hortons, a coffee-and-doughnut restaurant chain north of the border. Burger King, with 13,667 outlets in more than fifty countries, was much bigger than its new partner, Hortons, which had about 4,600 restaurants, almost all of them in Canada. Yet the company resulting from this deal, dubbed Restaurant Brands International, incorporated in Canada. Burger King was still managed from the same corporate office in Miami; it still celebrated the Fourth of July and Presidents' Day with big promotions across the United States; on paper, though, it became Canadian, which meant its profits were now to be taxed at the Canadian corporate income tax rate, 15%, as opposed to the 35% rate back home. Burger King's tax break was offset somewhat, though, because the province of Ontario charged another 11.5% in corporate tax.

The more important tax benefit seemed to be that the multibillion-dollar sums Burger King had been holding overseas could now be brought home to the United States, in various ways, without paying the U.S. income tax on that money. As a Canadian company, Burger King no longer had to pay U.S. tax when it brought foreign profits home. This is a standard, fundamental tax-avoidance aspect of inversion but not the most important one. The more valuable tax maneuver that American firms can and do employ after an inversion is a process called earnings skimming. For this one, the now-foreign company lends large sums to the parts of the firm remaining in the United States. The U.S. branch uses the borrowed money to pay its bills and makes an interest payment on the loan to the overseas "headquarters." Because this is considered a business loan, the interest can be deducted ("skimmed") from taxable earnings in the United States. In essence, a company borrows from itself, pays interest to itself, and gets a big deduction on its U.S. tax bill—for a transaction that may exist only on paper. Individuals can't use this trick to cut their tax bills, but it's legal for corporate taxpayers that are incorporated in a foreign country.

By early 2016, the inversion innovation had become so popular that the *New York Times* compared the surge in tax-avoiding corporations to the flood of immigrants pouring into Europe from the war-torn Middle East. "A Tidal Wave of Corporate Migrants Seeking (Tax) Shelter" read the clever *Times* headline. Almost any company in almost any industry was said to be considering a move to renounce the United States and move its titular headquarters offshore to duck taxes. Even firms that had profited from federal spending programs, government bailouts, or other significant benefits funded by U.S. taxpayers were willing to flee the country, and its 35% corporate tax, following the siren call of inversion.

Johnson Controls, for example, was a venerable American manufacturing concern—its founder, Warren Johnson, invented the thermostat in 1883—that became a major supplier (of passenger seats, batteries, and so on) to the auto industry. But in the Great Recession of 2008–9, with the Detroit automobile makers on the brink of bankruptcy, parts suppliers like Johnson Controls were in dire trouble. Johnson's president, Keith Wandell, went to Washington to plead for federal bailout money for his customers. "We respectfully urge . . . Congress as a whole to provide the financial support the automakers need at this critical time," he said. Sure enough, Washington came up with some $80 billion in emergency funding for domestic automakers—money that proved a lifeline not only to General Motors and Chrysler but also to their major suppliers, like Johnson Controls. (Johnson Controls later noted that it had asked Congress for bailout money only for the companies it supplied, not for itself.) In addition to this federal support, the company had received tens of millions of dollars of tax breaks from states where it had plants.

How did Johnson Controls demonstrate its gratitude for this timely help from American governments? In 2016, the company announced that it was selling itself to a firm incorporated in Ireland, Tyco International, and would no longer be a U.S. corporation. The firm estimated this move would cut its corporate income tax payments to the U.S. government by about $150 million per year. Tyco, incidentally, was itself a veteran of tax-avoidance inversion tactics, having moved its corporate domicile (on paper at least) from the United States to Bermuda to Switzerland to Ireland over a period of roughly twenty years.

Pfizer, the giant drug firm that makes such staples of the American medicine cabinet as Viagra and Preparation H, concedes in its reports to stockholders that its bottom line is heavily dependent on U.S. government programs financed by taxes. "Any significant spending reductions affecting Medicare, Medicaid, or other publicly funded or subsidized health programs . . . could have an adverse effect on our results," Pfizer noted in 2014. But this did not stop Pfizer from charging ahead with the biggest attempted inversion ever, in 2016, when it paid $155 billion for an Irish drug company called Allergan and announced plans (later scrapped) to move its corporate domicile to Ireland.

For the most part, the companies following the inversion route say that their move to a foreign jurisdiction is dictated by sound business considerations, not by tax concerns. That's exactly what Rick Gonzalez, the chief executive of an Illinois-based pharmaceutical firm called AbbVie, said when he announced that the U.S. firm intended to buy a drug company called Shire, which was headquartered on the island of Jersey, in the English Channel. AbbVie would then incorporate in Jersey and avoid much U.S. corporate tax. Gonzalez said, though, that this tax saving was not the reason for the planned merger; the company was moving to that island in the channel in order to provide better service to its customers. But then, before the purchase of Shire could be completed, the U.S. Treasury changed some of the rules surrounding inversions, and suddenly the tax benefits for AbbVie looked much smaller. AbbVie abruptly called off its proposed merger with Shire. Gonzalez issued an angry statement saying the Treasury had "interpreted longstanding tax principle in a uniquely selective manner designed specifically to destroy the financial benefits of these types of transactions." With that, AbbVie pretty much gave the game away. If the move to the isle of Jersey was not undertaken for tax reasons, why would a tax ruling "destroy the financial benefits" of the deal?[10]

Sometimes, the political or public relations cost of an attempted inversion turns out to be greater than the potential tax savings. The drugstore giant Walgreens found that out when it bought a stake in the European drugstore chain Alliance Boots and then proposed to move its legal domicile from Deerfield, Illinois, to Bern, Switzerland, where Alliance Boots was headquartered. The company was denounced by people who argued, fairly, that a famous American drugstore heavily dependent on taxpayer-funded Medicare prescription sales ought to be an American taxpayer. The *Chicago Tribune* came up with the term "Walgreed"; the business columnist Al Lewis called the plan an example of "the looting of America. . . . Yes, your corner drugstore would like to take your co-pay, bill your Medicare policy, and then pay its taxes in Switzerland," Lewis wrote. Under withering attacks from politicians, the press, and its customers, Walgreens had second thoughts and announced that it would retain its corporate presence in the United States.

ALL OF THE FIRMS cited here, and countless others, have been attacked by critics ranging from Bernie Sanders to Barack Obama to Donald Trump. They have been called "corporate traitors" and "Benedict Arnold companies" for shifting their tax burden out of the United States. They've been called outlaws and criminals for setting up such intricate structures to get around the tax code. In response to this calumny, the corporations reply that they are engaged in perfectly legal activity. They "minimize" their tax bills; they "avoid" paying taxes; but they do not "evade" taxes, because that would be against the law.

The distinction here is set forth in the definitive text *Tax Law Design and Drafting,* edited by the acknowledged master of the subject, Victor Thuronyi of the International Monetary Fund. (Dr. Thuronyi's magisterial study is priced at $560, so please stop complaining about the price you paid for this book.) That heavyweight piece of analysis defines tax "evasion" as a "clear violation of the tax laws, such as fabricating false accounts." Tax "avoidance," in contrast, is "behavior by the taxpayer that is aimed at reducing tax liability but that does not constitute a criminal offense." Avoidance can involve "abusing gaps or loopholes in the law" but falls short of "breaching specific statutory duties." And tax "minimization" is defined as "behavior that is legally effective in reducing tax liability," such as paying your January bills in December so as to get the deduction in the current tax year.

But of course these distinctions are not always so clear in practice. This has led to the cynical observation that "the rich avoid, the poor evade"; that is, rich taxpayers can afford to pay lawyers who will find a complicated but legal way to duck (that is, "avoid") taxes, while poorer people just cheat (that is, "evade"). Franklin Delano Roosevelt, no friend of those in the upper brackets, observed in 1935 that "tax avoidance means that you hire a $25,000-fee lawyer, and he changes the word 'evasion' into the word 'avoidance.'"

Defenders of tax avoidance tend to fall back on some favorite judicial utterances that seem to support the notion that a taxpayer is not obliged to pay one cent more than the minimum he can get away with under the law. In Britain, the champion of this position was Lord Clyde, the lord justice general, who famously declared in 1929 that "no man in this country is under the smallest obligation . . . to enable the Inland Revenue to put the largest possible shovel in his stores." In the United States, the preferred citation comes from the best-named magistrate in U.S. history, the federal circuit court judge Learned Hand. In one of the most widely cited opinions in the history of tax law, Judge Hand declared that "anyone may so arrange his affairs that his taxes shall be as low as possible; he is not bound to choose that pattern which will best pay the Treasury; there is not even a patriotic duty to increase one's taxes." In the same opinion, Hand even seemed to authorize both "avoiding" and "evading" taxes. "A transaction, otherwise within an exception of the tax law," he wrote, "does not lose its immunity because it is actuated by a desire to avoid, or, if one choose, to evade, taxation."

Learned Hand's mellifluous defense of tax avoidance is cherished by the lawyers and consultants who design "convoluted and pernicious strategies." What these lawyers and consultants generally don't mention is that in that case—it was *Helvering v. Gregory,* issued in

1934—Judge Hand also said that there are limits to how far you can go to avoid, or evade, taxes. In the *Helvering* case that tax lawyers love to quote, Learned Hand actually ruled in favor of the IRS and ordered the avoider to pay up.[11]

The case involved a wealthy Brooklyn socialite, Mrs. Evelyn Gregory, who was the sole owner of a company called United Mortgage Corporation. That firm, in turn, owned about $133,000 worth of stock in a separate company, the Monitor Securities Corporation. In 1928, Mrs. Gregory decided to sell the shares of Monitor Securities (it turned out to be a smart decision, because Monitor's shares lost virtually all their value in the 1929 market crash). Under the tax code, her profit on those shares would have been treated as ordinary income, and thus would be taxed at the top income tax rate. But if she could arrange the deal so that her profit was a "capital gain," she could cut the tax bill in half. To make this arrangement, Mrs. Gregory's lawyers created a shell corporation—no employees, no board of directors—in Delaware. That newly formed corporation received (on paper) the shares in Monitor, sold them, and distributed the proceeds to Mrs. Gregory. She put the money in the bank and dissolved the Delaware corporation six days after it was formed. She then told the IRS that her earnings on the Monitor shares were "capital gains." On this basis, Mrs. Gregory paid the tax on her profit at the lower rate. The IRS went to court, arguing that she should have paid at the higher rate for ordinary income.

In his oft-quoted opinion, Hand first lays out the principle quoted above: nobody has to pay a cent more in tax than the minimum required by law. But then he goes on to examine the dubious transactions—the empty corporate shell that existed for all of six days—Mrs. Gregory engaged in to take advantage of the lower tax rate. And he concludes that the whole complex operation was a "sham," designed only to evade taxes: "The transactions were no part of the conduct of the business of either or both companies; so viewed they were a sham." Because there was no legitimate business purpose for routing the shares the way she did, Mrs. Gregory had to pay the full amount the IRS demanded. "It is plain," Judge Hand decides, "that the taxpayer may not avoid her just taxes." A year later, the Supreme Court affirmed Hand's ruling; Mrs. Gregory's "sham" did not work.

It doesn't seem like too great of a stretch to suggest that some of the machinations employed by Google, Apple, and others to avoid ("or, if one choose, to evade") taxes might also fall into the "sham" category. For the most part, though, these companies have faced little or no trouble from the IRS. If some corporate treasurer can find a tax lawyer to design an intricate international arrangement that moves U.S. profits overseas and then cuts the tax bill, the IRS tends to stand aside and let it happen. This is partly because the corporations hire sophisticated tax accountants and law firms to make sure that maneuvers like the "Dutch Sandwich" fall within the precise parameters of the tax code.

But it's also because the IRS, facing budget cuts year after year from a hostile Congress, just doesn't have the firepower to take on rich, well-lawyered tax avoiders. The commissioner of the IRS, John Koskinen, essentially admitted that this is the case. "When Congress cuts our budget," the commissioner told me, "they say we have to do more with less. But the fact is, we're doing less with less because we don't have the resources to enforce the law the way we would want to." In the year 2015, the IRS reported that it performed fewer corporate audits than in any year since 2002, and the revenue generated from audits also hit a ten-year low.

There was considerable public consternation, in Congress and on the nation's editorial pages, about the surge of tax-ducking inversions that began in mid-2014. While members of Congress from both parties were lamenting this trend, nobody suggested that a gridlocked Congress might actually agree to do something about it. Accordingly, the secretary of the Treasury, Jacob Lew, stepped up three times—in the fall of 2014, and again in late 2015, and yet again in 2016—with new regulations designed to make inversions more difficult to pull off. Lew himself conceded that his proposals were weak reeds at best, but he said his actions went as far as he could go without congressional action. Tax accountants generally agreed that Lew's new rules would not stop the inversion craze among corporate treasurers. After Lew's second round of regulating, a *Wall Street Journal* headline neatly captured the business view: "'Inversion' Rule Changes Appear Minor." The only institution that punished U.S. companies for committing inversion was *Fortune* magazine, which refuses to list a company incorporated overseas in the famous Fortune 500 rankings. *Fortune* kicked out about ten companies, including Pfizer, which had ranked at No. 51 before it became an Irish corporation in order to cut its tax bill.

One company that did get in trouble with the IRS, and with criminal prosecutors, over its tax-avoidance efforts was Caterpillar Inc. After Caterpillar paid PricewaterhouseCoopers for figuring out the Swiss-subsidiary profit shift, it saved some $200 million each year in U.S. taxes for more than a decade. Things were going fine until the company ran into a buzz saw by the name of Carl Levin—and that convoluted tax diversion plan began to crumble.

Carl Levin, a Democratic U.S. senator from Michigan, served in Congress so long that he became chairman of an entity called the Permanent Subcommittee on Investigations. This is an obscure but powerful unit with a generous budget and a sizable staff that can probe, essentially, anything its chairman wants to probe. Levin chose to investigate tax avoidance by multinational U.S. corporations. This won the senator mixed reviews. The *New York Times* called him "a gift" to ordinary U.S. taxpayers; the *Wall Street Journal* called the same senator "a one-man wrecking crew of American job creation." Regardless, Levin pursued his tax probes with a passion. Thus it was, on an April morning in 2014, that the permanent subcommittee held a cantankerous hearing on the subject of "Caterpillar's offshore tax strategy."

Levin and his investigative staff laid out the history, in which some $8 billion of profits on spare-parts sales were transferred to a country that never designed, built, or warehoused a single spare part. Caterpillar executives responded, saying the profit shift to Switzerland was a "prudent, lawful business activity," carried out strictly for business purposes without consideration of the tax benefits. "We do not invent artificial business structures," said the company's vice president for financial services. Unfortunately for Caterpillar, the committee staff had obtained documents from PricewaterhouseCoopers that explicitly declared that the point of the Swiss transfer was to cut taxes. The smoking gun was an e-mail from a PwC tax partner that warned Caterpillar about the risks of its plan. "We are going to have to create a story," the tax man noted. "Get ready to do some dancing." As if that weren't bad enough, another PwC tax expert sent back a flip e-mail of his own: "What the heck. We'll all be retired when this comes up on audit."[12]

At the end of the hearing, Levin called on the IRS to investigate the Caterpillar maneuvers. Roughly a year later, Caterpillar announced that the IRS had dunned it for some $1 billion in back taxes and penalties for just one three-year period, from 2007 to 2009, because of improper shifting of profits to the Swiss subsidiary. The IRS was also probing the company's tax returns for other years. Meanwhile, federal prosecutors in Illinois subpoenaed corporate documents to determine whether the profit shifting violated federal law. And the Securities and Exchange Commission launched its own probe of Caterpillar's tax-avoidance efforts. To add insult to all these legal injuries, the *Wall Street Journal* reported that this flurry of investigations "threatens to become a serious embarrassment for Caterpillar, which has long projected a squeaky-clean Midwestern image."[13]

But such federal probes of tax-dodging efforts were hardly common. Most American companies that created an intricate avoidance apparatus were basically left untouched by the underfunded IRS and other U.S. agencies. The real heat over profit shifting, earnings skimming, and sweetheart deals with national tax agencies came from two international organizations, the OECD and the European Union. After years of study, the OECD in 2015 issued an "action plan" called BEPS—the Base Erosion and Profit Shifting Project—that gives countries various tools to prevent their companies from fleeing the nest to find a lower tax rate somewhere else.

Meanwhile, EU authorities had repeatedly expressed concern and anger about corporate tax-avoidance shenanigans, but their power to act was minimal, because it is a basic principle in Europe that the EU cannot dictate any country's tax rules or rates. If Switzerland wanted to offer a French company a special 2% tax rate, the EU commissioners in Brussels could only look on.

In 2014, though, the EU began pursuing tax dodgers under a new legal theory: the "state aid" rules. These regulations say that European governments cannot give their home-country companies special benefits that would give them an economic advantage over foreign competitors. For example, if France let some lumber company take timber from the national forests at no charge, that would be an unfair advantage over a German company that had to pay for its trees and would thus violate the "state aid" regulations. So the tax police in Brussels started citing certain countries—mainly Ireland, the Netherlands, Luxembourg, and Switzerland—for giving special low tax rates to certain companies; the regulators said those tax breaks amounted to "state aid" for the favored firms. And this had some impact. A few companies—Apple, Starbucks, and Fiat—were eventually required to pay back taxes to European countries that were found to have taxed them too lightly. In 2016, the EU ordered Apple to pay more than $14 billion in back taxes to Ireland—an order that was immediately challenged by Apple and the Irish government. The national tax authorities in several countries dropped some of the gimmicks they had used to lure foreign corporations; thanks to the European Union crackdown, the notorious "Double Irish" is no longer a viable path toward tax avoidance. Of course, the tax lawyers immediately started designing new ways for companies to duck taxation.

THE U.S. CORPORATE INCOME TAX is not working. We have a higher corporate tax rate than almost any other country, and we apply it to income earned anywhere in the world. And yet corporate income tax revenues have fallen so sharply that they now make up a fairly small share of the federal government's annual tax revenues. In the 1960s, the corporate tax brought in about 33% of U.S. tax revenues. Today, the same tax provides less than 9% of revenues; that means individual tax-payers have to take up the slack and pay more. Which we do. In the 1960s, the individual income tax and the Social Security tax consti-tuted about 50% of all federal tax revenues; today their share of the nation's total tax burden is more than 80%. Corporate tax revenues are plummeting partly because Congress has larded the corporate income tax with costly preferences and giveaways for corporations, and partly because American multinationals have become so successful at shifting income overseas. Hundreds of millions of dollars—money that might have gone to raising wages, or creating new medicines, or building factories—have been paid to tax lawyers for the creation of elaborate evasion schemes. The result is a complicated, unpopular, and stiff cor-porate income tax that actually doesn't do much taxing. "Both the high U.S. tax rate and the worldwide system of taxation have more bark than bite," notes the tax scholar Kimberly Clausing of Reed College.

What should we do? The solution proposed by politicians in both parties and by many (but not all) economists is to reduce that 35% rate. A lower rate would bring the United States more into sync with other wealthy countries. Reducing the corporate rate has been an international trend for the past three decades. Virtually all the other rich countries have done so, which is why it seems so attractive to American corporations to move their taxable income, or even their legal existence, overseas. If we were to follow the BBLR principle, we could almost certainly lower the rate of corporate tax without a loss of revenue.

The Government Accountability Office added up the cost of some eighty major business tax preferences and reported a tax loss for the year 2011 at $181 billion, which is not much less than the total revenue the corporate income tax brings in each year. Eliminating most of those deductions, exemptions, credits, and allowances would broaden the base significantly, so the rates could be lower. And many of these loopholes are indefensible. Why should a company be allowed to lend itself money, pay itself interest, and then take a tax deduction for the interest it paid to itself? No individual taxpayer could get away with that scam. But Congress lets corporations use that "earnings skimming" gambit every day of the year.

The most common proposals for cutting the corporate income tax rate call for a new rate in the range of 25%. President Barack Obama suggested cutting the rate to 28%, a proposal that was pronounced dead on arrival as soon as it reached Capitol Hill. The presidential candidate Donald Trump went further, of course, proposing a 15% corporate tax rate. A study by the Tax Analysis Center concluded that if all deductions, credits, and so on for business were eliminated, the IRS could collect the same revenue with a rate of 9% that it brings in now with the 35% rate. A rate that low, most likely, would take away the incentive to hire tax consultants and shift profits overseas.

The problem here is that if the United States cuts its rate, other countries might well respond by cutting their rates even lower. How low can you go? Congress might cut the U.S. corporate income tax rate to 12.5% to be competitive with Ireland. But then Switzerland, with its 8.5% rate, would still be a lure for chief financial officers looking to reduce the tax bill—not to mention Bermuda, New Zealand, and other countries where the corporate income tax rate is zero. And if the United States did agree to a large cut in the rate, other countries might well cut their tax rates even more sharply. This is a race to the bottom that nobody can really win.

How low does the tax rate have to go to stop corporations from devising intricate mechanisms to avoid paying? Great Britain, which reduced its corporate tax rate half a dozen times in the twenty-first century, now taxes profits at 20%. But that didn't stop Starbucks from creating an intricate multinational network to avoid tax in Britain. Starbucks had more than eight hundred outlets in Britain in the second decade of the twenty-first century, and the company repeatedly told financial analysts that the U.K. business was "profitable." But when it came time to pay the U.K. "company tax" on its income in Britain, those reported profits disappeared. Starbucks told the tax authorities that it had actually lost money for fourteen of the fifteen years between 1998 and 2013 and thus paid no U.K. tax.

Here's how: The Starbucks stores in the U.K. had to make royalty payments to Starbucks subsidiaries in other countries. Every time Starbucks sold a cup of coffee in Britain, it paid a royalty to a Swiss company called Starbucks Trading, which owned the rights to all coffee beans the company sold in Europe. There was a second royalty payment due to a Dutch company, Starbucks Coffee EMEA BV, which held the rights to all the "intellectual property" in a cup of coffee (presumably meaning the recipe for a Frappuccino or the trademarked logo on the paper cup).[14] And those royalty payments to other subsidiaries of the same company totaled more than Starbucks had earned in Britain. The upshot: no profit to report in Britain and thus no British tax. This neat arrangement caused such an uproar in the U.K. when it was reported (by Reuters, in October 2012) that Brits all over the country mounted a noisy, angry boycott of Starbucks. The protest campaign was so effective that Starbucks finally agreed to pay £20 million in U.K. tax—more than $30 million—in an effort to get its customers back.

Another approach to corporate tax reform would be to induce companies to bring home some of the money they have stashed away overseas. The amount at stake here is staggering: an estimated $2.3 trillion "permanently invested" outside the United States. Much of this money is actually held in bank accounts or investment funds within the United States, but on paper it is officially overseas and thus not subject to U.S. corporate tax. If all these profits were repatriated, and the full 35% tax were paid, the government would take in a revenue windfall of about $700 billion; that's enough to fund the entire defense budget, including the Middle East and Afghanistan, for a little more than a year. If all these profits were repatriated and corporations paid a tax of 15% on these earnings—roughly the effective rate they're paying now—the tax revenue would come to $300 billion, which would totally cover the government's combined annual spending for education, environmental protection, agriculture, housing, homeland security, national parks, and NASA.

To induce corporations to bring some of that money home—so that the government gets some tax revenue and the companies can have cash they could use to create new jobs or build new factories—many have proposed a tax holiday, in which the funds can be repatriated with a smaller tax bite. President Obama suggested a onetime cut to 19% for taxing profits brought home from overseas.

As a matter of fact, we tried the tax-holiday approach in 2004. After intense lobbying from American multinationals eager to bring their money back home, Congress passed a law optimistically titled the American Jobs Creation Act. One section of that law, known as the Homeland Investment Act, said that corporations could repatriate foreign-held profits and pay tax on them at a onetime rate of 5.25%—that is, about one-seventh of what they would have paid at the full corporate income tax rate. Wary of what corporate titans might do with this money, Congress specifically said that the repatriated funds could not be used to increase dividends to stockholders or to juice up executive pay. Instead, the money brought home was supposed to fund job creation, research, and capital investment here in the United States.

The government subsequently estimated that some $300 billion came home to the United States because of this break, generating about $16 billion in tax revenues. But the money didn't go where Congress had hoped it would.

"Repatriations did not lead to an increase in investment, employment or R&D—even for the firms that lobbied for the tax holiday stating these intentions," concluded a report from the National Bureau of Economic Research. "Instead, a $1 increase in repatriations was associated with an increase of approximately $1 in payouts to shareholders."[15] Beyond that, the tax holiday probably had the perverse effect of inducing corporations to keep more money overseas. "The provision also sends firms a strange message," noted Professor Clausing of Reed College; "they have an incentive to leave income abroad in the hope of similar holidays in the future."[16] Clausing concluded that the American Jobs Creation Act lived up to its name in one respect: "creating jobs for accountants and lawyers."

As the mountain of corporate cash piled up overseas grows higher and higher, some experts predict that American corporations will bite the bullet and pay the full rate of tax in order to get some of their money back home. "American corporations have been so proficient at shifting their earnings overseas . . . that today they're hoist by their own petard," notes Martin Sullivan, the highly regarded chief economist at the Washington firm Tax Analysts. "It's great to keep your profits out of the U.S. tax net, but as those piles of cash grow, you are missing more and more opportunities to employ that cash in the U.S. At some point, saving tax is not worth it."

From this point of view, Congress should hang tough—keep the corporate rate high, refuse to authorize another tax holiday—and sooner or later corporate America will bring its money home and pay the tax. Indeed, this has seemed to be the case in recent years. Economists estimate that some $300 billion was repatriated, at full tax rates, in 2015—about the same amount that came home following the 2004 tax holiday. When General Electric, under pressure from stockholders, decided in 2015 to repatriate $36 billion that had been held overseas for years, the *Wall Street Journal* reported that "GE's decision suggests more companies may be reaching a tipping point."[17]

LARGE QUANTITIES OF MONEY and effort—resources that might have been used for something productive—have been poured into "convoluted and pernicious strategies." Accordingly, some tax experts recommend that we eliminate the corporate income tax completely. Professor Laurence J. Kotlikoff of Boston University makes the case as follows:

Many economists . . . suspect that our corporate income tax is economically self-defeating—hurting workers, not capitalists, and collecting precious little revenue to boot. . . . The rich, including . . .
stockholders, can take their money and run. . . . To avoid our
federal corporate tax, they can, and often do, move their operations and jobs abroad. Apple . . . paid only 8.2 percent of its worldwide profits in United States corporate income taxes, thanks to
piling up most of its profits and locating far too many of its operations overseas.[18]

Those who agree on eliminating the corporate tax tend to disagree
on what should be done to make up for the lost revenue. On the left,
economists like Robert Reich of the University of California, Berkeley,
say corporate profits should still be taxed but not until the corporate
earnings have been distributed to stockholders. Then the government
can make the stockholder pay a higher rate of tax on the dividends or
on the increase in the value of the stock. The shortfall from lost corporate tax revenue would then be offset by the higher revenues from taxing the stockholders' dividend and capital gain income. Conservative
economists like N. Gregory Mankiw of Harvard argue that we should
stop trying to tax corporate earnings in any form and make up the revenue through "a broad-based tax on consumption."

Whatever changes we eventually make, almost every observer
agrees that the current corporate income tax is not working. The
corporate income tax, once a key source of funding for the U.S. government, has become just another minor revenue source. There are
already many of those.

THE SINGLE TAX, THE FAT TAX, THE TINY TAX, THE CARBON TAX— AND NO TAX AT ALL

Thomas Piketty's surprising bestseller, *Capital in the Twenty-First Century,* sold nearly a million copies in the year after its publication, a stunning development for a heavyweight economics tome. But Piketty is a piker compared with an earlier author who wrote a similarly hefty volume on the same subject. The newspaperman Henry George's economic magnum opus, *Progress and Poverty,* first published in 1879, sold more than three million copies in the late nineteenth and early twentieth centuries. It was translated into two dozen languages (there were three separate editions in German). The book made its previously unknown author one of the three most famous men in the United States (after Mark Twain and Thomas Edison); it spawned a national political movement (Georgism) that claims dedicated followers to this day. Literary titans including Leo Tolstoy, Arnold Toynbee, and George Bernard Shaw called George a crucial influence ("one of the greatest men of the 19th century," Tolstoy said). Dr. Sun Yat-sen, the leader of the rebellion that threw out China's last ruling dynasty, embraced Georgian tax policy for his (short-lived) new government. Franklin Delano Roosevelt and Martin Luther King Jr. cited Georgian principles in major speeches. To further their cause, George's followers in the early twentieth century created a board game designed to denounce the landlord class; this offshoot of Georgism lives on today as one of the world's most popular parlor pastimes. It's called Monopoly.

George's book became a surprise bestseller for essentially the same reasons that Thomas Piketty's did. Just as Piketty's book followed the Great Recession of 2008–9, *Progress and Poverty* came out in the wake of the national depression of 1873–77, a time when millions of working-class Americans felt they had been handed a raw deal by the economic and political establishment. Both books dealt directly with the gnawing problem of inequality; both came at a time when Americans were increasingly worried about the wealth gap and its impact on prosperity and democracy.

It is stunning to see how closely George's discussion of inequality in America tracks what is being said in the same country 140 years later. Although Henry George had a more florid style—"Amid the greatest accumulations of wealth," he wrote, "men die of starvation, and puny infants suckle dry breasts"—his book is studded with lines that would sound right at home in a 2016 campaign speech by Bernie Sanders.

> So long as all the increased wealth which modern progress brings goes but to build up great fortunes, to increase luxury and make sharper the contrast between the House of Have and the House of Want, progress is not real and cannot be permanent.

> Some get an infinitely better and easier living, but others find it hard to get a living at all.

> It is true that wealth has been greatly increased, and that the average of comfort, leisure, and refinement has been raised; but these gains are not general. . . . The tendency of what we call material progress . . . is still further to depress the condition of the lowest class.

It is true that disappointment has followed disappointment, and that discovery upon discovery, and invention after invention, have neither lessened the toil nor brought plenty to the poor.[1]

In another striking parallel with Piketty, Henry George came up with the same proposed tool to deal with the problem of inequality: taxes. Piketty calls for personal income tax rates as high as 80% and for an international wealth tax, like the one that's used in France, to extract even more from the richest taxpayers. George, in contrast, came up with a distinctive approach to taxation—indeed, an idea so radical it had not been tried before. This new system he called the Land Value Tax, or simply the Single Tax.

FROM THE ECONOMISTS, George took the basic principle that when you tax something, you generally get less of it. Therefore, a tax on labor—such as an income tax or a payroll tax deduction for Social Security—would lead people to work less and reduce overall productivity. A tax on commerce—such as a sales tax or a corporate profits tax—would diminish business activity and innovation. A tax on interest or dividends would discourage saving and investment. The only thing there wouldn't be less of if it were taxed, he concluded, is land. The quantity of land in any state or nation is fixed. It's not going away, no matter how steep the tax on landownership might be.

From the Bible, George drew the conviction that private ownership of land was contrary to God's word. (People can find almost anything in Holy Scripture, of course.) After all, it says right there in Psalm 115 that "the heavens are the Lord's, but the earth hath he given to the children of men." So, to Henry George, private landownership is sinful. Even worse, it is the source of the basic problem of economic inequality. When a small number of rich people own massive swaths of land—and the profit from rents and resources earned from their land—the privileged elite will consistently grow richer, while the masses struggle to get by. "Virtually all economic problems," George wrote, "arise from the fact that the land on which and from which All must live is made exclusive property of Some."

Logically, this might have led to a system that seized the land belonging to the Some and dispersed it equally to All. While Henry George was a radical, though, he was not so radical as to call for confiscation of private property. In his system, the rich could keep their land, but they were to be taxed to pay for this privilege. "The land belongs equally to all, and land values . . . should be shared among all." George proposed that governments impose a heavy tax on the value of land. In fact, this Land Value Tax was to be so heavy that the revenues would be enough to replace the income from all other forms of taxation. All governments would need only one form of tax. And because this Single Tax would be paid almost entirely by the landowning elites, working people would be free to spend and save their earnings without the need to fund government through other forms of taxation. The rich would pay more, the working class would pay less, and over time inequality of wealth would sharply diminish.

Could it have worked then? Could it work now? Even with a property tax regime at exorbitant rates, it is hard to see how a single tax on land could bring in enough money to finance every level of government. But in George's day, government—and thus the funding needed to pay for it—was vastly smaller than what we know today. When *Progress and Poverty* was published, in 1879, there was no Social Security, no Medicaid, no NASA, no Department of Transportation or Energy or Health and Human Services. Some economic historians argue that the Georgian Single Tax might have been adequate to maintain the relatively minimal governmental establishment of the 1880s.

THE SINGLE TAX WAS enormously popular in George's day, prompting Georgist movements to spring up around the world, and it continues to have prominent backers, both left and right. "In my opinion," declared the iconic conservative economist Milton Friedman, "the least bad tax is the property tax on the unimproved value of land, the Henry George argument of many, many years ago." And yet Henry George's "least bad tax" was never fully adopted anywhere. Some countries, though, have placed a heavy reliance on the land tax. Australia adopted unusually high property tax rates and has retained them to this day. In the United States, property taxes account for 17% of all tax revenue, and they are the main source of income for most cities, counties, and school districts. In most nations, though, the property tax remains a fairly small share of overall government revenues— about 5% in the richest countries and even less in poorer nations where land has less value, according to the International Monetary Fund. Tax authorities like the property tax, because it is hard to evade. You can move your family and your bank accounts to some low-tax haven. But you can't move your farm, or your beachfront hotel, or your twenty-eight-bedroom Palm Springs mansion across the border. Because a property tax imposes the heaviest burden on those with the biggest properties—that is, on the rich—it is also widely seen as a useful tool for fighting inequality. Accordingly, after the Great Recession of 2008–9, many countries raised their property taxes to make up for the decline in revenues from personal and corporate income taxes. Ireland reenacted a property tax that it had ended during the boom years of the 1990s. Some nations, such as Denmark, have enacted property taxes on a national basis; usually, though, the property tax is a local levy, used to fund schools, streets, and parks, and it is generally a minor aspect of a nation's overall tax structure. No country has ever been able to fund its governments with only the Single Tax on the value of land that Henry George envisioned.

OF COURSE, TAXATION IS an effective way for government to discourage people from doing things that are harmful to themselves or to society at large. As Henry George pointed out, property taxes don't reduce the amount of land; other than a land tax, however, taxing something leads to less of it. The classic success story here is the tobacco tax; heavy taxes on a pack of cigarettes, together with advertising restrictions and public education campaigns, have sharply reduced the rate of smoking in almost every nation. Thus encouraged, in the last few years many governments have turned their attention to reducing consumption of another popular product that is broadly considered harmful. Sugar has become the new tobacco.

Governments are popping the lid on a new type of tax designed to reduce drinking soda pop. One person knocking back one can of Red Bull is hardly a problem. But with billions of people consuming billions of cold cans of Coke and Pepsi every day, all those sugared sodas have led the World Health Organization to declare a global epidemic of obesity. First in the world's richest countries, and now in the poorer ("developing") nations as well, obesity and its derivative health problems, such as diabetes and heart disease, have become major national concerns. The sugar in drinks is also a major contributor to dental problems, particularly among children.

One straightforward approach to this growing concern would be to prohibit the sale of soda pop. It's a solution, though, that reeks of the nanny state and is proven not to work. One U.S. city famously tried prohibition, when Mayor Michael Bloomberg pushed through a regulation banning the sale of soft drinks larger than sixteen ounces anywhere in New York City. This effort ended in total failure; indeed, it was ruled invalid by the courts almost immediately on technical grounds. There were several problems with the Bloomberg approach. The regulation was poorly designed (for some reason, the sixty-four-ounce Big Gulp at 7-Eleven was exempt from the rule), it was imposed by a powerful mayor with little public input, and it was highly unpopular from the start. But the central issue was that Mayor Bloomberg used the wrong policy recipe to cut sugar consumption. Instead of outright prohibition, he could have achieved the same goal, without Big Brother–style dictates, through taxation.

That's what Mexico did. Our southern neighbor, a developing economy with a population of about 128 million, ranks roughly even with the United States for the dubious honor of being the world's fattest country. Year after year, Mexico and the United States report the world's highest rates of obesity. By several measures, in fact, Mexico is worse off on the body weight scale. About 70% of Mexican adults are designated overweight, and more than 12% of the population has diabetes—both alarming statistics significantly higher than the U.S. rates.

A major reason is sugared soda pop. A study by the American Heart Association found that Mexico had the world's highest rate of deaths due to diseases causes by sugared drinks (the public health experts call them SSBs, or sugar-sweetened beverages).[2] "We Mexicans are among the most avid consumers of soft drinks," notes the novelist David Toscana. "We swig a half-liter per person every day—thanks in part to the multinational beverage companies' distribution, advertising, and pricing strategies, but also because soft drinks, while not exactly nutritious, are at least (usually) free of germs. In Mexico, it is never easy to find water that is safe for drinking, and this is true in both the city and the countryside."[3]

To deal with both problems at once—the obesity epidemic and the lack of clean drinking water—Mexico in 2014 imposed a national tax on all drinks with added sugar or other high-calorie sweeteners. To make the idea palatable, its backers promised from the start to use much of the revenue to purify public water systems; supporters promised fountains bubbling with clean drinking water in the courtyard of every public school. Still, the legislation to create this new tax provoked a massive lobbying battle. Coca-Cola, Pepsi, and other soda sellers spent hundreds of millions of pesos fighting the tax; their money was countered, in part, by none other than Michael Bloomberg and his anti-obesity organization. Several TV networks refused to run Bloomberg's ads, so as not to offend the cola companies that advertise heavily on their air. But when the pro-tax ads did appear, they were potent. The most famous commercial, which almost all Mexicans still remember, showed a young girl sitting at a table with twelve spoonfuls of sugar in front of her. "Would anybody eat twelve spoonfuls of sugar?" the announcer asks, in incredulous tones. Then, as the girl casually pops open a can of cola, the announcer drops the bombshell: "We consume that much sugar every time we drink a soda." The law eventually passed, partly because of the ad campaign and partly because even the most conservative members of the federal Congreso saw the need for a dedicated revenue stream to improve the nation's drinking water.

Mexico's sugar tax makes a bottle of regular Coke about 25% more expensive than the sugarless version. To make this "fat tax" comprehensive, the law also imposed a new tax on junk food like chips, cheese curls, French fries, and candy bars—anything that had more than 275 calories per hundred grams (about three ounces).

Several studies carried out in the first two years after the "fat taxes" took effect suggested that they were having a significant, and healthy, impact. The giant Mexican Coca-Cola bottler, FEMSA, reported a sharp drop in sales of sugared products after the tax took effect. A nationwide household survey showed that consumption of sugared drinks fell by 6% in the first year of the tax—after rising, year after year, for decades before that. Sales of bottled water (sugar-free and thus tax-free) rose dramatically in the first two years of the tax; even the big soda pop makers put far more marketing oomph into their sugar-free offerings. And federal revenues from the tax hit $1 billion in the first year. In this chart, the two lines cross at the beginning of 2014, just as the soda pop tax took effect.

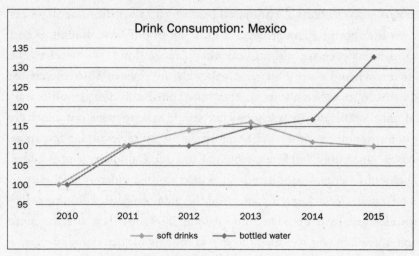

Source: Instituto Nacional de Estadistica y Geografía

Mexico's success prompted other countries to start taxing sugared drinks; Chile, Barbados, Dominica—all nations with untrustworthy public water systems—took up the idea in 2015; a year later, the idea spread to Europe. In presenting his budget for fiscal year 2016, Great Britain's chancellor of the exchequer, George Osborne, apologized to Parliament for not acting sooner. "We knew there was a problem with sugared drinks," the chancellor said. "We knew it caused disease. But we ducked the difficult decisions and we did nothing." But no longer: Britain passed a soda pop tax, to take effect in 2018, with the rate of tax rising depending on how much sugar the drink contains. Under the British formula, regular Coke, Pepsi, Red Bull, and such will incur the highest tax; less sugared recipes like Schweppes lemonade and Sprite will be taxed somewhat less. In the United States, there are diligent advocates of a fizzy-drink tax, but their efforts have fallen flat. Sugar-based taxes have been proposed in some thirty American cities; the soft drink industry has successfully fought them off almost everywhere. The exception was (wouldn't you know it?) Berkeley, California, a green, liberal bastion that imposed a penny-per-ounce tax on sugared drinks. This raised prices by $0.12 per can, or $0.68 per two-liter bottle. (The problem with a tax in one city, though, is that consumers eventually figure out they can go down the street to the next town and save $2.88 per case.) In the summer of 2016, the city of Philadelphia passed a soda pop tax but applied it to diet as well as sugared beverages; so Philadelphia's tax should raise revenue but may have no impact on the problem of obesity. In the 2016 election, a few more cities—including San Francisco and Oakland, California, and Boulder, Colorado—approved sugared-drink taxes aimed squarely at obesity.

Despite all the lobbying efforts of the soda companies, this looks like an idea that can't be corked up for long. The sugar tax, and the more extensive fat taxes, are likely to spread broadly in the next few years.

GOVERNMENTS AROUND THE WORLD have shown increasing interest in recent years in another form of FAT tax. This one is the "financial activities tax," although it has many other names. It's also known as an FTT, standing for "financial transactions tax" or "financial trading tax." This FAT tax is also widely called the "tiny tax," which seems unlikely but actually makes sense.

The financial trading tax that is about to take effect in the European Union has been dubbed the "Robin Hood tax," because it takes mainly from the rich. In the academic literature, economists generally refer to a tax on financial transactions as a "Tobin tax," in honor of the American economist James Tobin, a professor at Yale and a Nobel laureate in economics who began preaching the virtues of this form of taxation in the 1960s. When Bernie Sanders went around the country calling for taxes on financial trading during the 2016 presidential campaign—he said the revenue from this tax would finance his plan for free tuition at all public universities—he referred to his version of the FAT tax as the "Wall Street speculation tax."

The most basic form of a financial transactions tax is a sales tax applied to the purchase of financial instruments—stocks, bonds, options, foreign currencies, loans, insurance policies, and the more complicated securities such as derivatives that Wall Street traders keep dreaming up. This form of tax has been around a long time; Britain's stamp duty, which imposes a tax of one-half of 1% on all stock trades, has been in continuous effect since 1694. The United States had a tiny tax on stock market transactions from 1914 to 1966, until the growing political clout of the financial industry successfully pressured Congress to repeal the tax, which Wall Street had always hated. (But the Securities and Exchange Commission still imposes a fee—essentially, it's a tax—on stock trading, known as the Section 31 Fee, to finance its regulation of security markets.)

Italy, France, Switzerland, South Korea, and Taiwan all tax stock trades. Some countries put a tax on bond purchases and foreign currency exchange. About a dozen countries have bank account taxes; when you deposit money to your account, or withdraw it, the government takes a small portion of it in tax. Another common form of the Tobin tax—in fact, the type that James Tobin himself initially championed—is a tax on foreign currency transactions. In Brazil, for example, when you convert your dollars into reals, or vice versa, there's often a tax, ranging up to 6%, in addition to whatever fee the bank wants to charge.

One key problem with a FAT is that investors can carry out financial transactions almost anywhere today, and so they tend to buy stocks and bonds, or trade currencies, in the countries that don't tax those trades. This has made many nations reluctant to try this form of taxation. Sweden's experience was typical. When the government introduced a stock-trading tax in 1984, there was a burst of revenue in the first few years as Swedish investors continued, out of habit, to buy and sell on the Stockholm exchange, and thus pay the tax on each trade. Gradually, though, they started doing their trading through exchanges in Berlin, or Paris, or New York; it was just as easy, as computer trading became the norm, and the Swedish FTT did not apply. With the volume of trading plummeting in Stockholm year after year, the Swedes finally gave up and repealed their tax, in the hope of keeping some of the business at home.

In the aftermath of the global Great Recession of 2008–9, there has been renewed interest all over the world in some kind of Tobin tax. Amid the global downturn, governments everywhere had to use general tax revenues to bail out big banks and investment houses; now they want to impose some kind of tax on the financial industry that will pay for the next round of bailouts, if needed. Some economists argue as well that a well-designed tax could reduce volatility in securities markets and thus make financial crises less likely. Accordingly, national tax agencies and the big finance organizations like the World Bank and the IMF have launched new studies of the FTT. All over the developed world, universities and think tanks are holding learned seminars with clever titles like "Tobin, or Not Tobin?"

At a special meeting in Pittsburgh, finance ministers and Treasury secretaries from the Group of Twenty called on the International Monetary Fund to study and report back on "the range of options countries have adopted or are considering as to how the financial sector could make a fair and substantial contribution toward paying for any burdens associated with [saving] the banking system."[4] In plain English, governments wanted to know how to tax the financial industry to raise the money needed for future bailouts. The basic principle here is a familiar one to Americans. For decades, the government has been assessing a fee from every bank to pay for the FDIC program, the insurance plan that gives you back the money you had on deposit if your bank goes broke. In the same way, the FTT would tax the financial industry to build up an insurance fund that would cover any future government rescue of troubled firms.

But any financial transactions levy would face the same problem the Swedes ran into; in an era of electronic trading, financiers will just move their transactions to a jurisdiction that doesn't tax their stocks and bonds. For proponents of a Tobin tax, the answer to that problem is a multinational tax regime; that is, every country should institute an

FTT so that traders couldn't dodge the tax by setting up shop in a tax-free country. Like Professor Piketty's global wealth tax, that looks at first blush like one of those neat propositions that will never come to pass. But one wealthy, powerful league of nations has indeed agreed—well, sort of agreed—to institute financial transaction taxes that don't stop at the national border. The European Union, a political and economic conglomeration of twenty-eight countries stretching across the Continent from Ireland to the Russian border, has been working for years on plans for a pan-continental FTT. This effort took on new momentum after several European governments were forced to bail out big financial institutions in the wake of the Great Recession.

By 2013, eleven European Union member countries—including some of the world's richest nations, such as Germany, France, Italy, Belgium, and Spain—had agreed on a plan that taxed just about all financial trades. That's the so-called Robin Hood tax. To get around the problem of traders' simply shifting their business to tax-free jurisdictions, the EU tax applies regardless of where the transaction takes place; thus a German bank buying call options on the New York Stock Exchange would have to pay the transactions tax. Great Britain, in the midst of a strong anti-Europe swing in its domestic politics, opted out of the new tax. So did Luxembourg, a tiny but rich country where banking is the main industry. The remaining nations have repeatedly committed to move ahead with this tax. But this remains a controversial idea, and it has faced a relentless lobbying campaign from banks, brokerage houses, and hedge funds that would end up paying the tax. As a result, the EU's FTT keeps getting stalled. It was originally scheduled to take effect in 2013. This was delayed to 2014, then 2016. In the spring of 2016, the EU announced that the financial tax would be imposed starting in 2017. Definitely. No more delays. Of course, the EU has said that kind of thing before.

The striking thing is that the rates of FAT taxation are tiny. A standard sales tax in an American state might run about 8%; the value-added tax, a broader form of sales tax, runs about 18% to 25%

in countries around the world. In contrast, taxes on financial transactions are almost always less than 1%. The British "stamp duty" on stock trades, for example, is a tax of one-half of 1%. That proposed EU tax which has sparked so much controversy would be one-tenth of 1% for purchases of stocks and bonds and one-hundredth of 1% for derivative transactions (that is, one cent of tax on a $100 transaction). If a Frenchman, for example, bought a $3,000 wide-screen TV, the French value-added tax on that purchase, 20%, would come to $600; if the same Frenchman bought $3,000 of some company's stock, the tax would be all of $3. Even Bernie Sanders, in the midst of his soak-the-rich campaign for president in 2016, stuck to this tiny-rate formula when he proposed his FTT. He called for a tax of 0.5% on stock trades, 0.1% on bonds, and 0.005% on derivatives. At that tax rate—it is a tax of five cents on a $1,000 purchase—an investor buying a derivative contract worth $1 million would owe a total of $50 in tax on the purchase.

The reason proponents of FTTs opt for these tiny rates is that the dollar value of these transactions tends to be so huge—and there are so many of them, in an era of high-speed computer trading—that even a minuscule rate of tax can bring in serious money. The Tax Policy Center in Washington estimates that a U.S. financial transactions tax set at the tiny rate of one-tenth of 1% would bring in $66 billion per year; that's more than enough to run several cabinet departments. A *Wall Street Journal* headline nicely captured this basic fact about the tiny tax: "Small Fees, Big Bucks."

Proponents of the FTT say keeping the rates extremely low means there won't be much burden for the average investor, who makes relatively small trades now and then. The tax burden would fall, instead, on high-speed traders who move billion-dollar securities in a hundredth of a second and then move on to the next deal half a second later. So here's a tax that would fund much of the government but would be paid almost entirely by swashbuckling Wall Street 1-percenters. Politically, it sounds like a winner. And yet the idea has never gone far in the United States—despite the surprising popularity of the 2016 Sanders campaign—because major financial institutions argue that it would stifle the securities industry and make investing more expensive for everybody. And major financial institutions tend to get their way on tax issues in the U.S. Congress.

ANOTHER NEW FORM OF TAX that has been tested around the world in recent years is the carbon tax—that is, a tax on carbon-based fuels and emissions of carbon dioxide into the atmosphere. As with the soda pop and financial transaction taxes, the carbon tax has two purposes: it would raise revenue for government, of course, but it should also serve to offset the production of greenhouse gases (mainly, carbon dioxide) that promote climate change and accelerate global warming.

In the United States, the science around climate change is still a matter of political debate. In the other rich countries, though, it is accepted as fact that the average temperature of the planet is rising, that this will pose significant problems in the future, and that mankind's production of greenhouse gases—which prevent the earth's heat from escaping into the atmosphere—is a major reason for this climatic trend. Accordingly, most developed countries consider it essential to reduce carbon emissions; if they can bring in some additional tax revenue at the same time, all the better.

A 2015 study by the International Monetary Fund set forth the basic argument for the carbon tax in a nation (like the United States) that is running large government deficits:

> In the absence of mitigating measures, rising atmospheric concentrations of carbon dioxide (CO_2) and other greenhouse gases (GHGs) are projected to warm the planet by around 3.0 to 4.0°C by 2100 relative to pre-industrial times. Temperature increases of this magnitude . . . are very large by historical standards and pose considerable, and poorly understood, risks.

At the same time, the United States faces substantial fiscal challenges. . . . The federal debt-to-GDP ratio—already (at 73 percent) well above historical levels—is projected . . . to rise over the
medium to longer term because of higher interest costs and growing spending for Social Security and the government's major
health care programs. . . .

A carbon tax—that is, a tax on the carbon content of fossil fuels
(or on their carbon emissions)—could help address both of these
problems. Carbon taxes are potentially the most effective and
cost-effective policies for reducing CO_2 emissions. . . . These taxes
could also raise substantial revenues for easing fiscal pressures and/
or funding reductions in other taxes.[5]

Carbon taxes come in various shapes and sizes, but there are basically three ways to tax CO_2 emissions.

1. The *emissions tax* measures how much CO_2 pours out of the smokestacks of major producers, such as power plants and factories, and
   then imposes a tax on each ton of the stuff that is poured into the
   air. This approach requires fairly costly measuring devices to be
   installed and maintained. But it gives major emitters an economic
   incentive to invest in cleaner technology, or to use cleaner fuels,
   and thus reduce emissions, which cuts the tax bill.

2. The *fuel tax* imposes a special sales tax on the fossil fuels that cause
   CO_2 emissions when they are burned. Generally, this tax is higher
   for fuels that contain more carbon, so coal is taxed higher than
   crude oil, and oil is taxed higher than natural gas. Economists at
   the IMF prefer this form of carbon tax, which avoids the need to
   install complex emission gauges on smokestacks and such. Coal
   mines and oil wells already know how many tons or barrels they
   are selling to the power company, so it is easy to compute the carbon tax they have to pay. Because the coal and oil companies will

pass the tax on to their customers through higher prices, this type of tax gives those who burn carbon fuels an incentive to increase the fuel efficiency of their operations.

3. The *gas tax* increases the tax on gasoline and diesel fuel used in cars, trucks, and machines. This one is fairly simple to implement, because nearly every jurisdiction already has a gasoline tax and the pumps at every gas station are already equipped to calculate and collect the tax each time a motorist fills her tank. There is theoretically a lot of margin in the United States to tax carbon by increasing the gas tax, because America's taxes on motor fuel are much lower than those in most other countries. The *New York Times* columnist Thomas Friedman has been promoting higher gas taxes in the United States for years; he has proposed a $1 per gallon increase in the federal gas tax (it's 18.4 cents per gallon at present). To make this politically palatable, Friedman wants to call this levy the "anti-terror tax," because it would reduce gasoline consumption and thus reduce imports of oil from the Middle Eastern countries that finance terrorist groups.

A common way to implement the carbon tax is through a quasi-market mechanism called an emissions-trading system. There are dozens of these operating at the multinational, national, state, and local levels (the city of Tokyo, which uses more energy by itself than most countries, has an emissions market of its own). The basic design is that government gives (or sells) permits to each major source of emissions—power plants, refineries, manufacturing plants, automotive fleets, and so on—allowing it to pour out so many tons of CO_2 per month. That limit is called the cap. In order to reduce emissions over time, the amount of emissions permitted from each source is reduced every few years, even if the plant or factory increases overall output. If the emitter goes over the permitted cap in any year, it owes a fine to the government. Conversely, if a factory reduces its emissions and comes in under the cap, it can sell its excess permits to other companies so they can avoid the fine. Under an emissions-trading system, there's a public exchange in these permits, where companies can buy or sell (or "trade") the right to emit more tons of CO_2 than the cap would permit. Accordingly, this system is often called cap and trade. Because the fine imposed on sources that exceed the cap works just like a tax, opponents of these systems call them "cap and tax."

This kind of tax is broadly supported by economists, including American economists, of every political persuasion. Lawrence Summers, a Harvard liberal who held senior positions in both the Clinton and the Obama Democratic administrations, notes that "government debt and global climate change are two of the great problems of our time. Carbon taxation uniquely has the potential to address both." Summers's conservative Harvard colleague N. Gregory Mankiw, an adviser to many Republicans and chief of the Council of Economic Advisers under George W. Bush, agrees: "There is little doubt in my mind that for dealing with global climate change, the best policy includes a tax on carbon emissions."[6]

But bipartisan backing from academic economists doesn't necessarily make a difference when it comes to tax policy in the United States. In the U.S. Congress, the word "tax" is the kiss of death for almost any new idea, particularly among Republicans. Thus most efforts to create some form of a national cap-and-trade (or "cap-and-tax") scheme in our country—Bill Clinton tried it in 1993, and Barack Obama proposed it again in 2010—have been rejected. Still, there are emissions-trading systems operating today in the United States, ranging from the city of Boulder, Colorado (population 105,000), to the state of California, with 39.2 million people and thousands of emission sources subject to the state's caps. Ten U.S. states in the Northeast and the mid-Atlantic have created their own regional emissions-trading scheme (the Regional Greenhouse Gas Initiative). None of these plans have been big revenue raisers so far, but they could bring in significant money if expanded nationally.

Globally, dozens of countries now have cap-and-trade mechanisms in place. The world's biggest such market is the European Union's Emissions Trading System, known on the Continent as the ETS. It grants emission allowances to more than eleven thousand power plants and industrial sites in thirty-one countries; airlines are also covered. The system has had some serious problems since it started in 2005 and was almost given up for dead in 2013. By 2016, though, it was operating reasonably well. CO_2 emissions in Europe have fallen significantly since the ETS began, although some of that decrease stems from the Continent's prolonged economic doldrums. The EU now predicts that it will exceed the plan's original goal of reducing emissions by 20% from the 2005 level while bringing in billions in new tax revenues.

But even in Australia, a deeply green nation of twenty-three million environmentalists, a tax is still a tax, as the Australian Labor Party learned. "It's the kind of place where any tax to protect the environment ought to be a barn burner," explained the political reporter Malcolm Farr. "We've got a bloody big landmass and a bloody small population; it's a country the size of the United States with the population of Greater Los Angeles. And we all love our beautiful outback." Australians are devoted to the outdoors; almost every Aussie has (at least) one bicycle, and nearly all the bikes you see on the street are equipped with special racks for carrying golf clubs or surfboards. Indeed, nobody seemed particularly surprised when the nation's prime minister (Harold Holt) died in a surfing accident one choppy day off a beach on the Tasman Sea. "That's the kind of thing that happens to 'stralians," Farr told me, "even if you're prime minister."

Australia is also a major polluter. It's one of the world's leading producers and exporters of coal, and most of the nation's electric supply is produced by coal-burning power plants. The country rates among the world's top three nations for CO_2 emissions per capita. After the Kyoto accords on global warming, though, Australians became concerned about this; dealing with climate change became an important political issue in Australia. In the 2007 national election, both major parties supported a cap-and-trade system to reduce emissions. The mining and power companies fought back, and the 2008–9 global recession put the plan on hold. By the time of the 2010 election, the matter was so conflicted that Julia Gillard, the candidate of the Labor Party (the Australian equivalent of our Democrats), made a solemn pledge that "there will be no carbon tax under the government I lead."

So much for solemn pledges. When no party won a majority in the election, Gillard decided to cut a deal with the Green Party to form a coalition government that would make her prime minister. The price was straightforward: to get the Greens' support, Gillard agreed to pass a carbon tax, to be imposed on mines, power plants, factories, and airlines. This new tax took effect in July 2012 and had one immediate impact: everybody's electric bill went up. The monthly bills went up roughly 11% on average, and the electric companies thoughtfully noted on each bill that this increase was due to the new tax they had to pay. By some estimates, a typical Aussie family had to pay about $500 more per year for electricity. With that, cutting carbon emissions became a far less popular policy in Australia.

The opposition parties pounced. Because every home and business used electricity, they called the carbon tax "a great big new tax on everything." They labeled Julia Gillard "Ju-Liar Gillard" for going back on her no-tax promise. The media magnate Rupert Murdoch, whose newspapers reach 70% of the nation's households, mounted a fierce editorial crusade against the tax. The coal and electric companies threw their support to the political opposition, which is called the Liberal Party but is, in fact, Australia's equivalent of our Republicans. The Liberal leader, Tony Abbott, based his entire campaign on a promise to "axe the tax." The backlash against the carbon tax was so intense that Gillard's own Labor Party dumped her in 2013 and replaced her with a more popular former Labor prime minister. But it was too late. Abbott's party won the election, and the new conservative Parliament repealed the carbon tax just two years after it took effect.

The *Wall Street Journal* (another Murdoch property) warned that

Australia's action "could highlight the difficulty in implementing additional measures to reduce carbon emissions." Many Australians agreed, including those who had supported the carbon tax.

"What we have learned," said Professor Bill Butcher, a tax expert at the University of New South Wales in Sydney, "is that people are enthusiastic about environmental protection, but are not enthusiastic about paying for it."

BENJAMIN FRANKLIN'S FAMOUS OBSERVATION that "nothing is certain except death and taxes" has not entirely proven true. While no nation has yet managed to eradicate death, there are a few countries that have managed to operate without taxes, or at least with very few forms of tax. Of the planet's two hundred sovereign nations, about a dozen run their governments with almost no imposition of tax on their citizens. These tax-free states fall into two categories: oil-rich kingdoms, primarily in the Middle East, and vacation meccas that can get away with sticking the burden of taxation on their tourists.

Probably the least taxed nation on earth is the United Arab Emirates, a federation of seven sheikhdoms near the southeastern corner of the Arabian Peninsula. The U.A.E. is best known for its biggest cities, Abu Dhabi and Dubai (the site of the world's tallest building). It has five million residents, tens of thousands of square miles of sand, and some of the earth's richest deposits of oil. The income from this natural resource has meant the U.A.E. doesn't have to worry about the kinds of government revenues that have proven as inevitable as death almost everywhere else. The *International Tax Handbook,* an authoritative source on the different types of taxes found in every nation, lists the following for the U.A.E.:

Personal Income Tax: none
Corporate Income Tax: none
Property Tax: none

Capital Gains Tax: none
Sales Tax: none
Estate Tax: none
Wealth Tax: none

The Emirates' equally lucky Middle Eastern neighbors, Saudi Arabia (population 26.5 million), Oman (3.1 million), Qatar (1.95 million), Kuwait (1.5 million), and Bahrain (1.25 million), also get by with almost no taxes, as does the tiny sultanate of Brunei, a sliver of land on the northern coast of Borneo that is also blessed with petroleum deposits. None of these nations have personal or corporate income taxes or sales taxes. But several of them do have a form of Social Security tax, a levy that is withheld from wages to pay for the government-run health-care and pension systems. Because the Middle Eastern oil companies rely heavily on temporary immigrant labor, these payroll taxes are paid in large part by foreign workers.

There's one jurisdiction in the United States that has set up a tax regime something like those in the oil-rich Middle East. That would be oil-rich Alaska. In the 1970s, when it became clear that the frozen northern tundra of the forty-ninth state was situated over an enormous underground lake of crude oil, the state government had a long shopping list of ways to spend the severance tax revenue that began pouring in. But some farsighted political leaders decided—over loud opposition—to set aside a portion of the oil tax, invest the money, and save it for the future. This kind of rainy-day fund is formally known as a "sovereign wealth fund." But the one in Alaska bears an optimistic name—the "Permanent Fund"—on the theory that the money will always be there in time of need. In 1977, its first full year of operation, the Alaska Permanent Fund took in $734,000. By 2016, the fund totaled $53.7 billion and was making more each year on investment income than from oil revenues.

As the Permanent Fund began to grow in the late 1970s, Alaskans came to realize that oil revenues, and the income from investing the fund's assets, were big enough to replace the revenue from most state taxes. Alaska repealed its income tax in 1980 and has also eschewed, for the most part, sales and property taxes. Indeed, Alaska's oil fund works as a reverse income tax; each year, the government sends each resident a check, which is called the Permanent Fund Dividend, or PFD. (To qualify, you have to have lived in the state for an entire calendar year, January 1 to December 31. Every year a few people with bad luck or bad timing move to Alaska on January 2 or 3, only to discover that they'll have to wait two years to get the reverse income tax payment.) In 2015, the PFD payout came to $2,072 per person, or about $10,400 for a family of five. For many low-income Alaskans, the annual PFD check is a major portion of their annual income. Of course, Alaskans still have to pay federal income tax, and many use the Permanent Fund Dividend to pay what they owe Uncle Sam.

These tax-free arrangements can dry up rapidly if the oil runs out or if the price of oil plummets on world markets, as it did in 2014. The extended swoon in the price of crude oil over the next two years badly stretched government coffers in the Middle East, even among those farsighted countries that had set aside a chunk of their annual oil earnings in sovereign wealth funds, which act like national rainy-day funds. By 2015, several of the Middle East's no-tax territories were considering, or enacting, sales taxes, capital gains taxes, and tariffs on imported goods. In 2016, facing a severe budget deficit, Alaska cut its cherished Permanent Fund Dividend by 50%, setting a cap of $1,000 for each recipient; even more shocking, there was growing pressure to bring back a state income tax.

A few nations that lack oil but are blessed with swaying palms on sandy beaches or ski resorts amid snowcapped mountains have also managed for the most part to avoid taxing their citizens. Tropical escapes like the Bahamas, Bermuda, and the Cayman Islands have no corporate or personal income tax, no wealth tax, no property tax. Rather, they collect revenue from restaurant diners, hotel guests, Jet Ski riders, beach umbrella renters—that is, from foreign tourists.

Andorra, a no-tax smidgen of a nation (population 70,000) high atop the Pyrenees between France and Spain, thrives on skiers in the winter and on shoppers in the summer who cross the borders from the north and south to buy tobacco, liquor, perfume, and electronics that are free from the costly value-added taxes in France (VAT rate: 20%) and Spain (VAT rate: 21%). The Mediterranean getaway of Monaco funds its (small) government through tourism and a fee imposed on every bet placed in its famous Monte Carlo casinos. Macau, a quasi-independent Chinese enclave that bills itself as "the Asian Vegas," also uses casino fees to take the place of most taxes. Many of these postage-stamp-sized jurisdictions also take in a fair share of government revenues by printing and selling stamps that are prized by collectors around the world.

So why don't rich people just flock to these tax-free venues and hoard their wealth? It turns out that this is not simply a matter of packing a bag and renting a house on the beach in Bermuda. Any American citizen owes income tax to the Internal Revenue Service regardless of address. Some foreign earnings are excludable, and there is a credit for foreign taxes paid. But an American citizen who is willing to pick up stakes and move to Abu Dhabi is still legally required to file Form 1040 and pay up each year. You can avoid this requirement only by renouncing your U.S. citizenship. A few people actually do that; in fact, the number of Americans renouncing their native land just to dodge the tax man has grown somewhat in the past decade. To deal with this phenomenon, Congress in 2013 imposed a tax on renunciation. Yes, that's right: you get taxed for avoiding taxes. The expatriation tax—set forth in Section 877 and Section 877A of the Internal Revenue Code—is due from any U.S. citizen with assets greater than $2 million who turns in his passport and becomes a citizen of a foreign country. Naturally, the IRS has issued a complicated form (Form 8854) and instruction booklet (Publication 519) to collect the U.S. expatriation tax.

Beyond that, the no-tax countries do not always welcome tax-fleeing immigrants with open arms. To get a residence permit in

Monaco, you have to put half a million dollars in a bank there, and the money can't be withdrawn for years. Macau requires a down payment of roughly $375,000. The Cayman Islands ask for an investment of at least $500,000 in real estate or stock in a Caymans corporation. Andorra requires ten years' full-time residence before it will grant citizenship. And the Middle East sheikhdoms are not particularly welcoming to newcomers, except those who are male Muslims.

What many wealthy people would like to find, of course, is a way to duck taxes without the need to give up their passports and move to the parched deserts of Oman, where summer temperatures at midday run about 117 degrees. And we know that many of them manage to do so, hiding hundreds of billions of dollars, euros, pounds, and yen from the taxing authorities while living comfortably in their home countries. We know a great deal about how this is done and where the money is hidden. We know all this thanks to a huge journalistic scoop that hit the world's newspapers in the spring of 2016. It was a story that came to be called "the Panama Papers."

10.

THE PANAMA PAPERS: SUNNY PLACES FOR SHADY MONEY

n the spring of 2015, a newspaper reporter named Bastian Obermayer received an e-mail message. The sender was listed as "John Doe." The subject line contained one word: "Data." The message itself was cryptic: "Interested in data?"

For the recipient of that e-mail, this was all a little less obscure than it might seem. Bastian Obermayer is a financial correspondent for the great Munich newspaper *Süddeutsche Zeitung* (the name means "South German Newspaper"). He had been working for a few years on big stories exposing complex tax-avoidance schemes employed by European multimillionaires. Accordingly, Obermayer suspected from the start that the "data" from this "John Doe" might involve a few more cases of rich people hiding their money from the tax authorities. So the reporter e-mailed back, "How much data?" The answer, from the same John Doe, came back instantly: "More than anything you have ever seen."

This proved to be true. The data that John Doe was offering involved more than eleven million discrete documents from the confidential files of Mossack Fonseca, a flourishing law firm based in Panama City. The Mossack firm was virtually unknown in general legal circles, but it was nearly a household name among millionaires and billionaires, and their bankers, in much of the world. This obscure Panama City law firm had developed a lucrative specialty: helping the 1% hide their money. Sometimes it was a rich man trying to keep his holdings away from his ex, or his new spouse. Sometimes it was a surgeon who wanted to make her assets invisible because of a pending malpractice suit. It might be drug dealers, arms dealers, gambling professionals, or corrupt government officials who didn't want the police to track their illicit gains. But most often, it was a wealthy individual in a high-tax country who wanted to conceal money from the tax authorities. Mossack Fonseca had branch offices all over the world—including nine cities in China, which was its largest source of business by the second decade of the twenty-first century.

Over a period of weeks, John Doe funneled batch after batch of the firm's confidential documents—contracts, letters, e-mails, and tens of thousands of incorporation papers—to the German newspaper. Quickly, it became clear to Obermayer and his team that this trove of data was too big for any one newspaper to handle. By sheer number of pages, it was the biggest leak in history—the papers constituted about ten times as many documents as the notorious WikiLeaks revelations. There were so many clients and so many clandestine deals, and there was so much money secreted in anonymous bank accounts in so many countries, that the investigative reporters in Munich were quickly overwhelmed. Finally, they took a step that would be difficult for any scoop-hungry journalist: they decided to share the Panama Papers with other reporters around the world (they did not, of course, show the documents to any of their German competitors).

A Washington, D.C., organization called the International Consortium of Investigative Journalists put together an ad hoc team of some four hundred reporters and editors from a hundred media outlets in eighty countries; the group included the BBC and the *Guardian* newspaper in Britain, the French daily *Le Monde,* and the McClatchy chain in the United States, the owner of newspapers like the *Charlotte Observer,* the *Kansas City Star,* and the *Miami Herald.* The reporters held meetings in Munich, London, and Washington, D.C., and agreed that it would take months to track down all the information in the law firm's records. Accordingly, they made a pact that nobody would publish the story until all members of the team had finished reporting on Mossack Fonseca clients in their countries. Indeed, one of the most surprising things about this whole saga is that none of these reporters broke the self-imposed embargo.

Consequently, when the Panama Papers were finally made public, in the first week of April 2016, the story was a bombshell around the world. "The revelation of vast wealth hidden by politicians and powerful figures across the globe," the *New York Times* reported on its front page, "set off criminal investigations on at least two continents . . . as harsh new light was shed on the elaborate ways wealthy people hide money in secretive shell companies and offshore tax shelters."[1] For several days, the hashtag #PanamaPapers was the number one topic on Twitter. Columnists and editorial pages everywhere condemned the tax dodgers and the lawyers who helped them conceal their wealth. A few editorial pages took a different stance; the newspapers owned by the billionaire press magnate Rupert Murdoch generally said that tax avoidance was not such a big deal. "The mistake now," read the editorial in Murdoch's American flagship, the *Wall Street Journal,* "would be to narrow the focus prematurely, zeroing in on tax avoidance that is a hobbyhorse of the political class but in this case is a distraction."

The law firms' records provided strong confirmation of the widespread feeling, in the wake of the global recession of 2008–9, that the financial system was rigged in favor of the elites—that the very rich in almost every country could find ways to avoid the legal obligations (like paying taxes) that applied to ordinary citizens. The firm's clients included members of wealthy families as well as famous actors and athletes, marquee names like Jackie Chan and Lionel Messi. But the elite tax dodgers who made use of Mossack Fonseca's legal maneuvers also included dozens of public officials who had somehow become extremely rich while serving in government jobs. Family members or close friends of the former Egyptian president Hosni Mubarak, the Syrian president Bashar al-Assad, and China's president Xi Jinping were revealed to have hired the Panamanian firm to hide large sums of money. Several close associates of the Russian strongman Vladimir Putin showed up in the Panama Papers, including one Sergei Roldugin, a well-known friend of Putin's who listed his occupation as "cellist" but reportedly placed some $2 billion in offshore tax havens through the good offices of Mossack Fonseca. The prime minister of Pakistan and the son of the prime minister of Malaysia both had multimillion-dollar secret accounts arranged by the Panama law firm. Two days after the first news stories based on the leak, the prime minister of Iceland was forced from office after it was revealed that he and his wife had employed Mossack Fonseca to secrete millions of dollars in a shell corporation in the British Virgin Islands.

The British prime minister, David Cameron—a leader who had launched a high-profile campaign against tax avoidance in the U.K.—was embarrassed to see that his own wealthy father had hired the Panama City lawyers to create a secret offshore entity to hold his money. When reporters demanded to know whether the prime minister himself had any money stashed overseas, the PM's press secretary foolishly responded that this was a "private matter." This non-denial led to such widespread speculation in the ferocious British newspapers that Cameron felt the need to deal with the matter himself, making a personal declaration in Parliament that he had no overseas accounts. In Moscow, Putin's office declared that the whole Panama Papers story was simply an American plot. Russia's government-run TV news programs said that the "information war" against Putin was "the curatorial work of the U.S. State Department," a manifestation of continuing "Putinphobia" in the West. In China, President Xi's government reiterated its commitment to fight corruption but also banned any mention of the scandal in the news media and blocked all Internet searches that mentioned "Panama," "Papers," or the law firm. Back in Panama City, Ramón Fonseca, one of two name partners of the firm, said the law firm itself was the real victim. Because privacy had been the firm's most important product, it faced an angry backlash from clients whose secret fiscal maneuvers were suddenly bannered atop the front page.

The Panama Papers indicated that most of Mossack Fonseca's client list came from Europe, Asia, and Africa; there were not many names from the United States in the leaked documents. Still, the Internal Revenue Service issued a warning to any Americans who might have tried to salt away money in foreign accounts to avoid paying tax. "People hiding assets offshore should recognize," the IRS said, that such maneuvers were likely to be futile. "More than ever," the agency added, "their best option remains to come forward voluntarily and participate in the IRS Offshore Voluntary Disclosure Program." Naturally, the IRS has two different forms—Form 14437 and Form 14454—for Americans to use in revealing their offshore holdings. Just days after the first reports about the huge leak, the Justice Department announced that it had "opened a criminal investigation regarding matters to which the Panama Papers are relevant," which seemed to indicate that the feds were going after Americans mentioned in the papers.

When the story broke, the newspaper and broadcast accounts all referred to Mossack Fonseca as an "obscure" or "little-known" Panama law firm. And yet, the papers revealed, this unknown firm had more than fourteen thousand clients in more than a hundred countries, all of them willing to pay the Panama City lawyers hefty fees to salt their wealth away where nobody—and particularly no national tax agency—could track it.

The venues for this hidden money were countries—sometimes tiny countries with a national population smaller than an American small town's—that had written laws and regulations to permit people from any country to create corporations and/or set up bank accounts in complete secrecy. Such places are known in English as "tax havens." The French call them *paradis fiscaux,* or financial paradises; in Spanish, it's *asilos de impuestos,* asylums from taxation; the Italian term is *rifugio fiscale,* or fiscal refuge. Many of these refuges also happen to be sun-splashed tropical getaways, like Bermuda, the Cayman Islands, Panama, Belize, and Cyprus. That's because tax evaders sometimes need to visit their money—it's more private to go get the cash in person than to have the funds wired to your bank at home—and they like to take their families along for a beach vacation at the same time. Shady money is stashed in sunny places.

Mossack Fonseca worked with several of these tax havens to conceal their clients' funds. The Panama Papers showed precisely how this was done. In the early years—until the global crackdown on tax evasion began in the late 1990s—the firm sometimes just used the tried-and-true gambit of the numbered account at some international bank. The law firm would receive a large check from the client and deposit it in a bank in Switzerland, or Panama, or any other jurisdiction where secret bank accounts were legal. The bank's records for that account would show only a number—ZU456238, or some such. Frequently, the bank itself didn't know the identity of the depositor; only the law firm in Panama City had that information. Thus when the IRS or some other tax authority showed up at the bank with a warrant to search the accounts, the bank's officers could honestly say that nobody had any idea who really owned the money deposited there. For this service, the banks took some heat from governments and international organizations. But they were making good money on the business, receiving large deposits on which they paid little or no interest, and charging fees along the way. As long as the law firm's fees and the interest forgone cost less than the tax might have, the client was happy.

But the law firm also developed more sophisticated ways to conceal money, and this became important in the twenty-first century as rich nations began working together to crack down on secret bank accounts. Mossack Fonseca became a global leader in the practice of creating so-called "shell corporations"—that is, a "business" that does no business. A client—or his banker—would come to the law firm with, say, $50 million that he didn't want anybody to know about. The firm would then create a corporation with some anonymous name—something along the lines of "Panama 67453X," or "BVI48484JK," although some also took their names from characters or places in *Star Wars* or *Game of Thrones*—in a jurisdiction that was willing to issue a corporate license with no person's name attached. The client would then use his $50 million to buy stock in the do-nothing corporation. The stock certificates would be payable to "Bearer"—that is, whoever owned them. No names required. The money that purchased these anonymous stock certificates would be deposited in a bank account under the corporation's obscure name so that nobody could find it. Quite often, the bank would issue a Visa or Mastercard in the corporation's name, which the wealthy client could use to buy goods and services in her home country.

John Doe's trove of "data" suggested that setting up such legal creations—they're known as international business corporations, or IBCs—was an important line of business for Mossack Fonseca, and it clearly kept the lawyers busy. The Panama Papers indicated that the law firm created some 214,000 shell corporations—legal entities that had no employees, no officers, and no corporate activity except to serve as a clandestine repository for the money of wealthy tax dodgers. Sometimes, the firm put the money into "charities" or "foundations," which can also be used to hide funds. The firm worked with more than five hundred banks around the world.

This system required, of course, a legal jurisdiction that was willing to register a corporation or a foundation with no names attached. Mossack Fonseca's lawyers particularly favored the British Virgin Islands, a Caribbean archipelago that is home to thirty-two thousand residents, several large banks, and hundreds of thousands of registered corporations. But there were many accommodating venues for shell corporations—particularly Switzerland, Luxembourg, Panama,

Cyprus, and the Cayman Islands—which readily granted privacy in return for the incorporation fees and the banking business it generated. For that matter, the United States also served as a popular hiding place for money. In Delaware, Nevada, and South Dakota, it's legal to start a corporation anonymously, and there's no requirement that the new company transact any business.

In Nevada, for example, a corporate license requires no person's name; the state collects a "business license fee" of $500 per year, but this can be paid by a law firm or other go-between to preserve the privacy of the actual owner of the corporation. Generally, those who want to create a business in Nevada—legitimate or "shell"—hire a professional called a registered agent who files all the paperwork in return for a fee; the Nevada Registered Agent Association says this business supports a thousand jobs in the state. John Christensen, the British tax-reform advocate who tracks tax evasion around the world, told me that "the U.S. is a bitter adversary of tax-evasion schemes—when they take place in other countries. But, in fact, there's a big neon sign in several of your states saying, '**Open to tax cheats. Bring your money, and we won't tell.**'"

TWO WEEKS AFTER THE first media reports about the Panama Papers, representatives from forty nations gathered in Paris for an emergency meeting of an organization called JITSIC—the Joint International Tax Shelter Information and Collaboration Network. This international posse of tax officials had been working for more than a decade to crack down on tax-avoidance schemes like those set forth in the Panama documents. And JITSIC had made significant progress. All over the world, banks large and small had signed agreements promising to share information with tax authorities about their foreign customers and the money they had on deposit. But the Panama revelations suggested that international organizations like JITSIC still had a great deal of work to do.

The driving force behind JITSIC, and the acknowledged leader of the international push to police tax dodgers, was the U.S. government. Although the law firm responsible for the Panama Papers drew only a small share of its clients from the United States, rich Americans had been actively hiding their money from the IRS for decades. When reporters at the *Wall Street Journal* analyzed IRS records in the fall of 2015, they estimated that Americans had more than ten thousand hidden accounts holding more than $10 billion in just one country (Switzerland).[2] The amount of tax that could be collected, if the IRS could reach the hidden American money in every tax haven, is hard to measure (the IRS declines to give a figure). But congressional sources have estimated that the lost revenue is greater than $40 billion per year.

Motivated by numbers like that—the missing $40 billion could fund several entire federal agencies each year—Congress in 2010 enacted a tough new law forcing foreign banks, brokerages, and so on to report the names of all their American account holders and the amounts they had on deposit. The basic idea was to go after tax evaders by punishing the banks and law firms that kept their secrets. This statute, the Foreign Account Tax Compliance Act, or FATCA, has made a dramatic difference in the IRS's ability to find hidden hoards of American money. Consequently, the acronym "FATCA" has become a hated term among the kinds of wealthy clients who turn to Mossack Fonseca and similar firms to help hide their money.

Initially, the Obama administration sent out warnings to financial institutions around the world: if you help Americans hide their money to avoid taxation, you will be charged with a crime and liable to huge fines. For the first year or so after FATCA was enacted, this thinly veiled threat had only moderate impact. And then, in 2012, the Justice Department found a useful target and pounced. The U.S. attorney in Manhattan brought criminal charges against a Swiss bank—not just any bank, either, but Wegelin & Co., the oldest bank in Switzerland, with a proud pedigree of service to Swiss and foreign customers dating back 271 years (corporate slogan: "PrivatBankiers seit 1741").

The Swiss government issued an angry protest, and the bank itself, noting that it had no American branches, said it was outside the jurisdiction of U.S. criminal law. But Wegelin had several hundred U.S. depositors, whose secret accounts totaled some $1.2 billion that the bank had not reported. Testimony indicated Swiss bankers used all sorts of euphemisms to conceal what they were doing; when a U.S. customer wanted to withdraw some money, for example, she would ask the bank to "send me a postcard" or "download some tunes." A federal judge agreed that all this constituted a crime under FATCA, and the penalties were harsh. The bank paid a fine of $22 million, plus another $20 million representing the amount of U.S. tax that would have been collected if the IRS had known about the hidden money, plus a forfeiture of an additional $15.8 million representing the fees Wegelin had earned from its American customers. On top of that, the Justice Department seized $16 million that the firm had on deposit in a bank in the United States.

With its assets depleted, its age-old reputation for secrecy destroyed, and depositors fleeing, Wegelin & Co. went out of business. Some 245 of its American customers ended up paying $13 million in back taxes and penalties. On the steps of the courthouse, the U.S. attorney Preet Bharara issued a blunt warning to other foreign banks and to the American depositors who used them for tax evasion. "Wegelin has now paid a steep price for aiding and abetting tax fraud that should be heeded by other banks, bankers, and advisers who engage in the same conduct," he said. "U.S. taxpayers with undeclared accounts—wherever those accounts may be—should know that their bank may be next, and they should pay what they owe the IRS before we come find them."

And with that, the walls of secret banking started tumbling down. The United States indicted dozens of bankers, lawyers, and advisers in Switzerland for FATCA violations. By mid-2016, more than fifty Swiss banks had reached settlements with the Justice Department, agreeing to reveal the names of all American customers and to pay hefty fines for their secret deposits. The investigation caught more than fifty-four thousand U.S. taxpayers who had hidden money in Swiss banks, and it collected over $8 billion in back taxes and penalties from those would-be evaders. The biggest catch of all was the Swiss financial giant Credit Suisse, which pleaded guilty to criminal charges under FATCA in 2014 and paid a whopping $2.6 billion fine. Emboldened by the U.S. action, France, Germany, and other rich countries enacted their own versions of FATCA and went after banks in all the major tax havens. Under the auspices of the aforementioned JITSIC, countries beyond the United States and Europe joined the global war against tax havens; ninety-six nations signed on to an automated system of information sharing that would alert the tax authorities whenever their nationals deposited money in a bank overseas. Under intense pressure, some of the most recalcitrant champions of bank secrecy, including Cyprus, Luxembourg, Switzerland, the Bahamas, and the Cayman Islands, weakened their financial secrecy laws.

One major holdout was Panama, where the government recognized the work of the Mossack Fonseca firm and its affiliated banks as a significant portion of the national economy. The nation had entered into some bilateral agreements on financial data but did not join the JITSIC information-sharing system. But the storm of attention and criticism that followed the leak of the Panama Papers may have changed the country's stance. A week after the first news stories appeared, the Panamanian president, Juan Carlos Varela, announced the appointment of a national commission that was ordered to "strengthen the transparency of the financial and legal systems." The nation's cabinet chief announced that Panama no longer felt the need to stay outside the global system of banking transparency.

What was not transparent was the real identity of "John Doe," the source of the biggest global leak in journalistic history. Most observers guessed that the leaker of the Panama Papers was an embittered former (or, maybe, current) employee of the Mossack Fonseca firm. When Obermayer, the German reporter who received that first cryptic e-mail, asked his source why he was providing the flood of documents, the response seemed angry: "I want to make these crimes public." John Doe never asked for financial compensation, Obermayer said, and never tried to dictate what the newspapers would report. "My life is in danger," Mr. Doe told the newspaper. "No meetings, ever. The choice of stories is up to you." The law firm insisted that it had never done anything illegal and demanded a government investigation of the leaker who had hacked into the firm's records. But the government of Panama, facing a national embarrassment surrounding its eponymous "Papers," had more serious issues to worry about than the identity of John Doe.

11.

SIMPLIFY, SIMPLIFY

Every once in a while, the members of the U.S. Congress get mad at the Internal Revenue Service. Reacting to some bureaucratic bungle, real or imagined, the senators and representatives launch a round of angry speeches in their respective chambers. Then they order IRS officials to appear at a hearing before one of the congressional oversight committees—a session that is generally marked by scorching rhetoric, hostile questions, and furious accusations, as long as the TV cameras are on. Finally, the members put out a fiery report denouncing the tax code and the IRS staffers who administer it. Then they move on to the next target.

There's a strong kill-the-messenger flavor to these periodic outbursts of manufactured rage. Members of Congress love to harangue the IRS bureaucrats about lengthy tax forms and unfair rules and complex instructions—but of course the IRS isn't responsible for the length, the fairness, or the complexity of our tax code. It is Congress that writes the tax laws. It's Congress that adds hundreds of new exemptions, allowances, credits, and calculations to the tax code every year. It was Congress that decided to give the IRS responsibility for managing the health insurance subsidies flowing to millions of Americans under the Affordable Care Act (ObamaCare)—and then cut the agency's staff after assigning it this major new task. It was Congress that assigned to the IRS the management of the earned income tax credit (EITC), which has become one of the nation's largest support programs for low-income Americans. It was Congress that crafted the much-hated alternative minimum tax, which spawned whole new dimensions of complexity, and hours of additional work, for millions of families. And yet congressmen and senators can't seem to resist pointing angry fingers at the IRS, as if somebody else had created the legislative monster that is the U.S. tax code.

This form of political showmanship reached its zenith in the spring of 2016, when a group of Republican backbenchers mounted a quixotic effort to impeach the commissioner of the IRS, John Koskinen. This idea—the first time Congress had ever tried such a thing—was doomed from the start, because the leadership in both houses opposed it, viewing the whole exercise as an empty gesture. But the critics were determined to proceed, in large part because Koskinen—who came out of retirement in his seventies to run the agency and thus had no fear of snippy young congressmen—had never treated the august members of Congress with the respect and deference they had come to expect from bureaucrats. Indeed, Koskinen generally displayed thinly veiled contempt for committee members when he was hauled into a congressional hearing. Whenever the members starting griping about the complexity of the tax system, Koskinen would shake his head and steer the complaint right back at them. "I didn't write the tax laws, Congressman," he would say. "You did that." When Congress scheduled a hearing in mid-2016 on the impeachment resolutions, Koskinen rather blatantly thumbed his nose: the IRS sent word that the commissioner was too busy to make the one-and-a-half-mile ride to Capitol Hill to testify. The impeachment resolutions didn't come to a vote in either chamber.

Generally, a congressional inquisition of the IRS leads to nothing more than a fleeting moment on the evening news and a committee report that is put on a shelf and forgotten. But occasionally, this burst of congressional rancor prompts new legislation designed to deal with whatever problem sparked the anger in the first place. One such moment came in 1998, following a series of heated congressional hearings on the way IRS agents were treating (and sometimes mistreating) taxpayers who had run afoul of the code. The result was the IRS Restructuring and Reform Act of 1998, a voluminous and hugely complex new law, which included the laughable "anti-complexity clause"—that is, Section 7803(c)(2)(B)(ii)(IX). Another part of that same law—to wit, Section 7803(c)(I)(B)(i)—created a new office within the Internal Revenue Service, to be known as the Office of the Taxpayer Advocate. The national taxpayer advocate was based on a position found in the national tax agencies of several foreign countries: the ombudsman. The taxpayer advocate's main job is to be a helping hand for harried taxpayers facing an audit or a penalty fee or a levy from the IRS. This ombudsman is to work within the IRS but not under the control of the commissioner; the advocate is appointed by the secretary of the Treasury to an unlimited term and can be removed only by the secretary. Congress did not stint on resources, either; the taxpayer advocate has a staff of two thousand people, with offices in every state, who are empowered to jump in whenever a taxpayer complains of being mistreated.

Lawrence Summers, who was the last Treasury secretary of the Clinton administration, made an inspired choice when he named the first national taxpayer advocate in 2000. He picked Nina Olson, a tough, feisty tax lawyer and single mom who had spent the bulk of her career as an accountant, doing the books for a series of one-person or mom-and-pop businesses. Seeing all the trouble her clients had in filing their taxes, Olson went to law school at night and then earned a master's degree in tax law at Georgetown University. She was perhaps the only graduate of that elite program who did not use her degree to represent an upper-bracket clientele. Instead, she opened a clinic in Richmond, Virginia, to help low-income people who had tax problems but nowhere near enough money to hire a tax lawyer.

Having spent years watching her clients fall into despair as they struggled with endless IRS forms and incomprehensible IRS instructions, Nina Olson was ready, willing, and able to take on the agency from the inside when she was asked to become the taxpayer advocate. "The thing is, they had to listen to me, and they couldn't fire me, no matter how mad they got," Olson told me one day in her impossibly cluttered office at IRS headquarters. As of the publication of this book, Nina Olson is still the national taxpayer advocate—the only person ever to hold the job.

In addition to standing up for harried taxpayers, the taxpayer advocate was given a series of further responsibilities by the IRS Restructuring and Reform Act of 1998. Among other things, the law—this would be Section 7803(c)(2)(B)(ii)(III)—requires that she report to Congress regularly on "at least 20 of the most serious problems encountered by taxpayers." This she has done every year, and nearly every year she has listed the same issue as the number one most serious problem facing American taxpayers. That problem is the complexity of the tax code.

"Every year, I tell them that the tax system is just too complicated— that people have to pour all sorts of time and money into the task of filing their taxes," Olson told me. "And of course that makes people hate the system, and hate the IRS, and feel that the other guy is cheating while they have to pay full freight. I mean, it undermines the whole idea of voluntary compliance with the tax code!

"So every year I tell them about this problem, and every year they make the problem worse. Why did they ask me to file a report on serious problems facing taxpayers, if they just go on doing the same thing? Sometimes I feel like Cassandra."[1]

NINA OLSON KEEPS WARNING CONGRESS that the steady stream of revisions and additions to the tax code can only exacerbate the problem of complexity. But Congress doesn't listen. Commerce Clearing House, a publisher that tracks developments in the tax laws, has estimated that there are about 420 significant changes to the tax code every year, many of which require new forms, new rules, and whole books of instructions for taxpayers to follow.

"One of the most surprising, most disappointing things I found when I got this job," said John Koskinen, who was named commissioner of the IRS in 2013, "is the way Congress just changes the tax code willy-nilly, without ever thinking about it. People keep adding stuff without ever thinking, is this going to be easy to deal with? Is this going to make taxes more complicated? Because they are way too complicated already."

The national taxpayer advocate set forth the familiar complaint in significant detail in her annual report to Congress for the year 2012. "The most serious problem facing taxpayers—and the IRS—is the complexity of the Internal Revenue Code," Olson reported. She went on to list some of the implications of this complexity. The tax code, she wrote,

• "Makes compliance difficult, requiring taxpayers to devote excessive time to preparing and filing their returns;

• "Requires the significant majority of taxpayers to bear monetary costs to comply, as most taxpayers hire preparers and many other taxpayers purchase tax preparation software;

• "Obscures comprehension, leaving many taxpayers unaware of how their taxes are computed and what rate of tax they pay;

• "Facilitates tax avoidance by enabling sophisticated taxpayers to reduce their tax liabilities and by providing criminals with opportunities to commit tax fraud;

• "Undermines trust in the system by creating an impression that many taxpayers are not compliant, thereby reducing the incentives that honest taxpayers feel to comply; and

• "Generates tens of millions of phone calls to the IRS each year, overburdening the agency and compromising its ability to provide high-quality taxpayer service."

The U.S. tax code has grown so huge that nobody really knows how long it is. During the 2016 presidential campaign, candidates routinely cited a figure of seventy-three thousand pages—a number that seems to include about thirty-five hundred pages of the law itself, plus another seventy thousand pages of regulations. The Republican candidate Carly Fiorina said she could reduce that "down to about three pages," although the proposal she made for tax simplification would have replaced only Subtitle A of the code (there are ten more sections, Subtitles B through K, that presumably would have remained intact under the Fiorina plan).

When Nina Olson's staff copied the entire Title 26 of the U.S. Code (that's the Internal Revenue Code) into a Microsoft Word document, the program's "Word Count" feature found a total just under four million words.

The IRS likes to boast that it is a highly efficient government agency, and this is accurate, in a sense. In fiscal year 2015, the agency spent $11.4 billion and brought in revenues of $3.3 trillion; that is, the service spends just thirty-five cents for every $100 it brings in. Another measure of efficiency is revenue per employee. The agency has a staff of about seventy-six thousand to raise that $3.3 trillion, which means the average IRS employee takes in more than four hundred times her government salary.[2] On both measures—cost of collection and revenue per employee—America's IRS ranks at or near the top for sheer efficiency among the taxing agencies of the world's rich countries.

But the IRS achieves this noteworthy status by imposing much of the cost of the tax system on taxpayers. In other rich countries, as we'll see shortly, the tax collector shoulders much of the burden that is borne by individual and corporate taxpayers in the United States.

The IRS, in contrast, pushes those costs onto us. While the tax agency spends $11.4 billion, American taxpayers end up paying vastly more just to file their annual returns. The Office of the Taxpayer Advocate says American families spend 3.16 billion hours each year getting their taxes done—gathering the data, keeping records, and filling out forms; businesses spend about 2.9 billion hours on the same tasks (a figure that does not include all the time required for the tax-avoidance gymnastics). At an average wage, those six billion hours devoted to filing tax returns represent about $400 billion per year of working time; six billion hours is the equivalent of 3.1 million people working forty hours per week, fifty weeks per year. In terms of time and cost, just paying our taxes has become one of the biggest industries in the United States.

Because the system is so complicated, hardly any Americans still fill out Form 1040 by themselves. Just two decades ago, pulling out the shoe box full of receipts and filling in the tax forms was a standard, if not particularly pleasant, rite of spring for most U.S. families. Today, barely 10% of Americans do their own tax returns. About 60% of all individual taxpayers hire tax-preparation agencies to do the work for them; another 30% buy tax-preparation software each year to get them through the process. The IRS says an average family at the median income shells out about $260 per year for tax-preparation services; those with higher incomes can easily pay ten times as much. Including the hours needed just to gather the records, Americans spend about three times the IRS budget just to file their returns. "The current tax code imposes huge compliance burdens on individual taxpayers and businesses," the Office of the Taxpayer Advocate says.

Filling out a tax return in the United States can resemble solving an absurdly difficult word puzzle. The hundreds of different IRS forms are studded with thousands of instructions and precautions that people have to read two or three times to figure out. When I was writing the first chapter of this book, I asked Nina Olson to help me find a standard IRS instruction that is so complicated it would seem ludicrous. She replied, "But there are so many of those!" Eventually, we settled on the instruction found in chapter 1 of this book: "Go to Part IV of Schedule I to figure line 52 if the estate or trust has qualified dividends or has a gain on lines 18a and 19 of column (2) of Schedule D (Form 1041) (as refigured for the AMT, if necessary)."

That one comes from IRS Form 1041, but Nina was right. There are countless instructions and directions that could give you a good laugh—if you didn't have to figure out what they mean:

- "If you are a single-member LLC that is disregarded as an entity separate from its owner (see *Limited Liability Company (LLC)* on this page), enter the owner's SSN (or EIN, if the owner has one). Do not enter the disregarded entity's EIN. If the LLC is classified as a corporation or partnership, enter the entity's EIN."[3]

- "If you are considered the owner under the grantor trust rules of any part of a domestic liquidating trust under Regulations §301.7701-4(d) that is created under chapter 7 or chapter 11 of the Bankruptcy Code, you do not have to report any specified foreign financial asset held by the part of the trust you are considered to own."[4]

- "Enter 6% (.06) of the smaller of line 40 or the value of your Archer MSAs on December 31, 2015 (including 2015 contributions made in 2016). Include this amount on Form 1040, line 58, or Form 1040NR, line 56."[5]

- "The recapture amount that you must include on line 1 will not exceed the amount of your early distribution; and, for purposes of determining this recapture amount, a rollover amount (or portion of a rollover) will only be allocated to an early distribution once."[6]

Among tax experts and aficionados, there is a friendly competition going on to come up with a nutty but fictitious instruction that sounds so authentically convoluted that it is hard to differentiate the phony from the real thing. One professor of tax policy gave his students the following quiz:

Which of the following is NOT a genuine IRS instruction?

a. Combine Lines 1 through 17. Enter here and on Schedule M-3, Part II, Line 27, reporting positive amounts as negative and negative amounts as positive.

b. Enter the number of vehicles for categories A–V in the applicable column. Add the number of vehicles in columns (3a) and (3b), categories A–V. For category W, enter the number of suspended vehicles in the applicable columns.

c. Enter 18.2% (.182) of line 37(b) or the total of your monthly electric bills for the tax year (excluding December, January, and February), whichever is greater.

d. If you received a Form 1099-INT that reflects accrued interest paid on a bond you bought between interest payment dates, include the full amount shown as interest on the Form 1099-INT on Schedule B (Form 1040A or 1040), Part I, line 1.*

One of the more pernicious aspects of the complexity problem is that some of the most opaque provisions of the tax code apply to people in the lowest income brackets—the taxpayers least able to afford a tax accountant to help them navigate this regulatory swamp. For example, the earned income tax credit is a reverse income tax through which the federal government gives money to working people whose income is below the median (the cutoff is about $15,000 per year for single people and $50,000 per year for a family of four). The instruction book for low-income taxpayers hoping to get this benefit (Publication 596) is fifty-nine pages long. The book lists fifteen separate conditions, spread over three chapters, that you have to

---

*The correct answer (the fake instruction) is c.

meet to claim the credit. "If you meet all seven rules in this chapter," states the introduction to chapter 1, "then read either chapter 2 or chapter 3 (whichever applies) for more rules you must meet." And even that warning is incomplete, because the first sentence of chapter 4 reads, "You must meet one more rule to claim the EIC." The whole thing is so complicated that the error rate is 27%, which means one out of four filers, and the IRS, have to spend even more time trying to get it right. This has prompted a mini-industry of tax fraud, with shysters going door-to-door in low-rent neighborhoods offering to fill out the EITC forms (for a fee, of course) whether the client actually qualifies or not. Similarly, the tax credits for people buying health insurance on the ObamaCare exchanges are generally aimed at low-income taxpayers and are also ridiculously complicated.

There's another significant cost as well to all this complexity. A tax code so byzantine that people can't understand how much they have to pay badly undermines the spirit of voluntary payment that is essential to a successful tax regime. Economists talk about a concept called "tax morale," which means people's willingness to pay for the services government provides. If the public services are popular, and if the tax code feels fair, then tax morale is high and people are willing to pay. But a tax code that nobody can understand reduces tax morale. Then people are not so willing to pay, and they look for ways to avoid paying what they owe.

"Complexity obscures understanding and creates a sense of distance between taxpayers and the government," the taxpayer advocate says, "resulting in lower rates of voluntary tax compliance. . . . Taxpayers who believe they are unfairly paying more than others inevitably will feel more justified in 'fudging' to right the perceived wrong. . . . Simplifying the tax code so tax policy choices and computations are more transparent would go a long way toward reassuring taxpayers that the system is not rigged against them."

For all these reasons, Nina Olson incessantly urges Congress to simplify the tax code with BBLR reforms.

Eliminating all those complex tax preferences will make the whole process of filing and paying taxes vastly easier, for both the taxpayer and the tax collector. Every deduction and exemption that is eliminated means one less line on the tax return, or one less form, and one less booklet of obscure instructions. Nina Olson concedes that following the path of simplification—of BBLR—might not be simple as a political matter. "In concept, most of us agree that the tax code is too complex, and that broadening the tax base by eliminating existing tax breaks in exchange for lower rates would improve the system," she wrote in her 2012 report on the most serious issues facing taxpayers. "In practice . . . the threatened loss of existing tax breaks raises immediate concerns. And the lower we want tax rates to be, the more of these tax breaks we have to be willing to give up."

It doesn't have to be this way. Countless other countries like ours—advanced, high-tech, free-market democracies—have found ways to collect the tax revenues they need without imposing long hours of tedious labor and large tax-preparer fees on their citizens. Their parliaments and their tax collectors are no smarter than their counterparts in the United States. The difference is, those countries make a genuine commitment to simplification of the tax code. The U.S. Congress, in contrast, likes to talk about simplification but has shown no commitment to do anything about it (except once every thirty-two years). In many countries, the tax agency ombudsman— in essence, the equivalent of Nina Olson—has the power to order changes in the system, while Olson is stuck making endless futile pleas to Congress.

According to the Algemene Fiscale Politiek, the Netherlands' counterpart of the IRS, the average time for a Dutch taxpayer to complete both federal and local returns is fifteen minutes. That's partially because there's really only one return. To make things easier for tax-payers, the Dutch have established a "unified" tax system such that the national and provincial governments use the same form to collect income taxes. But even the Netherlands is a piker in this field compared with Estonia, a former Soviet satellite that has leaped enthusiastically into the digital age. Estonia's tax agency says the average time to complete its federal tax return is seven minutes. Estonia's tax agency doesn't want to waste any time reviewing tax returns on paper, so all returns must be filed online. The small cohort of Estonians who still don't have a computer are invited to go to an office of the tax agency, where a helpful clerk will complete the online form for you.

For Japanese wage earners, the task of paying income tax is even easier. Japan's equivalent of the IRS, Kokuzeicho, gathers all the pertinent data for each worker—income, taxable benefits, number of personal exemptions, tax withheld, and so on—and then computes how much the worker owes in tax, down to the last yen. Because Japan uses a system known as "precision withholding," with the amount changing whenever pay goes up or down, most people withhold the exact amount due. In early March, Kokuzeicho sends a postcard to every citizen that sets forth all this information: how much you earned, how much tax you owe, how much tax you've already paid through withholding. If you've paid in more tax than you owe, Kokuzeicho deposits the refund amount in your bank account; if you did not withhold enough, the agency takes the tax that's due from your bank account. If the figures on the postcard from Kokuzeicho look about right, the taxpayer does nothing. The tax has been computed and paid already. If the numbers look wrong, you go into the local tax office and try to straighten things out. As a result, paying income tax is a totally automatic process for about 80% of Japanese households, requiring no more work than reading a postcard once a year. When I told my friend Togo Shigehiko that Americans spend hours or days gathering records each year and filling out the forms, he was incredulous. "Why would anybody want to do that?" he asked me.

Britain's version of the IRS, Her Majesty's Revenue and Customs, maintains a full-time bureau called the U.K. Office of Tax Simplification, or OTS.[7] Its mission statement is similar to that of the Office of the Taxpayer Advocate at the IRS: "There is already evidence that simpler taxes encourage compliance: taxpayers find it easier to comply and have greater trust in the system. That implies reduced scope for avoidance." But OTS has a track record that would make Nina Olson dark green with envy; the office has made some four hundred formal proposals to simplify either the tax code or the tax return forms, and 50% of them have been implemented, at least in part. The U.K. has established a system rather like Japan's, with Her Majesty's Revenue and Customs filling in the tax return with data it has received from employers, banks, brokerage houses, charitable recipients, and so on. The Brits also use a "precision withholding" system, called Pay as You Earn, or PAYE, which takes into account wages and benefits, Social Security and health-care deductions, student loan deductions, and various other adjustments to income. With that, most British wage earners find their yearly total of tax withholding just about equals the tax they owe; in 2014, according to the Office of Tax Simplification, only one in five Brits had to file a tax return.

There's a pattern to the simplification of taxation in the Netherlands, Japan, Britain, and several other countries—including Denmark, Sweden, Spain, and Portugal—that have taken similar steps. In each case, the government does the work of filling out the tax return. The taxpayer just checks the numbers—sometimes with a beer in hand, as with my Dutch friend Michael—and confirms that the tax agency got things right. And if the agency got something wrong, there's a mechanism for the taxpayer to make the correction. To make this work, the taxing authority has to know all the relevant information: wages, bonuses, benefits, bank and brokerage accounts, mortgage payments, charitable contributions, educational spending, and the like. As a rule, all payers and all recipients of money that might be deductible are required to report what they paid you, or received from you, to the government. In Britain, for example, charities report all contributions to Her Majesty's Revenue and Customs, so the tax agency knows how much you gave and can compute the appropriate deduction for you.

The tax authorities refer to this type of system as "pre-filled forms" or "pre-populated returns." (In the United States, it is sometimes called "return-free filing," which is a misnomer, because there's still a return. It's just that the taxpayer doesn't have to fill it out.) This approach is obviously simpler for the taxpayer. Beyond that, experience has shown that it leads to fewer errors; generally, the government's computers don't transpose digits when entering a number and don't enter data on the wrong lines, as ordinary taxpayers sometimes do. Of course pre-filled forms work better when the tax system is simpler; if there's no deduction for a home mortgage, for example, or no credit for buying a hybrid car, the tax agency doesn't have to check with every mortgage company and every auto dealer to fill out the forms.

Could pre-filled forms work in the United States, with its convoluted rules on what constitutes "income" and its endless roster of credits, deductions, exemptions, and allowances? In a limited sense, it already does work here. California has launched what it calls an "experimental" program known as CalFile in which the revenue department will send you a state tax return that is already filled in; if the numbers look right, you sign it, and the work is done. If they don't, you send back the return with your changes. The state has never spent much money to publicize this system, so it is poorly known and little used. But of the ninety thousand Californians who did file through this pre-filled form in 2012, 98% subsequently told pollsters that they loved it and would definitely use it again. When California asked users for comments on the system, the replies were downright ecstatic. "THIS IS THE BEST SERVICE I HAVE EVER SEEN BY THE GOVERNMENT," one taxpayer said.

There are advocates, both in academia and in government, who would like to see a pre-filled form system for the federal income tax in the United States. It's clear that the IRS already has much or all of the necessary data for a large number of American taxpayers. Anybody who has received a thick envelope in the mail from the IRS, raising questions about last year's return, can see that the agency seems to have records on every payment (be it wages or self-employment income), every investment account, every bank account, and so on.

When I got such a letter—it was a CP2000 Notice, which is one step before an official audit—the document said, "The income and payment information we have on file from sources such as employers or financial institutions doesn't match the information you reported on your tax return." With some chagrin, I had to admit that the IRS was right, for the most part. I had received a fourteen-page year-end statement from my brokerage firm, full of different numbers for different investment accounts, some taxable and some not. I was supposed to figure out which data were relevant and where to enter them on my tax return. I got it wrong, which was why that CP2000 Notice showed up in the mail a few months later. And I thought, if the IRS has all this stuff in its computers, how come I had to dig through this fourteen-page statement to tell the IRS what it already knows? If I hire a tax preparer to do my tax return, why should I pay her to give the IRS information that it already has?

Questions like that have prompted several members of the U.S. Congress to champion pre-filled forms. Senators Ron Wyden (D-Ore.), Dan Coats (R-Ind.), and Elizabeth Warren (D-Mass.) and Representative Jim Cooper (D-Tenn.) are among the sponsors of legislation to create such a system. Given the current tax code, the IRS estimates that it has all the necessary information to prepare a completed Form 1040 for about 30% of American taxpayers; other estimates range as high as 40%. Over time, with stronger reporting requirements and a simpler tax code, that number could increase sharply, perhaps approaching Japan's rate of 80% of taxpayers who simply get a postcard from the government each March. But even at the 30% rate that the IRS estimates, pre-filled forms could save American families one billion hours of work each year and $10 billion in tax-preparation costs.

If this system, already in place in many other advanced democracies, could save Americans such large amounts of time and money, why don't we use it? The answer is pure politics. It turns out that the complexity of the U.S. tax system is a moneymaker for some large companies. So they have lobbied strenuously, and successfully, against all efforts to simplify the tax code. The "Tax Complexity Lobby," as *Forbes* magazine called it, includes tax-preparation firms like H&R Block and Jackson Hewitt, as well as companies that make tax-preparation software.

The biggest spender in the anti-simplification camp is Intuit, the maker of TurboTax, the top-selling tax software program. The firm's lobbying disclosure forms in Washington show that it has spent millions of dollars to persuade members of Congress to "oppose IRS government tax preparation." (Intuit has also lobbied, without success, to shut down California's pre-filled form system.)[8] Intuit's main argument seems to be that tax returns prepared by the IRS and then reviewed by the taxpayer would be less accurate than a return filled out by the taxpayer. "Relying on an actual withholding or government reconciliation tax system, eliminating or curtailing citizen participation in the taxation process, has far-reaching implications for accuracy in public tax expenditures, which are often targeted by policymakers to those lower and middle income citizens with the simplest returns," the company says.

On Tax Day in 2016 (it was April 18 that year), Intuit placed a full-page ad in the *New York Times* headlined "Tax Simplification: A National Imperative." "Simply put, our tax code is mind-numbingly complex," the advertisement reads. "No one set out to create an incomprehensible tax code—it just happened, little by little, over a period of decades. . . . It will take a determined effort to tackle the resulting complexity and make common-sense tax simplification reform a reality." Intuit's advertisement did not mention that Intuit has spent millions of dollars fighting the "tax simplification reform" of pre-filled forms.

———

IN ADDITION TO the familiar approaches to simplifying the tax code—things like BBLR and pre-filled forms—there is a school of thought which holds that the personal income tax can never really be simple, because the lobbyists and politicians will perennially add complex new provisions that benefit one interest group or another. Those who hold this view, accordingly, want to scrap the income tax altogether, or at least make it a much less important part of the government's overall revenue-raising apparatus. To do that, these advocates propose a new form of tax that has been adopted, successfully, in some 175 countries around the world—but never tried in the United States.

THE MONEY MACHINE

As a boy growing up on his father's coffee plantation outside Saigon—in a country known then as French Indochina—Maurice Lauré liked to spend his evenings in the community library. The volume that young Maurice liked best was an oversized picture book showing the uniforms of French government officials. As a country that reveres its civil servants, France provided impressive uniforms not only for the military, police, and firefighters but also for customs agents, bank inspectors, drain commissioners, public health officers, mayors, municipal band leaders, and others.

The outfit that made the greatest impression on young Maurice Lauré was the uniform of the *inspecteur des finances,* or tax collector. Going back to the eighteenth century, agents of the French national tax authority wore an impressive blue suit with a yellow stripe down each leg and a golden epaulet on the right shoulder. "It seemed to me to be a terribly important corps with influence in all things," Lauré recalled in an interview some fifty years later. "So I told my mother I would like to be an inspecteur des finances. She thought it was an excellent idea."[1]

After a detour into the army's engineering corps during World War II, Lauré did, in fact, join La Direction Générale des Impôts, the French equivalent of the IRS; sadly, that "very fine" uniform had been retired by the time he arrived. By the early 1950s, he was co-director of the agency, and one of the major problems he addressed was non-compliance by business taxpayers. France at the time imposed a tax on commercial activities of the type known as a turnover tax or a gross receipts tax. It was a complex edifice and fairly easy for businesses to avoid, which they regularly did. So Lauré, the engineer turned tax man, rolled up his sleeves and designed a new kind of tax, a levy that applied to virtually every business transaction but that was easy for tax collectors to track and thus hard for taxpayers to duck. In 1953, he published his seminal book, *La taxe sur la valeur ajoutée* (The tax on added value).

Drawing on earlier work by the German economist Wilhelm von Siemens and the American Carl S. Shoup (who had proposed a value-added tax for Japan during the American occupation after World War II), Lauré's new tax on commercial transactions worked so well that it began to spread to other countries; Europe's nascent Common Market (which became the European Union) made the value-added tax mandatory for all its member nations in 1967, on the theory that a unified market should have a unified tax structure. Fairly quickly, the idea was taken up in South America and Africa, in the fast-growing "Tiger economies" of East Asia, and then, somewhat later, in former British colonies like Australia, New Zealand, and Canada. By 2016, some 175 of the planet's 200 countries had a value-added tax or a goods and services tax, which is another name for the same thing. This form of taxation brings in about 20% of all the government revenue in the world; among the members of the OECD, the club of rich nations, VAT payments constitute 33% of all tax revenue. For many countries, the VAT has become the most important single tax; in France, Lauré's invention generates about 40% of revenues.

"The rise of the value-added tax," observed the economic historian Liam Ebrill, "was the most dramatic—and probably most important—development in taxation in the last half of the twentieth century." The law professors Alan Schenk and Oliver Oldman noted that "the VAT has spread more quickly than any other new tax in modern history."[2]

The International Fiscal Association, a global think tank on government finance, has created the Maurice Lauré Prize to recognize the most innovative proposal put forth each year to improve tax collection. "If you look at the economic history of the last half century or so," said Professor Richard Bird of the University of Toronto, "the VAT is one of the world's biggest fiscal stories." Professor Bird, who has helped design tax regimes for numerous countries, told me that "a VAT, or its twin, a GST, is an absolutely essential element of any tax structure today. To set up a tax system anywhere that didn't include a VAT would be malpractice; it would be like creating a health-care system without hospitals. That's why every responsible Finance Ministry has used it."

Professor Bird's comment is a backhanded slam at the United States, because our country is the only developed nation that has missed the boat on this successful new innovation. Almost all economists who've looked at the U.S. tax code, almost every blue-ribbon study commission, almost all presidential candidates who bother to propose a program of tax reform, agree that some version of the value-added tax could increase the fairness and efficiency of our tax system and reduce its mind-boggling complexity. And yet the United States stands alone among the world's rich nations in refusing to implement this common levy.

It's one of the curious manifestations of the concept of "American exceptionalism," the idea that there's no country like the United States of America. Of course we're proud of the freedom and opportunity the United States offers its citizens and its immigrants. There may not be another country where the son of a visiting student from Kenya, raised by a single mother in modest circumstances, could grow up to be elected the head of state; there may not be another country where the son of an immigrant restaurant worker from Syria could create the company called Apple. There are unique aspects of the American way that make these success stories common, and nobody wants to lose the things that make our country exceptional. The problem comes when U.S. politicians are so determined to be exceptional, to do things our own way, that they refuse to implement a valuable idea that almost every other country on the planet has embraced to its benefit. This makes us exceptional, but not in a way that any other country would choose.

THE VALUE-ADDED TAX IS essentially a sales tax—like the retail sales tax most Americans pay at the store every day—but one that is applied to every stage of commerce, not just to the final sale at the retail store. To see the difference, let's imagine an American, whom we'll call Mrs. Buyer, purchasing a dining-room table—a handsome mahogany table, stained a dark reddish brown—at a local emporium called the Acme Furniture Store.

Under the retail sales tax that is familiar to Americans, the transaction works like this: The retail price of the table is $600. But the customer, of course, has to pay more than that. If the local sales tax is 8%, Mrs. Buyer has to pay $648 for the table—the retail price, plus the 8% tax. The customer pays the tax; the furniture store plays the role of tax collector, taking in the $48 and sending it on to the local department of revenue. It's important to note here that Mrs. Buyer doesn't know whether the furniture store actually remits the tax payment to the government and doesn't much care, either. It makes no difference to her.

Under a VAT regime, the government receives the same amount of revenue as the retail sales tax, but the collection process is different.

• It starts when the owner of Mahogany Forests Inc. sells the raw timber to a wood-finishing company that we'll call Elite Wood Products. Elite pays the forest company $150 for the timber, plus a value-added tax of 8%, or $12; the forest company is required to remit this tax to the government.

• Elite Wood Products cleans and sands the wood and applies that dark reddish-brown stain. Elite then sells the finished pieces of wood to a furniture maker that we'll call Distinguished Tables Inc. The price is $250, plus a value-added tax of 8%, or $20; Elite is obliged to remit the tax it collected to the government. But it can take a credit for the amount of tax it previously paid—that is, the $12 in tax it paid to the forest company—so that Elite's actual tax payment to the government is $8.

- The skilled workers at Distinguished Tables use the dark-stained wood purchased from Elite to build a beautiful table, with carefully finished corners and striking carved legs. Distinguished, the table maker, then sells the table to a wholesaler, an outfit that we'll call Wholesale Furniture Trading Inc. The wholesale company pays $400 for the finished table, plus a value-added tax of 8%, or $32. Distinguished Tables is required to remit this tax payment to the government, but it gets a credit for the amount of tax it previously paid—that is, the $20 in tax it paid to Elite Wood Products. So Distinguished, the table maker, actually pays the government $12 in tax.

- Wholesale Furniture Trading sells the table to the retail store, the Acme Furniture Store. The price is $450, plus a value-added tax of 8%, or $36. The wholesaler is obliged to remit this tax to the government, but it can take a credit for the tax it paid—that is, $32—to the table maker. So Wholesale Furniture Trading pays the government $4 in tax.

- Acme Furniture sells the table to Mrs. Buyer for $600, plus the 8% tax, for a total of $648. Acme is required to remit this $48 in tax to the government, but it gets a credit for tax it paid—that is, $36—to the wholesaler. So Acme actually pays the government $12.

With the credits for taxes already paid, each link in this chain of production and merchandising ends up paying tax only on its contribution to the product along the way. That is, the value-added tax does what its name suggests: it taxes each link in the chain only on the amount of value it added toward the final product.

If you add up all the tax payments—$12 from the forest company, $8 from the wood products company, $12 from the furniture maker, $4 from the wholesaler, and $12 from the retail store—the government collects a total of $48 from the sale of this table. That's precisely the same amount it would receive from an 8% tax applied only on the retail sale. But the chain of payments that take place under a VAT makes the VAT system work better—from the government's standpoint, at least.

With a retail sales tax, Mrs. Buyer paid Acme Furniture $48 in tax, which the store is supposed to remit to the government. For the tax collector, an important aspect of this common transaction is that Mrs. Buyer has no incentive to find out whether the retailer actually forwarded this $48 to the department of revenue. It's all the same to her whether the owner of Acme Furniture pays the tax or pockets the money. To economists, this is a fundamental flaw with a retail sales tax: nobody has an incentive to see that the tax is actually paid. And this was Maurice Lauré's great gift to tax collectors all over the world; in his VAT system, everybody has an incentive to report the taxes that are due.

With a VAT, each buyer along the chain gets a credit for the sales tax it already paid. And thus each buyer has an incentive to report that tax payment to the government. In the example we just considered, Distinguished Tables reports that it paid a tax of $20 to Elite Wood Products; Distinguished reports that $20 so it can get the credit against the tax it owes. As a result, the tax agency knows that Elite received $20 in tax and should have remitted that $20; if Elite failed to pay the tax, the government will know about it and start collection procedures. Because every buyer along the chain has an incentive to report the tax he paid to his supplier, no supplier can get away with ducking the tax. In essence, the VAT is self-policing, which makes it a much harder tax to evade than a simple retail sales tax.

Beyond that, the VAT provides a more even flow of tax revenue to government coffers than a retail sales tax. Some products can take months or years to move from raw material to final retail sale. Under the retail sales tax, the government won't get a penny of revenue until the retail customer makes that final purchase. With a VAT, in contrast, each step along the way from forest to furniture store triggers a tax payment.

Economists, too, think the VAT is a "good" form of taxation—or at least one that has fewer negative side effects than a tax on personal or corporate income. Because (almost) every government has to collect tax, economists want to see it done in a way that minimizes economic distortion. The VAT meets that test in several ways:

• It's a tax on spending, not on labor or savings or investment. As we've seen throughout this book, it's a basic economic principle that if you tax something, you get less of it. A payroll tax penalizes work; in theory, people will work less if their earnings are taxed. A tax on dividends or interest penalizes saving; a tax on capital gains penalizes investment. So if a nation can use VAT revenues to reduce the burden of other taxes, the undesirable side effects of other types of taxes will be reduced.

• The amount of consumption in an economy tends to be more constant than the amount of labor. When recessions hit, and people lose their jobs, they no longer have wages and salaries to be taxed. But to some extent, people keep buying things. So a consumption tax like the VAT is less variable and thus more dependable as a source of revenue, particularly when the overall economy slows.

• Because everybody buys stuff, everybody pays a tax on purchases. This is appealing to those who worry about the so-called 47% problem—that is, the significant number of people who don't pay income tax. In the United States in recent years, the number of households exempt from the federal income tax—because their income is below the basic threshold where the tax kicks in—has run about 47%, as Mitt Romney famously complained during the 2012 presidential campaign. (Of course, the 47-percenters still have to pay Social Security tax, Medicare tax, gasoline tax, and so on.) A consumption tax like the VAT is paid by everybody, including those who pay no income tax and those who are in the country illegally.

- With a VAT, particularly if imposed at the national level, it is no problem to apply the tax to online purchases. This eliminates the disadvantage the brick-and-mortar stores face when they have to pay a local sales tax while the distant Internet seller can price the same product without including local tax.

- Most VAT systems do not charge a tax on the final sale of an item that is exported. This means the seller can quote a tax-free price to his export customer. For a trading country that has no VAT—that is, the United States—that creates a competitive disadvantage for domestic companies, which are already facing a corporate income tax higher than that of most of their foreign competitors. If VAT revenues were used to reduce the corporate income tax rate, the combination should enhance exports and thus improve the national balance of payments.

ON THE OTHER HAND, there are also economic problems associated with a value-added tax—problems that prompt furious opposition whenever somebody proposes a VAT for the United States.

The VAT often works as an "invisible" tax. That is, the amount of tax is included in the retail price of the item, so the purchaser isn't reminded that she's paying a tax every time she buys something.

If you buy a book for $25.00 in the United States, you actually have to pay more; if the sales tax is 7%, the total price of that book will be $26.75. Because the price tag said $25.00, the buyer knows with every purchase that she's paying a tax. But if you buy a book for €25.00 in France, you'll pay only €25.00. The book was actually priced at €20.83; the 20% VAT, €4.16, is included in the retail price. So the buyer thinks she's paying for a €25.00 book, as if there were no tax.

This system makes it easier for countries to raise their taxes; because the tax is invisible, consumers don't know when taxes have gone up. If the VAT on that book goes from €4.16 to €4.66, the purchaser will now be charged €25.50. The customer may not be pleased about it, but she's likely to blame the publisher or the bookstore for this increase.

Governments use this ploy all the time. Britain's Conservative Party has always held itself out as the small-government, low-tax party. But after the Great Recession slashed government revenues, the Conservative government raised the national VAT rate from 17.5% to 20%. This increased the cost of almost everything Brits went to buy, but the tax increase was hidden in the retail price of each item. At the next election, in 2015, British voters told pollsters they still considered the Conservatives the low-tax party—a major reason the Tories won a big electoral victory that year.

To the economists, an invisible tax is a bad idea. People should know how much they're paying—whether they are buying books or governmental services. I asked the policy director of the Netherlands' national tax bureau about this aspect of the Dutch VAT, which is folded into the retail price and thus hidden from consumers. "As an economist, of course I deplore an invisible tax," Michiel Sweers told me. "As a tax collector, I'm all for it."

Of course, the VAT need not be invisible. Canada's GST is applied like an American sales tax; there's a pretax retail price for the product, and the sales clerk then adds the tax to the total due at time of purchase. So Canadian consumers are reminded of the tax with every *ca-ching* of the cash register. But Canada is the only country so far to reject tax-inclusive pricing.

Because it tends to make raising taxes so easy—and so free from consequences for the party responsible—champions of lower taxes consider the value-added tax anathema. Conservatives argue that the VAT is a "money machine" designed to churn out increasing revenue to pay for more and more government. The *Wall Street Journal* neatly set forth the anti-VAT line of argument in an editorial:

> It's the hottest trend among tax collectors, raising a gusher of revenue for spendthrift governments worldwide. We refer to the value-added tax (VAT). . . . Americans, be warned.
>
> The VAT is a sort of turbo-charged national sales tax on goods and services that is applied at each stage of production, not merely on retail transactions. Politicians love it because it is the most efficient revenue-raiser known to man, and its rates can be raised gradually to finance new entitlements or fill budget holes. The VAT is typically introduced with a low rate but then moves up over time until it swallows huge chunks of national economies. . . .
>
> Because VATs are embedded in the price of products, they can often rise unnoticed by the consumer, which is why liberals love them as a vehicle for periodic stealth tax hikes. . . .
>
> [T]he VAT . . . makes every business an aggressive tax collector. . . . The businesses get a rebate on the portion they paid when they remit to the government the sums they collected, so the system motivates all companies to ensure taxes are paid in full.
>
> The U.S. is a rare industrial nation that doesn't have a VAT, though don't think it can't happen here. Liberals campaign on soaking the rich, but they know there're only so many rich to soak. . . . [T]hey need a new broad-based tax that hits the middle class, where the big money is.[3]

The *Journal*'s observation about who ends up paying a value-added tax—that is, everybody who buys things, rich or poor—points to another downside of the value-added tax. It can be regressive; that is, it can have a bigger impact on low-income people than on the wealthy. People in the lower brackets spend a higher share of what they earn on basic consumption than the wealthy do, which means the VAT is proportionally a heavier tax on those least able to pay.

There are different approaches to dealing with the regressive nature of a VAT. One is to make certain items tax-free—items that are essential for life and make up a major share of purchases by lower-income consumers. Typically, countries will exempt groceries, medicine, and school supplies from the tax. Some places say that work clothes or cleaning supplies or pet food should be taxed at a lower rate than less essential items. But this becomes another instance of a problem we've seen throughout this book: equity in taxation often comes at the price of simplicity. Once you start varying the rates, or exempting certain purchases completely, the tax regime gets complicated fairly quickly. Many countries apply the full VAT to restaurant meals—on the theory that the rich are more likely to dine out—but do not tax groceries that are to be consumed at home. That means a clerk should not collect tax on the sale of eight ounces of ham, but she should on three ounces; in the eyes of the law, the former is a grocery sale and the latter is lunch. Canada's VAT applies to one to five doughnuts—that's considered "immediate consumption"—but not to six, which are classified as "basic groceries" to be taken home.[4] It becomes a complicated mess for some guy who's just trying to make a living selling doughnuts.

A simpler way to deal with this problem—the method recommended by the International Monetary Fund and other tax-advisory organizations—is to charge the same VAT for everything but then to give a credit to low-income people through the income tax. This, too, can get complicated. But because most developed countries already have special income tax provisions for low-income families—such as the earned income tax credit in the United States—it's something tax authorities know how to do. New Zealand has chosen to deal with the problem of regression this way: Its 15% GST applies to virtually everything, including the goods and/or services provided in a brothel. But it has mechanisms to refund the GST payments for people in the lowest brackets.

The system of tax collections and credits for every link in the production chain is not simple. There's a definite cost involved in setting up a VAT regime, and there are compliance costs for those who have to pay the tax. Once the system is in place, though, it should be cheaper and easier than what we've got today. The economists Joel Slemrod and Jon Bakija reviewed several studies on administrative costs of different tax regimes. They concluded that "a broad-based, single-rate VAT could involve considerably lower enforcement and compliance costs than the current income tax in the United States."[5]

Beyond that, imposing a VAT raises prices, which is likely to deter consumption and stifle economic growth. The Japanese learned that the hard way. After the burst of the "bubble economy" of the 1980s, business activity and tax revenues fell sharply. The Japanese government began running up huge annual deficits. More revenues were needed, so the government implemented a VAT in 1989 and raised it in 1997. This made the recession worse. The price of everything went up. People stopped shopping. The economy slumped even further. It took years before economic activity returned to pre-VAT levels. To avoid a repeat of that disaster, Japan's prime minister decided in 2016 to cancel a scheduled increase in the VAT rate.

ALTHOUGH THE BASIC STRUCTURE of VAT/GST all over the world is essentially the same thing that Maurice Lauré implemented in France in the 1950s, there is a broad range of tax rates and regulations governing this consumption tax. In the European Union, member nations are required to have a VAT of at least 15% so that no member tries to lure shoppers into its stores with a sharply lower sales tax. (The EU also allows countries to set reduced rates on items like food, medicine, and books.) Most EU members impose a tax higher than that; in 2016, the average rate in Europe was 21%. As we've seen earlier, the current world champion at gouging shoppers is Hungary, with a standard rate of 27%.

Hungary offsets this severe tax bite with lower rates for certain basic commodities, like food and medicine. Many other countries do the same. Going in the other direction, some nations impose a higher VAT for luxury goods like perfume and jewelry; the luxury VAT can run as high as 85% (in Chile), which the buyers of diamond-encrusted watches and pearl necklaces can presumably afford.

Here's a list of various countries and their standard VAT rate, as of 2016:[6]

Nation	Standard VAT/GST rate
Argentina	21%
Australia	10%
Belgium	21%
Canada	9.975% to 15%
Chile	19%
China	17%
Denmark	25%
Egypt	10%
Finland	24%
France	20%
Germany	19%
Hungary	27%
Ireland	23%

Nation	Standard VAT/GST rate
Italy	22%
Japan	8%
Malaysia	6%
Mexico	16%
New Zealand	15%
Norway	25%
Russia	18%
South Africa	14%
Sweden	25%
U.K.	20%
United States	0%

Because the VAT is such a ubiquitous aspect of daily life, the consumption tax has predictably become the focus of furious political battles. Moviemakers in Japan, arguing that the nation's once great film industry was dying, lobbied for years to get movie tickets exempt from the VAT (and won). Under similar lobbying pressure, France sharply cut the VAT on restaurant meals in 2009, and Germany cut the tax on hotel rooms in 2010; in both cases, subsequent studies showed that only a small fraction of the savings was passed on to consumers through lower prices.[7] Poland applied a zero rating (that is, no VAT) on disinfectants and had to fight the Brussels bureaucracy all the way to the European Court of Justice (in essence, the EU's Supreme Court) to defend it. All over Europe, women's groups have launched prolonged battles against applying the VAT to tampons, calling this a tax on women. Results to date are mixed: women have won a zero rating for tampons in Ireland and reduced tax rates in Britain, France, the Netherlands, and Spain. But most European countries still tax tampons at the full rate, which means Hungarian women get to pay 27% over the retail price every time they stock up.

STUDY AFTER STUDY and blue-ribbon panel after blue-ribbon panel have concluded that a VAT would work in the United States. If the revenues were used to eliminate, or at least reduce, the tax on interest, dividends, and capital gains, the consumption tax might encourage savings and investment. There would be a definite start-up effect, both in administrative costs and in higher retail prices, but over time these impacts should disappear. For this reason, presidents from Nixon to Obama have thought out loud about establishing a VAT.

The most ambitious recent study came from the George W. Bush administration. Just after his reelection in 2004, Bush created a study commission, the President's Advisory Panel on Federal Tax Reform, with instructions to leave no stone unturned in search of ways to make the U.S. tax code fairer, simpler, and more efficient. The group allocated a great deal of debate, and a full chapter in its final report, to the idea of a federal VAT. It concluded that such a tax would allow for a substantial reduction of income tax rates, with no loss of revenue. In an earlier section of its report, the advisory panel had proposed a revamped federal income tax, with a progressive rate structure of 15% for the lowest brackets and then additional brackets of 25%, 28%, and 33% for people at higher incomes. But if the United States adopted a 15% VAT on purchases, the income tax could be slashed to two brackets: 5% for lower-income families and 15% for taxpayers above the median income. With a top rate of 15%, few taxpayers would find it necessary or productive to invest in complicated tax-avoidance schemes, so compliance would go up and IRS administrative costs would go down. Accordingly, the panel reported that imposing a federal VAT could be a key element of successful tax reform.

But this study took place in 2005, when the polarization and division that mark American politics today were already starting to take root. Sure enough, the President's Advisory Panel on Federal Tax

Reform was so badly divided that it couldn't muster a majority to support any plan. On the VAT, the final report said, "Panel members recognized that lower income tax rates made possible by VAT revenues could create a tax system that is more efficient and could reduce the economic distortions and disincentives created by our income tax. However, the Panel could not reach a consensus on whether to recommend a VAT option.

"Some members of the Panel who supported introducing a consumption tax in general expressed concern about the compliance and administrative burdens that would be imposed by operating a VAT," the report explained. "Some members were also concerned that . . . the VAT would be a 'money machine.' . . . Others expressed the opposite view and regarded the VAT as a stable and efficient tool that could be used to reduce income taxes, fund entitlement programs, or serve as a possible replacement for payroll taxes."[8]

One substantive objection to a national VAT or GST in the United States is the federal system. There are thousands of state, county, city, and special district governments that must raise revenues themselves, and many of them do it through a retail sales tax; Professor Jay Rosengard of Harvard's Kennedy School estimates there are more than six thousand different sales taxes in place in the United States today. In most communities, they accumulate atop each other. The sales tax in Denver, where I live, is fairly typical. Denver's 7.62% sales tax is a combination of state, county, and city levies, along with an additional 1% for the local transit district, 0.1% to pay for the Denver Broncos football stadium, and another 0.1% for something called the Scientific and Cultural Facilities District, which pays for museums, libraries, zoos, and the like. If the United States were to add a significant new value-added tax on top of all those local sales taxes, we'd be approaching European levels of tax on most purchases.

President Bush's advisory panel worried about this aspect of a federal VAT. "Coordinating between states' retail sales taxes and the VAT would be a major challenge," its report said. "States likely would view a VAT as an intrusion on their traditional sales tax base."

Around the world, though, the existence of local sales taxes has not been an insurmountable obstacle to imposing a federal VAT. Several countries have done exactly that, including New Zealand, Australia, and Great Britain. In some countries, the federal government collects all the tax and then distributes it to local governments. In others, there's a tax like the combined sales tax I have to pay in Denver, with part of the take going to the local government and part going to the national tax agency. That's the system Canada has set up, although getting there wasn't a particularly easy process.

For decades, Canada imposed a tax on manufactured goods called the manufacturers' sales tax (MST). Most Canadians were unaware of its existence, even though it was passed on to consumers through higher prices. The business community fought consistently for its repeal. Economists, too, opposed this tax; after all, it was a penalty on producing things, something any developed economy should encourage, not penalize.

As in the United States, there were advisory panels and study commissions on tax reform at regular intervals. As in the United States, nearly all of them urged the country to adopt a value-added tax at the federal level. By the start of the 1990s, with federal deficits increasing and the MST getting stiffer—the rate went from 5% to 13.5% in a dozen years—it was clear, even to the antitax Conservative Party, that the time had come. The Conservative prime minister, Brian Mulroney, muscled a consumption tax through the Parliament. Following New Zealand's example, Mulroney called it a GST. It took effect on January 1, 1991, and was immediately unpopular.

A major reason was that nearly all Canadians were already paying a sales tax. Every Canadian province except one had a retail sales tax in effect at the time. When the GST came along, people suddenly found themselves paying a new tax, piled on top of the provincial sales taxes already in place. Three provinces went to the Supreme Court to fight this new federal impost. To duck the tax, Canadians by the millions started traveling south to make major purchases (a practice that ended after 9/11, when crossing any U.S. border became much more difficult). Although the 1991 GST brought in significant revenues to pay for popular government services, Canadians were still furious in 1993, when the Conservative government had to stand for reelection. The Liberal Party leader, Jean Chrétien, based his entire campaign on the new tax—the Liberals' slogan was "Axe the tax"—and won such a huge victory that Mulroney's Conservatives saw their sixty-nine seats in the Parliament reduced to two.

In fact, though, the Liberals couldn't "axe the tax." By the time Chrétien came to power, revenues from the GST were such an important part of the federal budget that the new levy simply had to stay in place. Chrétien offered voters an apology but then started negotiating with the provinces on a consumption tax that combined the provincial and federal taxes. The result was a new levy, the harmonized sales tax (HST), with proceeds split between the national and the provincial governments. Nearly all the provinces have gone along; 80% of the Canadian economy today operates under the GST/HST arrangement. Both Conservative and Liberal governments have backed this regime for more than two decades. In 2016, the federal portion of this tax was 5%; provincial rates, added to the federal levy, ranged from 4.75% to 10%. "Canada's experience shows that you can impose a federal VAT on top of local sales taxes and make it work," said Professor Bird of the University of Toronto. "And it might even be easier in the [United] States, because you could learn from our example."

The major problem facing a VAT or GST in the United States is not so much administrative as political. The tax is known as a "money machine," and that in itself is enough to make it a bad idea for many American political leaders. It would bring in more revenue, which could fund more government. Grover Norquist, the founder of the tax-cutting lobby group Americans for Tax Reform, likes to say that "VAT is French for big government." Daniel Mitchell of the Cato Institute has said the term "VAT" evokes certain other terms, including "Bad! Europe! France! Greece! Ebola virus!"[9] Some politicians who might favor a VAT because it taxes consumption, not labor or thrift, have been scared away by the potential political cost. On Capitol Hill, the very idea of a VAT tends to bring back scary memories of a U.S. representative from Oregon, a Democrat named Al Ullman.

When I was covering Congress, Ullman was a powerful figure: a twelve-term veteran who was chairman of the House Ways and Means Committee, the tax-writing committee. A former teacher, he was a serious student of tax policy. When I would interview him, he showed no interest in sports or hobbies or the politics of his sprawling eastern Oregon district; he liked to talk tax. After conferring with countless economists, Ullman became Congress's leading champion of a national VAT and proposed such a tax in 1979. Ullman saw the VAT as a way to cut personal and corporate income taxes; the Republicans saw it as a new tax on hardworking Americans and poured money into his district to defeat him. Sure enough, he lost the 1980 election, although it's hard to say the VAT was the only reason; Ronald Reagan carried his district by a whopping margin that year. But ever since, any mention of a VAT on Capitol Hill has prompted the comment "Remember Al Ullman." Another top Democrat, Senator Byron Dorgan of North Dakota, used to tell his colleagues, "The last guy to push a VAT isn't working here anymore."

And yet you can make a strong case that the guys on Capitol Hill—particularly conservatives—should be pushing a VAT.

"The irony is that the VAT is probably the ideal tax from a conservative point of view," wrote the Republican tax expert Bruce Bartlett, who oversaw tax policy in the Treasury Department under the first president Bush. "As a broad-based tax on consumption it creates less economic distortion per dollar of revenue than any other tax—certainly much less than the income tax. If Republicans are successful in defeating a VAT, the alternative will inevitably be significantly higher income taxes, which will do far more damage to the economy than a VAT raising the same revenue.

"I myself opposed the VAT on money-machine grounds," Bartlett continued. "I changed my mind when I realized that there was no longer any hope of controlling entitlement spending before the deluge hits when the baby boomers retire; therefore, the U.S. now needs a money machine."[10]

Bartlett is not alone in his party. Alan Greenspan, the Federal Reserve chairman who endorsed the Bush tax cuts at the start of this century, has argued that a VAT is the "least worst" way to raise taxes. Now and then Republicans propose a VAT/GST or a similar form of consumption tax, operating on the theory that it's better than the personal and corporate income tax regimes we have in place today. During the 2016 presidential primaries, several of the GOP candidates suggested plans—although they were not always crystal clear—for a national consumption tax. The most fully developed was a classic value-added tax put forth by the Texas senator Ted Cruz, who offered himself as the most conservative of all the sixteen Republican hopefuls.

Cruz, of course, did not use the tainted words "value-added tax." He called his plan, alternately, the "simple flat tax" or the "16% business flat tax" (BFT). He promised that his new tax would eliminate the corporate income tax, the estate and gift tax, the ObamaCare taxes, and the payroll taxes that pay for Social Security and Medicare ("while maintaining full funding for Social Security and Medicare"). He insisted that his plan would allow Washington to set everybody's personal income tax rate at 10%—a major tax cut for most Americans—while maintaining the tax deductions Americans like best. To do all that, Cruz proposed a 16% value-added tax on businesses. He said that every business should file a quarterly tax return listing its total revenue for the quarter but subtracting its total purchases (but not wages). "This would tax companies' gross receipts from sales of goods and services, less purchases from other businesses, including capital investment," Cruz wrote. The difference between a company's revenues and its purchases—that is, the amount of value added by that company—would be taxed at 16%. Because each company would report to the government how much it paid to all of its suppliers, the tax would be self-policing.[11] And by the way, Cruz added, "the business flat tax in my proposal is not a VAT."

Economists from the left and the right begged to differ. All of them gave Cruz credit for laying out a tax plan in detail, something few of his rivals for the presidency in either party were willing to do. But the economists agreed that the business flat tax was, in fact, a VAT, because it tallied the difference between a company's output and its input—that is, the value added—and taxed that amount. Professor Len Burman, a tax economist and head of the Tax Policy Center, called the Cruz tax plan "a textbook example" of a VAT. Alan Cole, an economist at the corporate-funded Tax Foundation, agreed: "This is definitely still a value-added tax."[12]

Cruz felt a need to deny that his BFT was really a VAT, because the money-machine view of that tax makes it a nonstarter for small-government advocates. In fact, though, it's not so clear that this form of tax is necessarily a recipe for bigger government. "In most countries," noted Professor Bird, the VAT or GST "has not resulted to any significant extent either in higher taxes or bigger government, but rather in governments being able to finance their expenditures in economically less damaging ways."[13] In Britain, for example, the increase in VAT from 17.5% to 20% was followed by a significant cut in government employment and welfare spending. (The government used most of the increased revenue to shore up the National Health Service, the country's most popular public program.)

———

WHETHER IT'S A VAT, a GST, a BFT, or any other three little letters, can a national consumption tax ever be enacted in the United States? The former Treasury secretary Lawrence Summers offered a tongue-in-cheek prediction of when that could happen. "Liberals think the VAT is regressive," Summers said, "and conservatives think it's a money machine. If they reverse their positions, the VAT may happen."

EPILOGUE:
THE INTERNAL REVENUE
CODE OF 2018

Ah, the blithe joys of springtime in the United States of America: azaleas in bloom at the Masters, school trips to the state capital, big sales at the garden stores, baseball's opening day, picnics in the park on bright, breezy April afternoons—and the ordeal of Form 1040, with instructions like this one from the Internal Revenue Service: "If you determined your tax in the earlier year by using the Schedule D Tax Worksheet, or the Qualified Dividends and Capital Gain Tax Worksheet, and you receive a refund in 2016 of a deduction claimed in that year, you will have to recompute your tax for the earlier year to determine if the recovery must be included in your income."[1]

The U.S. tax code often seems to be at war with the taxpayers. The tax law has become so stuffed with obscure provisions that were important to some group or other at some point in time that the mess just becomes too difficult for anybody to understand or to manage. The resulting complexity—made worse by the so-called anti-complexity clause that Congress threw into the stew some years back—has reached absurd dimensions. When I asked the commissioner of the IRS whether anybody in his agency has read all seventy-three thousand pages of IRS regulations, he laughed at the very suggestion.

At the same time, the tax code often seems to be at war with itself.

There are many provisions, for example, that provide benefits or preferences for families that have a child. The problem is that the different
sections of the Internal Revenue Code can't agree on what constitutes
a "child" for tax purposes. There's a "child credit" in the personal
income tax that applies to any person under the age of seventeen. But
there's also a separate "child and dependent care credit," which de-
fines a "child" as somebody under thirteen. For families getting the
earned income tax credit (that's the reverse income tax that sends
checks to taxpayers who have low-paying jobs), a "child" is any person under nineteen—unless the person is a full-time student, in which
case a "child" is anybody under twenty-four. Every time Congress
decides to give a tax break for having a child, it just picks some definition of "child" and stuffs that language into the tax code, regardless
of how many other designations of "child" have been stuffed in the
code somewhere else.

This has been going on since the birth of the federal income tax a
century ago. And history has shown that every three decades or so the
tax code becomes so huge and complicated and contradictory that the
only way to fix it is to scrap the whole mess and start over. The thesis
of this book is that, by looking at other industrialized democracies
that have faced the same tax questions we're dealing with, we can
decide what should be in this new tax code and what should not.
That's why the U.S. Treasury secretary in 1984, Donald Regan, dispatched his policy experts to look at other systems and bring back the
best ideas—a process that ended with the dramatic tax changes of
1986, widely recognized as the most sweeping, and most admired,
reform in the history of the U.S. tax code.

Here at home, our political leaders talk about fixing the tax code
all the time. But their proposals involve incremental change to the
existing system, and incremental change, over the decades, is what
got us into the fine mess we're stuck with today. These approaches to
tax reform, including the plans we heard during the 2016 presidential
campaign, all suffer from the same problem: they're too timid.

They all have a rearranging-the-deck-chairs quality at a time when the whole structure is sinking from its own weight. As we've seen in other countries, the way to bring about fundamental change in a dysfunctional tax code is to start over—to rewrite from scratch. In chapter 4 of this book, the New Zealand parliamentarian Maurice McTigue explained why his country was able to scrap a decrepit, inequitable, inefficient tax code and replace it with a system that has won plaudits from tax experts everywhere. "A key reason was that we did it big," McTigue said. "They changed almost everything at once. And that's an important lesson: if you're going to do tax reform, you'd better make it a large reform. That way, for every change a taxpayer doesn't like, there's something else in the package that he wants." It's the same conclusion the former senator Bill Bradley drew from our country's successful revamp of the Internal Revenue Code in 1986. "You can't just tinker," Bradley said then. "Facing a huge, almost incomprehensible system, you have to take it on. Your goal has to be to fix the whole damn thing."

For the U.S. personal income tax, fixing the whole damn thing means that the whole boatload of exemptions, exclusions, and tax-free income clauses should be jettisoned. If the employer pays part of a worker's health insurance premium, that's a fine thing, but the payment should be taxable income to the worker. If a taxpayer decides to buy a $105,000 electric-powered sports car, that's great, but we shouldn't give her a $7,500 tax credit to honor this indulgence. This is the "broad base" element of BBLR—broad base, low rates—which is the essential formula for successful tax reform.

Would American taxpayers go along if Congress eliminated all their deductions and credits? That's where the "low rate" side of the BBLR equation sinks in. To win support for eliminating the giveaways, Congress cuts everybody's tax rates. As we saw in this book, the Treasury Department says every individual and corporate tax bill could be cut by 37% if all the exemptions and such in the tax code were eliminated. Beyond that, getting rid of all the exemptions and such would make filing taxes vastly easier. So the average American would get a much lower tax rate and wouldn't have to pay H&R Block to fill out all the forms.

Moving to BBLR is an area where purity is essential; we need to get rid of all the "tax expenditures" in the code—not just some of them—no matter how widely used they are. Then the tax writers in Congress can say to any lobbyist pushing for a particular loophole, "We don't do that anymore. If you want to keep that deduction, we'll have to raise the rates for everybody." To emphasize this point, we should eliminate the two most popular deductions in the personal income tax: (1) the deduction for mortgage interest, which reduces revenues some $100 billion each year and provides the most benefit to taxpayers who need it least, and (2) the deduction for contributions to charity, which costs the government $50 billion per year and is even less defensible. It gives the biggest breaks to the richest taxpayers and assumes, incorrectly, that Americans won't give money to good causes unless they get a tax break for it.

The same principle—BBLR—must apply to a revamp of the corporate income tax. As we've seen in this book, this tax just doesn't work. American corporations that abide by the law end up paying a higher rate of tax than their competitors in other rich countries. Eliminating the hundreds of special provisions in the corporate tax code that benefit particular industries—or, sometimes, single companies—would broaden the base. The Government Accountability Office reported that the lost revenue from the eighty biggest corporate tax preferences in 2011 was $181 billion. Eliminate those, and the United States could bring in more corporate tax revenue with significantly lower rates. If the tax rate were lower, corporations would not find it worthwhile to indulge in convoluted schemes of avoidance; it would be cheaper and simpler just to pay the tax than to pay Pricewater-houseCoopers for a plan to duck it. If the preferences were eliminated from the corporate income tax so the tax rate could be reduced from the current 35% to 25% or less, this tax would almost surely produce more revenue with much less economic disruption.

"Warren Buffett paid a lower tax rate than his secretary." This bumper-sticker slogan (which Buffett has confirmed to be true) captures a major problem with the current U.S. tax code. The picture of a billionaire paying a lower rate of tax than a middle-class working family runs counter to basic notions of fairness. The system of progressive taxation, of asking the richest to chip in the most to the common treasury, is even more important in these first decades of the twenty-first century because of the looming problem of inequality—"the defining challenge of our time," as Barack Obama put it. Since the end of the Great Recession of 2008–9, virtually all of the increase in wealth in the United States has accrued to the wealthy. The rich are getting richer, and most others are not. A family at the median income takes in little more income today than it did ten years ago. This is gnawing away at the general population's sense of optimism. The traditionally American notion that tomorrow will be better, that our kids will be better off than we've been, has become something of a sardonic joke for a considerable segment of the population. Naturally, politicians of every stripe have figured this out. When political leaders—ranging from Elizabeth Warren and Bernie Sanders on the left to Donald Trump on the right—declare that the American economic system is rigged against the average worker, millions of average workers roar their agreement. A progressive tax code can be a crucial tool for fighting the national problem of inequality.

Some American politicians—including several Republican presidential candidates in 2016—have called for a flat-rate income tax, in which the billionaire and the guy who pumps gas into her limousine both pay income tax at the same rate. But the flat tax just doesn't bring in enough money, and a flat rate of tax fuels greater inequality. It means big savings for the rich, and higher rates for average people to make up for the shortfall. So the U.S. income tax should continue to keep a progressive set of rates. Indeed, the experience of other countries would suggest that we should make the highest marginal tax rate kick in at a lower income level than it does now. Other rich nations apply the highest rate of tax to about half of all taxpayers; in the United States, the top rate of 39.6% applies only to income above $418,400—which is to say, less than 1% of tax returns.

A tax code designed to offset (somewhat) the overall inequality of wealth and income should not give special tax breaks to the wealthiest. The "carried interest" provision—the clause that lets Warren Buffett get away with a bargain-basement tax rate—is indefensible. That's why no other country permits this loophole for financiers and why both Donald Trump and Hillary Clinton promised to end it. It would also make a lot of sense to tax income earned from financial transactions (capital gains, dividends, and so on) at the same rates as income from wages and salaries. When Ronald Reagan included that change in the famous tax reform of 1986—capital gains were taxed at 28%, the same tax burden as the highest marginal rate on earned income—it had almost no impact on stock markets; the argument that rich investors need a lower rate of tax to put their money into the markets has not been borne out in history. Finally, there's the estate and gift tax—adroitly nicknamed the "death tax" by its opponents, although the burden of it actually falls on the living people lucky enough to receive a multimillion-dollar inheritance. This has been an important tool for making the richest Americans help pay for the things we choose to do collectively through government. It's a tax that doesn't penalize work; if you worked for the money you received, by definition you don't owe any estate tax. The estate tax should be retained, and probably increased, as a further weapon against inequality.

Two other major innovations, the VAT and the FAT, would give the federal government even more room to reduce both personal and corporate income tax rates. The value-added tax has been the most successful taxation innovation of the past sixty years. It has been adopted in every major nation on earth and in most small nations as well. The absence of a VAT is the most glaring hole in America's tax code; we should use the occasion of a top-to-bottom tax reform to implement this tax and use the money it raises to cut taxes on work and savings. Countries like Australia, Canada, and the U.K. can show us how to harmonize a national consumption tax with state and local sales taxes.

The United States should follow the lead of the European Union and many other countries by enacting one particular form of a consumption tax, the financial activities tax. As we saw in chapter 9, the tax rate for this kind of levy can be tiny—$1 on a million-dollar trade. Because of Wall Street's current obsession with high-speed trading—buying securities, selling securities, swapping securities, all in a few millionths of a second—this tax can add up to significant revenue while adding an infinitesimal cost to each transaction.

Taking the BBLR approach as the guiding principle of tax reform will go far to simplify the tax laws. If the tax code treated all income as income, and got rid of all the loopholes, the whole process of paying tax would be vastly simpler. And tax rates could be drastically cut. In addition, getting rid of all those preferences for specific taxpayers would mean we could eliminate the alternative minimum tax, a much-despised provision that forces several million taxpayers each year (both individual and corporate) to complete their tax returns twice, using different rules and rates each time.

Beyond that, the Internal Revenue Service should take over most of the work it now sticks on the taxpayer. Because of the reporting requirements it imposes on employers, banks, investment managers, local governments, and the like, the IRS already knows virtually every number on almost every tax return. The service could fill out your tax return for you and send it to you by e-mail so you could check it for accuracy. Assuming the IRS gets the figures right—and audits show that it does, 99.9% of the time—filing your taxes could be reduced to a single click.

IF WE HAD THE GOOD SENSE, and the political courage, to undertake this top-to-bottom housecleaning of our tax code, the benefits would extend far beyond relieving American families of the annual April ordeal surrounding Form 1040. A new tax system built along the lines of successful tax codes in other rich democracies could enhance every corner of the national economy. It would give people the freedom to make big choices—Should I take that job? Could we buy that house? Should we choose that school for the kids? Can I start that business I've been dreaming of? Where should we invest our money? How much should we contribute?—without worrying about the tax complications. It would enhance the global competitiveness of American corporations and allow them to keep their money at home, to be used for investment or higher wages or bigger dividends to investors. Both individuals and corporations could invest their money in plans and projects and funds based purely on business considerations, rather than studying obscure implications of the capital gains tax. Even with significantly lower rates, the IRS could bring in just as much or more revenue as the current system, producing billions of dollars for new government programs, deficit reduction, or both. A revamped code would mean a federal tax system that works against inequality in a land where everyone is created equal. The enormous sums that Americans hand over today to consulting firms and tax lawyers for the design of "convoluted and pernicious" tax-avoidance schemes could be turned instead to productive uses that enhance the nation's wealth and well-being. The billions of dollars and billions of hours that ordinary taxpayers must spend today just to calculate their tax bill would be available for more enjoyable and beneficial family pursuits. And April 15 could be just another sunny spring day.

The task ahead of us, therefore, is clear: the United States needs a completely new Internal Revenue Code, built around the principles that have made the tax codes in other advanced nations fairer, simpler, and more efficient than the one we're stuck with today. For tax codes, there comes a point where the sheer accumulation of complicated and contradictory stuff requires that the "whole damn thing" be replaced.

In the past, we've scrapped our tax code, and started over, every thirty-two years. The last time that happened was 1986, when Congress produced a much-praised act of tax reform. Which means the time has come again to scratch that thirty-two-year itch. To fix our costly, complex, inequitable monster of a tax system, the United States needs a new beginning: the Internal Revenue Code of 2018.

AFTERWORD:
THE TAX CUTS AND JOBS ACT

Late in 2017, BBLR came to Washington. Briefly.

As we've seen throughout this book, economists around the world agree that the basic formula for an effective tax code is "BBLR"—that is, Broaden the Base in order to Lower the Rates. This means that if the tax base—the total amount of income that is taxable—is kept as large as possible, then the tax rate—the percentage of income that people have to pay the government—can be kept low, with no loss of revenue.

As soon as the Republican Party took control of Congress and the White House in 2017, GOP leaders started talking about a major tax reform built around this respected formula. Kevin Brady, the plain-speaking Texan who chaired the House Ways and Means Committee, promised that the Republican tax plan would "eliminate all sorts of exemptions and loopholes so that we can cut rates and make taxes simpler for middle-class American families"—which is a plain-speaking way to say "BBLR."

And in fact, Brady's initial reform bill—it was titled the Tax Cuts and Jobs Act and given the vaunted legislative number H.R. 1—was a definite step in the BBLR direction. The plan eliminated some of the most egregious tax preferences cited in this book—including that

$7,500 credit for people who buy $100,000 hybrid sports cars—and cut rates for almost all businesses and individual taxpayers.

But as the tax bill made its way from the House of Representatives to the Senate and back again, most of the base-broadening reforms were lost amid furious lobbying and vote trading. In the end, the Republican tax bill—signed into law by a delighted President Trump on December 22, 2017—put far more emphasis on the Low Rates part of the equation than on the Broad Base.

Contrary to the leadership's promises, the new law made the tax code not simpler, but more complex and confusing; it was quickly dubbed the "CPA Relief Act" because of all the extra fees it would mean for tax accountants. And the big winners were not "middle class American families," but rather corporations and the richest 1% of federal taxpayers. Congress's Joint Committee on Taxation estimated that, of the $1.4 billion in tax cuts provided by the 2017 tax bill, 10% would go to families earning between $20,000 and $100,000; the bulk of the savings would go to corporations, business partnerships, and taxpayers earning $500,000 or more per year.[1]

Corporate and Business Taxes

The main thrust of the 2017 tax bill was reducing taxes for American businesses, to make them more competitive with competitors overseas. The top corporate income tax rate was cut from 35% to 21%, giving major companies a cumulative tax savings estimated at $1 trillion over ten years. Proponents argued that this sharp reduction would stop American corporations from shifting profits overseas—but it's not clear this will work. That's because the new law also sets a lower tax rate—effectively 10.5%—for corporate profits earned overseas, creating an incentive to shift operations abroad.

The tax bill takes an innovative approach to the huge sums—

perhaps $2.3 trillion—that U.S. corporations stashed overseas to avoid the 35% tax. The bill called for a "tax holiday," taxing that cash at a bargain rate of 15.5%. But this would not be a voluntary "holiday." The law imposes a new idea called "deemed repatriation"—which means the United States will consider all that money to be "repatriated," so companies would have to pay the tax whether they bring the cash home or not. The result: most of the overseas funds will probably come home, providing a tax windfall in the range of $300 billion for the Treasury. The downside is that offering a tax holiday may encourage companies to keep more profits overseas in the future, on the theory that the government will eventually offer another such "holiday" a few years from now. And there's no requirement that companies use these repatriated funds for investment or job creation; preliminary indications were that most would be used to enhance stock-market values—and thus benefit top executives and investors.

Another boon to business in the law is the elimination of the corporate Alternative Minimum Tax. That will provide major savings for the thousands of companies that had to pay this extra levy, and it makes things simpler for corporate tax departments. But the same bill also makes things more complicated for many companies by adding two new taxes. These were given creative acronyms: the BEAT (Base Erosion and Anti-Abuse Tax) and the GILTI (Global Intangible Low-Taxed Income tax). They represent an attempt to combat the convoluted strategies—as seen in chapter 8 of this book—that multinational companies have employed to shift profits overseas.

H.R. 1 also provided big tax cuts for the self-employed and for business partnerships, whose owners pay tax on their earnings by "pass-through" to the personal income tax. The law lets most pass-through taxpayers shield 20% of their earnings from taxation. For a lawyer, say, or a doctor making $250,000 per year, that would cut the tax bill by some $17,500. This will likely prompt upper-bracket wage earners to look for ways to portray their salaries as "pass-through" earnings, and thus get that 20% break. By early 2018, accountants were already proposing such schemes to their clients; a headline in *The Economist* captured the mind-set nicely: "Let the Games Begin."

Personal Taxes

The 2017 bill also provides reduced rates for individuals and families paying their taxes through Form 1040. It retains the basic structure of seven different tax brackets, with the rate increasing progressively for higher incomes. But it reduces the tax rate in every bracket; under the new law, the top marginal rate drops from 39.6% to 37% for earnings over $500,000 (or $600,000 for couples). In a major step to simplify the tax return, the plan doubled the standard deduction to $24,000 for couples. This means that a large number of families—more than 70%, by some estimates—would no longer have to calculate how much they paid in mortgage interest, student loan interest, charitable contributions, state sales tax, etc. That higher standard deduction means a couple can immediately subtract $24,000 from its taxable income—and pay tax on the lower amount. The law also doubled the credit for each child to $2,000, yet another reduction for families. These cuts, though, are partly offset because the law eliminates the personal exemption; that change will increase taxable income by $8,300 for a couple, and by $16,600 for a family of four.

As with the corporate tax proposals, the plan's changes to the personal income tax are also designed to give the biggest breaks to the richest taxpayers. The plan would sharply reduce the bite of the Estate Tax—sometimes called the "Lucky Rich Kids' Tax" because it is only paid by people who inherit millions. It doubles the amount that people can inherit tax free; now nobody will pay tax on an inheritance less than $11.2 million. As we saw in chapter 7, this is a boon to a super-rich smidgen of Americans; President Trump's family, for example, will save millions through this change. The bill also cuts back the Alternative Minimum Tax, a levy that hits only upper-bracket families. And, contrary to repeated promises from the president and Republican leaders, the tax plan did not eliminate the so-called "carried interest" clause, which allows multimillionaire investment bankers and hedge fund executives to pay tax at a lower rate than their secretaries or chauffeurs.

The personal income tax cuts meant that almost every American would pay less on their 2018 tax return—the one that's due on April 15, 2019. But those cuts won't last. To reduce the drain on federal revenues, Congress had to make some of the cuts in the new law temporary. Reflecting the basic pro-business direction of the new law, it terminates all the personal income tax reductions after seven years, in 2025. The corporate tax cuts, though, were made permanent.

Broad Base

As Ways and Means Chairman Kevin Brady had promised, his original bill, introduced in September, made serious strides in broadening the tax base by taking away a number of exemptions and deductions, which cost billions in lost revenue. Over the next two months, an army of lobbyists went to work, and they managed to kill most of the base-broadening provisions Brady had championed. Even that $7,500 credit for those who could buy a $138,000 hybrid car was retained in the final version of the bill.

Still, a few costly tax preferences were targeted. The new bill put a limit of $10,000 on the deduction for state and local taxes, a change that will raise taxes for some wealthy people in high-tax states. The bill also limited, slightly, the write-off for mortgage interest. And it took away a loophole that let fans of major college sports teams deduct 80% of the cost of season tickets.

But this was a scattershot, and incomplete, approach to Broadening the Base. H.R. 1 kept in place scores of tax expenditures. It retained some of the most expensive in the existing IRS code, including the deduction for charitable contributions and the exclusion of employer-paid insurance premiums. As we saw in this book, the right way to broaden the tax base is to get rid of all deductions, exemptions, credits, etc.; the new law falls well short of that goal.

To win the votes of wavering senators, and to please their electoral base, Republican leaders tossed a few stray provisions into the law that had little to do with taxation. H.R. 1 specifically authorizes oil drilling in some parts of the Arctic National Wildlife Refuge in northeastern Alaska. It eliminates, as of 2019, an unpopular provision in the Affordable Care Act ("ObamaCare") that requires people to buy health insurance and thus take responsibility for their own medical bills. It imposes a new tax on Ivy League universities and a few other rich schools that have billion-dollar endowments. And it creates a hefty new "excise tax" (21%) on tax-exempt schools, hospitals, and charities if they pay any executive more than $1 million annually; so a college football coach or a hospital CEO with a $5 million salary will cost the institution an additional $1.05 million per year in taxes.

Not Ronald Reagan's Tax Bill

To promote their reform proposal, Republican leaders invoked the memory of their beloved former president, Ronald Reagan, who championed the nation's last major tax reform in 1986. Standing at the very table where Reagan signed that bill into law, Chairman Brady said the new GOP proposal closely tracked the "fundamental principles" of the Reagan reforms.

Well, not exactly. The 2017 tax law is actually the opposite of what Ronald Reagan did for taxpayers.

As we saw in chapter 4 of this book, that Reagan reform in '86 reduced taxes for almost every American family—and made up for the lost revenue by raising taxes on corporations. In contrast, the Republicans' 2017 plan offered huge permanent tax cuts for corporations and business partnerships—and made up for it by giving smaller, temporary benefits to families. In essence, individuals get a smaller tax break so that corporations and partnerships can get the biggest cuts.

In another break with the "fundamental principles" of the 1986 tax reform, H.R. 1 was specifically designed to lose money for the government—and thus increase the deficit. Ronald Reagan promised that his tax reform would be "revenue neutral"—that the increased taxes on corporations would make up for the tax cuts given to families. (Deficits did go up under Reagan, but that was due mainly to increased spending, not tax changes.) In 2017, in contrast, Republican leaders openly admitted that their plan would add some $150 billion to the deficit each year for the next ten years. And some outside estimates showed the cost to the Treasury would be considerably greater.

That was a sharp turnabout for the GOP, which had preached fiscal responsibility for decades. Even Rupert Murdoch's media outlets—the *New York Post*, *The Wall Street Journal*, and Fox News—became big boosters of government deficits, arguing that the lost government revenue in the tax plan would generate economic growth. For some reason, they never made that argument when Democrats were running up the deficits.

Every thirty-two years, the United States has seen a major reform of its tax code. With the sweeping new tax bill that took effect on January 1, 2018, Congress and the president continued that cycle. But this latest version of tax reform largely ignored the fundamental principle of BBLR.

THANKS

It would be taxing beyond measure to list all the institutions and experts around the world who helped me in reporting and writing *A Fine Mess*. A battalion of economists, academics, reporters, diplomats, tax accountants, tax collectors, and salt-of-the-earth taxpayers generously shared their experience and wisdom to steer an ink-stained reporter through the intricacies of taxes, tariffs, exemptions, exclusions, VAT, FAT, FTT, and so on. I wish I could give all of them a tax credit for their kindness; at least I can give them credit here for their contributions to this book.

Several international organizations and think tanks study the good, the bad, and the ugly of tax systems around the world; a number of them gave me the benefit of their expertise and their multinational surveys. I'm particularly grateful to the Organization for Economic Cooperation and Development (OECD), the World Bank, the International Monetary Fund (IMF), the Brookings Institution, the Urban Institute, the American Enterprise Institute (AEI), the Tax Foundation, the Canadian Tax Foundation (in Toronto), the Tax Justice Network (in London), the Grattan Institute (in Melbourne), and the Institute for Fiscal Studies (IFS; in London). The scholars who found time to help me included Aparna Mathur at AEI, Will McBride at the Tax Foundation, Henry Aaron at Brookings, John Daley at Grattan, Larry Chapman at the Canadian Tax Foundation, and Paul Johnson at IFS.

Professor Jay Rosengard's course on comparative tax policy and administration at the John F. Kennedy School of Government at Harvard was a brilliant introduction to the policy issues pondered in this book. Several of the professors in that course became my gurus throughout the research and writing. I'm particularly grateful to Professors Brian Arnold, Richard Bird, and Eric Zolt. Other economists who offered insightful advice along the way included Alan Krueger, Peter Orzag, and Uwe Reinhardt (who was a gold mine of knowledge on a previous book of mine as well).

Executives at the revenue bureaus of many countries were kind enough to explain the art and science of tax collection in a broad variety of political settings. I owe special thanks to Michiel Sweers, the policy chief at the federal tax agency in the Netherlands, and Achilles Sunday Amawhe (the man who gave me the FIRS baseball cap) of the Federal Inland Revenue Service in Nigeria. In addition, John Paul Liddle of Scotland, Nuno Reis of Timor-Leste, José Zorrilla Rostro of Mexico, and David Trony of Angola helped me to understand the fine balancing act of collecting taxes without sparking a revolt among taxpayers. In the United States, the commissioner of internal revenue, John Koskinen (a colleague of mine eons ago when we were both, briefly, lawyers), and the IRS's indomitable national taxpayer advocate, Nina Olson, gave me advice, information, and encouragement while this book was in the works.

In almost every country I visited, smart foreign service officers at U.S. embassies provided precious insights into local politics and policy; I was repeatedly impressed by the breadth of knowledge shown by the (generally young) political and commercial officers at our embassies. I would particularly like to thank Steve Butler, Colin Crosby, Mal Murray, Robert King, and Brett Baeker for their help. Because of our country's deplorable tradition of rewarding fat-cat political contributors by making them ambassadors, U.S. ambassadors around the world are often far less qualified than the career foreign service officers who work under them. In reporting this book, though, I received thoughtful help from some American ambassadors who knew what they were doing—notably Philip Lader in London, Walter F. Mondale in Tokyo, and Norman Eisen in Prague. I was particularly impressed with Theodore (Tod) Sedgwick, our country's much-esteemed ambassador to Slovakia, who seemed to know every person and every policy issue in that nation's government. With some trepidation, I asked

Ambassador Sedgwick if he might possibly help me get an interview with Slovakia's finance minister, Peter Kažimír. The ambassador replied, "I play tennis with Peter every week, so I think that can be arranged."

Political reporters, with their inbred blend of cynicism and idealism, are also insightful observers of government policies and policymakers; many of my fellow reporters helped me in my study of tax systems around the globe. I would particularly like to thank Tom Allard, Fleur Anderson, Adi Bloom, Phil Coorey, Malcolm Farr, Anna Fifield, Jon Freedland, and Tony Wright. A great reporter and a great friend of mine, Togo Shigehiko, showed me precisely how Japan manages to collect trillions in taxes in a system where 85% of the workers never file a tax return. I relied on the reporting of my former colleagues Alan Murray and Jeffrey Birnbaum in *Showdown at Gucci Gulch,* the definitive chronicle of America's 1986 tax reform, and on the work of my former competitor Steve Weisman in *The Great Tax Wars,* his fascinating history of the U.S. income tax.

And in each country where I did the reporting for this book, I was lucky to find economists, accountants, and officials who were willing to answer a nondepreciating list of questions from an inquiring American. It would double the length of this book to list them all. In addition to those named above, though, I am particularly grateful to Steven Rogers and Professors Graeme Cooper, Michael Walpole, and Bill Butcher in Australia; John Christiansen and Professor Judith Freeman in Britain; Larry Chapman and Professor Glenn Jenkins in Canada; Rahim Bohacek and Petr Guth in Czechia; Juri Kalda, Mart Larr, and Professor Viktor Forsberg in Estonia; Antoine Reillac, Guy Carrez, and Professor Martin Collett in France; Ridha Hamzaoui in the Netherlands; Maurice McTigue, Sir Graham Scott, and Professors Bob Buckle and Norman Gemmell in New Zealand; and Peter Kažimír, Ivan Mikloš, Ludovic Ódor, Ján Oravec, and Vladimir Vano in Slovakia.

It must be said that these people don't always agree with one another on particular aspects of tax policy, and they don't always agree with me. So any mistakes in this book are my fault, not theirs.

Even in our intensely digital age, libraries serve as immensely useful vaults of information and analysis. I'm grateful to many libraries, public and academic, that allowed me access to their materials on taxation around the world. Those I used the most were the Kennedy School and Widener libraries at Harvard, the Firestone and Stokes libraries at Princeton, the Dewey Library at MIT, the Anderson Academic Commons at the University of Denver, the Auraria Library at the University of Colorado, the law library at the University of New South Wales, the wonderful Westminster Research Library on St. Martin's Street in London, and the Denver Public Library. I'm deeply grateful to researchers at several of these institutions who found all the obscure books and studies I requested. At one point I needed a particular volume on tax reform in New Zealand; in the entire United States there was a single copy—and the research desk at the University of Denver library managed to borrow it for me.

I hit the jackpot on this project when I hired a brilliant and diligent researcher, Chris Steele, who teaches history at Regis University in Denver. At the start of this project, Chris barely knew the difference between an excise tax and an import duty; by the end, he was teaching me about the intricacies of national tax regimes.

I'm grateful to many friends who tolerated years of questions and complaints from me and provided valuable advice at various stages of the project. These cherished kibitzers include Bill Bradley, Jay Brown, Ricki Hadow, Marc Hecht, Ted Hoster, Bert Kerstetter, Walter Isaacson, Wendy Liu, Sachiko Nakahira, Joe Ptacek, John Rollins, Ann Saybolt, Ed Stein, Cheryl Stevenson, Kirsten Thistle (who wanted to title this book *The 32-Year Itch*), and Yoshida Makiko.

As she has done before, the genius literary agent Gail Ross figured out what this book was about before the author did, and kept me on course over the years. As she has done before, the genius editor Ann Godoff shaped a rather chaotic manuscript into a coherent volume. Casey Rasch Denis of Penguin Press skillfully supervised its transformation into a finished book.

Last but foremost, McMahon Thomas Homer Reid, O'Gorman Catherine Penelope Reid, and Erin Andromache Wilhelmina Reid put up with the author and the manuscript in good spirits for years—a task far more demanding than writing any book.

Denver, Colorado, 2013–2017

NOTES

Chapter 1: Policy Laboratories

1. This quirk of the tax code, known to economists as "the mysterious 60% band," is explained at www.milnecraig.co.uk/the-60-income-tax-band/.

Chapter 2: "Low Effort, Low Collection"

1. You can find the Gallup poll results for 2015 at "More Than Half of Americans Say Federal Taxes Too High," www.gallup.com/poll/168500/half -americans-say-federal-taxes-high.aspx.
2. World Bank, "Tax Capacity and Tax Effort" (Policy Research working paper 6252).
3. OECD, Taxation of Wage Income 2000–2013.
4. Compiled by Ernst & Young; www.cato.org/sites/cato.org/files/pubs/pdf/tbb -066.pdf.
5. Sales Tax Institute, www.salestaxinstitute.com.
6. EY, Worldwide VAT, GST, and Sales Tax Guide, at www.ey.com/Publication /vwLUAssets/Worldwide-VAT-GST-and-sales-tax-guide-2015/$FILE /Worldwide%20VAT,%20GST%20and%20Sales%20Tax%20Guide %202015.pdf.
7. Kyle Pomerleau, "How High Are Other Nations' Gas Taxes?," Tax Foundation, Mar. 3, 2015.
8. Liz Emanuel, "State Cigarette Tax Rates in 2014," Tax Foundation, July 2, 2014, http://taxfoundation.org/blog/state-cigarette-tax-rates-2014.
9. *Le Monde Diplomatique,* Dec. 2014, 3.
10. "Las aventuras de Ivo la Chinchilla," www.planetasii.cl.

Chapter 3: Taxes: What Are They Good For?

1. Mark 12:41–44; Luke 21:1–4.
2. For example, Joel Slemrod and Jon Bakija, *Taxing Ourselves* (Cambridge, Mass.: MIT Press, 2008), 44: "Indeed, the progressive rate structure might be regarded as the reason for the existence of the income tax."
3. 275 U.S. 87 (1927).
4. OECD, "General Government Fiscal Liabilities as a Percentage of GDP," www.oecd-ilibrary.org/economics/government-debt_gov-debt-table-en.
5. "The War of 1812," *Smithsonian Magazine,* July–Aug. 2014, 40.
6. Sven Steinmo, *Taxation and Democracy* (New Haven, Conn.: Yale University Press, 1993), 1, 3.
7. "Mulled Wines," *Economist,* Dec. 21, 2013, 62.
8. Slemrod and Bakija, *Taxing Ourselves,* chap. 4.
9. Richard M. Bird, *Tax Policy and Economic Development* (Baltimore: Johns Hopkins University Press, 1992), 7.
10. F. A. Hayek, *The Constitution of Liberty* (Chicago: University of Chicago Press, 2011), 316.
11. Edwin R. A. Seligman, *The Income Tax,* 2nd ed. (New York: Macmillan, 1914), 4–5.
12. Ibid., 368.
13. *Pollock v. Farmers' Loan and Trust Co.,* 157 U.S. 607 (1894).
14. An excellent history of the first U.S. income tax can be found in Steven R. Weisman, *The Great Tax Wars* (New York: Simon & Schuster, 2002).
15. Liz Alderman, "In Pursuit of Greek Tycoons and Tax Cheats," *New York Times,* Feb. 26, 2015, B1.
16. Lucy Martin, "Taxation, Loss Aversion, and Accountability" (Yale University, Department of Political Science, 2014).

Chapter 4: BBLR

1. Union des Associations Internationales, *Yearbook of International Organizations, 2014–2015* (Brussels: Brill, 2015).
2. John Maynard Keynes, *The General Theory of Employment, Interest, and Money* (London: Macmillan, 1936), 372.
3. James R. Hines Jr., "Do We Really Want a Tax System with a Broad Base and Low Rates?" (PowerPoint presentation, Dec. 9, 2014).
4. OECD, *Choosing a Broad Base–Low Rate Approach to Taxation* (OECD Tax Policy Studies 19, 2010), 11.
5. Johan Christensen, "Bringing the Bureaucrats Back In: Neo-liberal Tax Reform in New Zealand," *Journal of Public Policy* 32, no. 2 (Aug. 2012): 141.
6. Steinmo, *Taxation and Democracy,* 163.

7. John Witte, *The Politics and Development of the Federal Income Tax* (Madison: University of Wisconsin Press, 1985), 380.
8. Bradley wrote a postmortem on the success of the 1986 reform in "Tax Reform's Lesson for Health Care Reform," *New York Times,* Aug. 30, 2009, 30.
9. Jeffrey Birnbaum and Alan S. Murray, *Showdown at Gucci Gulch* (New York: Random House, 1987), 5.

Chapter 5: Scooping Water with a Sieve

1. Stanley Surrey, "Tax Incentives as a Device for Implementing Government Policy: A Comparison with Direct Government Expenditures," *Harvard Law Review* 83 (1970): 705.
2. Internal Revenue Code Section 179.
3. OECD, *Choosing a Broad Base–Low Rate Approach to Taxation,* 38.
4. Congressional Record, U.S. Senate, July 6, 2011.
5. OECD, *Choosing a Broad Base–Low Rate Approach to Taxation,* Annex A.
6. IRS, Publication 15-B, 2015, 19.
7. Peter Klenk, "Maximizing Charitable Income Tax Deductions When Donating Art," at www.klenklaw.com.
8. Patricia Cohen, "Writing Off the Warhol Next Door," *New York Times,* Jan. 11, 2015, Sunday Business, 1.
9. www.irs.gov/Charities-&-Non-Profits/Search-for-Charities.
10. Stephanie Strom, "Grab Bag of Charities Grows," *New York Times,* Dec. 3, 2010.
11. OECD, *Choosing a Broad Base–Low Rate Approach to Taxation,* 81.

Chapter 6: Flat Broke

1. Robert E. Hall and Alvin Rabushka, *The Flat Tax* (Stanford, Calif.: Hoover Institution Press, 1995). You can read most of Hall and Rabushka's text at www.hooverpress.org/productdetails.cfm?PC=1274.
2. Steve Forbes, *Flat Tax Revolution: Using a Postcard to Abolish the IRS* (Washington, D.C.: Regnery, 2005).
3. Milton Friedman, *Capitalism and Freedom* (Chicago: University of Chicago Press, 1962), 35–36.
4. Paul Belien, "Walking on Water: How to Do It," *Brussels Journal,* Aug. 22, 2005, 202.
5. "The Case for Flat Taxes," *Economist,* Apr. 16, 2005, 11.
6. See Mart Laar's blog: blog.irl.ee/Mart/.
7. Andreas Peichl quoted in *Bloomberg Businessweek,* May 15, 2013, www.bloomberg.com/news/articles/2013-05-15/flat-tax-wave-ebbs-in -eastern-europe.

Chapter 7: The Defining Problem; the Taxing Solution

1. "New Data, Old Story," *New York Times,* Aug. 17, 2014.
2. *CBS Morning News,* June 10, 2014, www.cbsnews.com/news.
   /goldman-sachs-ceo-lloyd-blankfein-income-inequality-is-destabilizing/.
3. The White House, "Remarks by the President on Economic Mobility,"
   Dec. 4, 2013.
4. Matt Ridley, "Start Spreading the Good News on Inequality," *Times* (London),
   June 2, 2014.
5. "Progressive Kristallnacht Coming?," *Wall Street Journal,* Jan. 24, 2014.
6. Jonathan Alter, "Schwarzman: 'It's a War' Between Obama, Wall St.," *Newsweek,*
   Aug. 15, 2010.
7. Joseph E. Stiglitz, *The Price of Inequality* (New York: W. W. Norton, 2012), 273–74.
8. Geert De Clercq, "Inequality Guru Sees 'French Roosevelt' in Hollande,"
   Reuters, Apr. 17, 2012.
9. http://ucfs.nek.uu.se./digital/Assets/129/129492_wp200913.pdf.
10. *L'affaire Depardieu* is discussed in detail in Lauren Collins, "L'Étranger," *New
   Yorker,* Feb. 23, 2013, 58.
11. Seligman, *Income Tax,* 5.
12. Tax Policy Center, "Historical Federal Income Tax Rates for a Family of Four,"
   www.taxpolicycenter.org/taxfacts/displayafact.cfm?Docid=226.
13. Peter Cohan, "Trump Is Right About Carried Interest Deduction," Forbes.com,
   Sept. 17, 2015.

Chapter 8: Convoluted and Pernicious Strategies

1. Minutes of Caterpillar Board of Directors Meeting, Feb. 8, 2012, in "Caterpillar's
   Offshore Tax Strategy," U.S. Senate Permanent Committee on Investigations,
   Apr. 1, 2014, p. 411.
2. The PwC recommendation, and Caterpillar's decision to follow it, are set forth in
   "Caterpillar's Offshore Tax Strategy," U.S. Senate Permanent Subcommittee on
   Investigations, Apr. 1, 2014.
3. Corporate Tax Rates, 2015: www2.deloitte.com/content/dam/Deloitte/global
   /Documents/Tax/dttl-tax-corporate-tax-rates-2015.pdf.
4. "Corporate Income Tax: Effective Tax Rates Can Differ Significantly from the
   Statutory Rate" (GAO report GAO-13-520, May 2013).
5. "U.S. Corporations Pay 35%," *Wall Street Journal,* Oct. 27, 2013, www.wsj
   .com/articles/SB10001424052702303902404579152271744452490.
6. *Offshore Profit Shifting and the U.S. Tax Code—Part 2 (Apple Inc.),* U.S. Senate
   Permanent Subcommittee on Investigations, May 21, 2013, 152–91.
7. Jesse Drucker, "'Dutch Sandwich' Saves Google Billions in Taxes," *Bloomberg
   Businessweek,* Oct. 22, 2010. Another excellent explanation of Google's "Double
   Irish" system can be found in Cyrus Farivar, "Silicon Valley Fights to Keep Its
   Dutch Sandwich and Double Irish Loopholes," *Ars Technica,* Jan. 20, 2014.

8. *Offshore Profit Shifting and the U.S. Tax Code—Part 1 (Microsoft and Hewlett-Packard)*, U.S. Senate Permanent Subcommittee on Investigations, Sept. 20, 2012, 180–81.
9. Shayndi Raice, "Behind the Surge in a Hot Trend: Skadden Arps's M&A Lawyers," *Wall Street Journal*, Aug. 6, 2014, B1.
10. "AbbVie Chief Blames US Treasury," *Financial Times*, Oct. 21, 2014, B1.
11. *Helvering v. Gregory*, 69 F.2d 809 (2nd Cir. 1934).
12. "Caterpillar's Offshore Tax Strategy," 54–55.
13. James R. Hagerty, "Caterpillar Faces Pileup of Probes and Inquiries," *Wall Street Journal*, Feb. 18, 2015.
14. This is a simplified explanation of a highly complex set of intercorporate transactions. Professor Edward D. Kleinbard wrote a thirty-page study of Starbucks's tax strategy in the U.K., setting forth the arrangement in significant detail. Edward D. Kleinbard, "Through a Latte, Darkly: Starbucks's Stateless Income Planning," *Tax Notes*, June 24, 2013, 1515–35.
15. Dhammika Dharmapala, C. Fritz Foley, and Kristin J. Forbes, "Watch What I Do, Not What I Say: The Unintended Consequences of the Homeland Investment Act" (MIT Sloan Research Paper 4741-09, Apr. 27, 2010).
16. Kimberly Clausing, "The American Jobs Creation Act of 2004: Creating Jobs for Accountants and Lawyers" (Urban-Brookings Tax Policy Center, Tax Policy Issues and Options No. 8, Dec. 2004).
17. John D. McKinnon, "In Biting Tax Bullet, Move to Help Fund Share Buybacks," *Wall Street Journal*, Apr. 10, 2015.
18. Laurence J. Kotlikoff, "Abolish the Corporate Income Tax," *New York Times*, Jan. 6, 2014.

Chapter 9: The Single Tax, the Fat Tax, the Tiny Tax, the Carbon Tax—and No Tax At All

1. All these quotations come from Henry George, *Progress and Poverty: An Inquiry into the Cause of Industrial Depressions and of Increase of Want with Increase of Wealth* (New York: Robert Schalkenbach Foundation, 1955).
2. Gitanjali M. Singh et al., "Global SSB-Related Morbidity and Mortality," http://circ.ahajournals.org/content/circulationaha/early/2015/06/25/CIRCULATIONAHA.114.010636.full.pdf.
3. David Toscana, "Mexico's Soda-Tax Gimmick," *New York Times*, Nov. 5, 2013, 22.
4. Thornton Matheson, "Taxing Financial Transactions: Issues and Evidence" (International Monetary Fund working paper 11/54, Mar. 2011).
5. Ian Parry, Adele Morris, and Roberton C. Williams III, eds., *Implementing a US Carbon Tax* (New York: Routledge, 2015), xxiii.
6. Summers and Mankiw quoted in ibid., frontispiece.

Chapter 10: The Panama Papers: Sunny Places for Shady Money

1. Steven Erlanger, Stephen Castle, and Rick Gladstone, "Airing of Hidden Wealth Stirs Inquiries and Rage," *New York Times,* Apr. 6, 2016, 1.
2. Laura Saunders, "Inside Swiss Banks' Tax-Cheating Machinery," *Wall Street Journal,* Oct. 22, 2015, B1, www.wsj.com/articles/inside-swiss-banks-tax -cheating-machinery-1445506381.

Chapter 11: Simplify, Simplify

1. This erudite reference invokes Greek myth. Cassandra, a Trojan princess, had an affair with the god Apollo but then spurned him. To punish her, Apollo gave Cassandra a cruel gift: she could foresee the future, but nobody would believe her when she told them what was coming. During the Trojan War, the Greek soldiers besieging the city of Troy appeared to give up and go home and left a big wooden horse outside the city walls. Cassandra could see the truth, and she warned her countrymen to have nothing to do with this Trojan horse ("Beware the Greeks bearing gifts"). But nobody believed her, and the Trojans happily hauled the wooden horse inside their city walls. Late at night, a troop of Greek soldiers led by the intrepid Ulysses emerged from their hiding place inside the horse and pillaged the city.
2. Internal Revenue Service, *IRS Data Book* (2015), www.irs.gov/uac/soi-tax -stats-irs-data-book.
3. IRS Form W-9, 3.
4. IRS Cat. No. 55389W, Instructions for Form 8938, 7.
5. IRS Form 5329, pt. 6, line 41.
6. IRS Cat. No. 13330R, Instructions for Form 5329 (2012), 3.
7. It's at www.gov.uk/government/organisations/office-of-tax-simplification.
8. The lobbying efforts against tax simplification have been documented by the reporters Liz Day of the ProPublica news service (www.propublica.org/article /how-the-maker-of-turbotax-fought-free-simple-tax-filing) and Louis Serino of the Sunlight Foundation (http://sunlightfoundation.com/blog/2013/04/15 /tax-preparers-lobby-heavily-against-simple-filing/).

Chapter 12: The Money Machine

1. "The Alchemist at Société Générale," *Euromoney,* Oct. 1981, 176.
2. Both quoted in *Encyclopedia of Management* (Detroit: Gale, 2009), 987.
3. "The Global VAT Craze," *Wall Street Journal,* Mar. 21–22, 2015, A10.
4. Richard M. Bird, "The GST/HST," in *After Twenty Years: The Future of the Goods and Services Tax,* ed. J. M. Mintz and S. R. Richardson (Toronto: Canadian Tax Foundation, 2014), 17.
5. Slemrod and Bakija, *Taxing Ourselves,* 247.
6. The global accounting firm EY compiles this list each year. To see more countries, go to www.ey.com/Publication/vwLUAssets/Worldwide-VAT

-GST-and-sales-tax-guide-2015/$FILE/Worldwide%20VAT,%20GST%20and
%20Sales%20Tax%20Guide%202015.pdf.

7. Alain Charlet and Jeffrey Owens, "An International Perspective on VAT,"
   Tax Notes International, Sept. 20, 2010, 950.

8. President's Advisory Panel on Federal Tax Reform, Final Report, Nov. 1,
   2005, http://govinfo.library.unt.edu/taxreformpanel/final-report/index
   .html, chap. 8.

9. Max Ehrenfreund, "The Three Dirtiest Letters in the GOP Primary," *Wonkblog*
   (blog), *Washington Post,* Feb. 19, 2016.

10. Bruce Bartlett, "VAT Time?," *Forbes,* June 5, 2009.

11. Cruz described his plan in some detail in the *Wall Street Journal.* Ted Cruz, "A
    Simple Flat Tax for Economic Growth," *Wall Street Journal,* Oct. 29, 2015, A17.

12. Ehrenfreund, "Three Dirtiest Letters in the GOP Primary."

13. Bird, "The GST/HST," 4.

Epilogue: The Internal Revenue Code of 2018

1. IRS Publication 525, Taxable and Nontaxable Income, 23.

Afterword: The Tax Cuts and Jobs Act

1. "Middle Class Gets 10% of Cut," *The Wall Street Journal,* December 19, 2017, p. A5.

Index

Abbott, Tony, 190
AbbVie, 157
accelerated depreciation, 55, 62
Affordable Care Act, 209, 218, 246
Afghanistan, 79, 167
Africa, 152, 201, 228
airline industry, 189–90
Alaska Permanent Fund, 192–93
alcohol tax, 37–38, 40, 105
Alliance Boots, 157–58
allowances, 2, 52–53, 60–61, 70, 72, 74, 165–66, 209. *See also* depletion/depreciation allowances; tax breaks
alternative minimum tax, 210, 255
Amawhe, Achilles, 35, 47
American Jobs Creation Act, 168–69
Americans for Tax Reform, 245
America We Deserve, The (Trump), 98
ancient Rome, 30, 34
Andorra, 194–95
Apple Inc., 145, 148–51, 153–54, 161, 164, 170, 229
appraisers/appraisals, 83–84, 124, 129–30
Argentina, 145, 239
art, 83–84, 124, 133
Asia, 59, 201
audits, 40, 55, 143–44, 161, 163, 211, 223, 255
Austen, Jane, 121
austerity measures, 34, 42, 52, 112, 127, 129
Austin, Texas, 26
Australia
    and carbon tax, 8, 189–91
    tax deductions in, 36, 41, 89–90

tax rates of, 19, 21, 146, 175
tax revenues of, 15, 17
VAT in, 228, 239, 243, 255
Austria, 14, 17, 19–20, 44, 78, 86, 132, 146
automobile industry, 21, 39–40, 71–74, 156, 164.
    See also cars

Bahamas, 193, 207
bailouts, 116, 122, 156, 182–83
Baker, James, 66–67
Bakija, Jon, 43, 238
Balzac, Honoré de, 121
banks, 89, 181
    bailouts of, 122, 182–83
    in eastern Europe, 95, 103
    and filing returns, 220–21, 223, 255
    and governments, 33–34, 129
    secret accounts of, 198, 200–207
    and tax avoidance, 147, 160, 167, 200–207
    See also savings
Bartlett, Bruce, 245–46
Belgium, 14, 16–18, 38, 50, 87, 133, 136, 146, 164, 183, 239
Bermuda, 151–52, 156, 166, 193–94, 202
Bharara, Preet, 206
Bird, Richard M., 44, 139, 229, 244, 247
Blankfein, Lloyd, 117
Bloomberg, Michael, 176–78
Bloomberg Businessweek, 153
Boháček, Radim, 94, 108–9
Boulder, Colorado, 180, 188
Bradley, Bill, 66–68, 251

Brazil, 39, 181
British Virgin Islands, 200, 203
broad base, low rates (BBLR)
    advocates for, 56, 91, 218–19
    explanation of, 52–57
    in New Zealand, 57–63, 79, 86, 136
    as successful formula, 48, 251–52
    and tax breaks, 81, 86, 91, 109
    and tax reform, 125, 225
    in U.S., 66–70, 73, 165–66, 236,
        251–52, 255
brokerages, 65, 183, 205, 221, 223
Buffett, Warren, 136–38, 253–54
Bulgaria, 106, 110
Bush, George H. W., 101, 245–46
Bush, George W., 42–43, 56, 88, 101, 108,
    131–32, 241–43
Bush, Jeb, 43, 138
business flat tax (BFT), 246–48

Cain, Herman, 96, 108
California, 20, 60, 149, 170, 179–80, 222, 224
Cameron, David, 200
Canada, 9, 21, 36–38, 57, 122, 132
    and charitable donations, 24, 86
    corporate taxes of, 146, 155
    GST in, 228, 235–37, 239, 243–44, 255
    tax deductions in, 86, 89–90
    tax reform in, 69–70, 243–44
    tax revenues of, 15, 17
    and U.S. corporations, 154–55
cap-and-trade system, 188–90
capital gains tax, 88, 133, 256
    explanation of, 17–19, 69, 233
    increasing rate of, 137, 170
    in Middle East, 192–93
    reduced rate for, 70, 124, 136–39, 160, 241
    and the rich, 70, 99, 124–25, 132, 136–39
    and tax reform, 68–70, 254
Capital in the Twenty-First Century (Piketty), 115,
    121–25, 128, 136, 139, 171–73
capital investment, 23, 56, 102, 114, 123,
    136–39, 168
capitalists/capitalism, 29, 94, 101–3, 114, 170
carbon tax, 8, 133, 185–91
carried-interest preference, 137–39
cars, 107–8, 128
    electric, 36, 71–73, 80, 251
    fuel efficiency of, 21, 39–40
    tax breaks for, 71–74, 80, 81, 122, 222, 251
    See also gas tax
Carson, Ben, 8, 95
Caterpillar Inc., 141–45, 148, 153–54, 162–63
Cayman Islands, 117, 139, 193, 195, 202,
    204, 207

CEOs, 98–99, 117, 122, 128, 150, 154
charitable contributions, 36, 203
    of Americans, 13, 24, 53, 138
    deductions for, 1, 8–9, 40–41, 53, 55, 61, 69,
        79, 81–87, 221, 252
    problems with, 82–87, 90
Chicago Tribune, 158
children, 36, 53, 55, 70, 78, 80, 176, 250, 256
Chile, 14, 16, 25, 51, 120, 146, 179, 239
China, 22, 32, 149, 171, 198, 200, 239
*Choosing a Broad Base–Low Rate Approach to
    Taxation* (OECD), 57
Christensen, John, 204
Chronicle of Philanthropy, 82
churches, 24, 53, 61, 82–84, 93
cigarette tax, 10, 21, 37–38, 40, 176
citizenship, 28–30, 36–37, 46–48, 194–95
Clausing, Kimberly, 165, 169
climate change, 185, 188–89
Clinton, Bill, 101, 188, 211
Clinton, Hillary, 138, 254
Clyde, Lord, 159
Collet, Martin, 125–26, 128
Commerce Clearing House, 212–13
commodities, 18–21, 37–39, 123, 237,
    239–40
Common Market, 228
community programs/services, 27–33
commuting to work, 10, 36, 40, 80
*Compañía General de Tabacos de Filipinas v.
    Collector of Internal Revenue*, 30–32
competition, economic, 106, 108–10, 112, 127,
    145, 164, 234, 256
conservatives, 43, 119, 133, 170
    on flat tax, 100, 104, 108
    on progressive taxes, 44–45, 62, 112
    on tax reform, 64–67
    on VAT, 235–36, 243–46, 248
    See also Republicans
Constitution of Liberty, The (Hayek), 45
consumer spending, 41–42, 57, 114, 174,
    233–39, 243
consumption tax, 35–39, 170, 233–34, 238–48,
    255. *See also* value-added tax (VAT)
Cook, Tim, 150–51, 154
corporate income tax, 75, 128, 154, 156, 173,
    191–92, 233
    avoidance of, 22–23, 31, 54, 139, 142–70, 252
    elimination of, 150–51, 169–70, 246
    and flat-rate tax, 96–97, 108
    in flat-tax nations, 110
    higher in U.S., 13, 21–22, 145, 148, 164–65,
        234, 252
    lowering of, 11, 21–22, 64, 69, 145, 148,
        165–66, 234, 245, 251–54

in other nations, 21–25, 36, 110, 142, 145,
    149, 166–67, 175, 252
  reform of, 164–70, 252–53
corporations, 11, 63, 74, 122, 214, 256
  back taxes paid by, 163–64
  bailouts of, 123, 156
  in eastern Europe, 95, 106
  overseas profits of, 22–23, 81, 141, 143–58,
    161–62, 165–70
  and repatriated profits, 167–69
  tax breaks for, 56, 59, 68–69, 72, 74, 148,
    155–56, 165–70, 252–53
corruption, 46–47, 100, 198, 200
Crassus, Marcus Licinius, 29–30
credits, 2, 5, 41, 55, 71–72, 218
  addition of, 64, 70, 209
  in corporate tax code, 22, 36, 148, 165–66
  elimination of, 56–57, 62, 69, 81, 91, 165–66,
    251–52
  for low-income people, 237–38
  in other nations, 78, 89–90
  for political contributions, 36–37
  and taxable income, 52–53, 59–60
  and tax expenditures, 74–77
Credit Suisse, 207
Cruz, Ted, 8, 95, 246–47
CSARL, 143–45
currency, 29, 32–33, 51, 58, 103, 110, 181,
    197–208
custom duties, 34–35, 50
Cyprus, 129, 202, 204, 207
Czech Republic, 15, 18–19, 93–94, 106, 108–11,
    113, 132

"death tax," 131–32, 254. *See also* estate tax
debts/deficits, 33–34, 41, 51, 64, 71–72, 81, 96,
    185–86, 193, 238, 243, 256
deductions, 17, 40–41, 55, 103, 155, 159, 246
  and corporate taxes, 22, 165–66
  elimination of, 56, 60–62, 67–70,
    81–82, 97, 100, 109–10, 165–66, 219,
    222, 252
  explanation of, 72–78
  itemized, 87–88
  and the rich, 82–83, 86, 88–90
  standard, 83, 89
  and taxable income, 52–53
  and U.S. Congress, 5, 10
See also charitable contributions; mortgage
    interest
deductions; tax breaks
Delaware, 19, 160, 204
Democrats, 43, 60, 64–68, 117, 132, 148, 162,
    188, 190, 245
Denmark, 38, 102, 105, 120

government spending in, 23, 126
  high tax rates of, 17, 19
  property taxes in, 175
  simple tax returns of, 221
  tax revenues of, 14, 16, 79, 126
  VAT rates of, 239
Depardieu, Gérard, 133–34, 139, 151
depletion/depreciation allowances, 64–66,
    69–70
derivatives, 181, 184
dividends, 6, 9, 23, 36, 55, 70, 111, 147, 168,
    170, 173, 193, 233, 241, 254, 256
"Double Irish with a Dutch Sandwich," 151–53,
    161, 164
Douglas, Roger, 60–61
dynamic scoring theory, 101

earned income tax credit (EITC), 210, 217–18,
    238, 250
East Asia, 21, 23, 228
eastern Europe, 93–95, 101–14
economic growth, 16, 36, 41–43, 50, 52, 55, 91,
    101, 104–8, 114, 120, 124, 136, 238
economic impact of taxes, 16, 95, 100–101
Economic Recovery Tax Act of 1981 (ERTA), 64
Economist magazine, 58, 104, 126
education, 36, 44, 53, 63, 70, 79, 84, 105,
    117–18, 123, 126–27, 168, 175, 180, 221
Egypt, 200, 239
Eisenhower, Dwight, 2
electronic trading, 181–84
emissions. *See* carbon tax
Energy Improvement and Extension Act of
    2008, 71–73
environment, 51, 168, 189, 191. *See also*
    carbon tax
Environmental Protection Agency, 39–40
equality, economic, 120, 124
estate tax, 6, 45, 129–32, 192, 246, 254
Estonia, 15, 94, 102–11, 113–14, 220
e-tax system, 105
European Union, 110, 112
  Emissions Trading System (ETS) of, 189
  and FTT tax, 180, 183–84
  members of, 95, 103, 108, 125
  tax dodgers pursued by, 163–64
  and VAT, 228, 239–40
exemptions, 1–2, 5, 17, 80, 84–85, 103,
    130–31, 220
  addition of, 64, 70, 209
  in corporate tax code, 22, 148, 165–66
  elimination of, 55–57, 97, 100, 109–10,
    165–66, 219, 251–52
  explanation of, 76–78
  and loss of revenue, 41, 78

exemptions *(cont.)*
  in paying income tax, 233–34
  and taxable income, 52–53, 59–60
  and tax expenditures, 74–77
  See also tax breaks
expatriation tax, 194
exports, 34, 59–60, 106, 189, 234

Fair Tax Act, 67–68
Farr, Malcolm, 189
fast-food chains, 154–55
fat tax, 38–40, 177–80
FAT tax (financial activities tax), 180–85,
  254–55
Federal Deposit Insurance Corporation (FDIC),
  34, 182
Fico, Robert, 112
Field, Stephen J., 46
filing returns, 1–2, 214
  complexity of, 5–7, 40, 97–98, 211–15,
    219, 224
  by governments, 219–22, 224, 255
  high expense of, 5–6, 212–15, 219, 223–24,
    252, 256
  online, 105, 220, 255
  by precision withholding, 220–21
  by pre-filled forms, 221–25
  and seven income brackets, 97
  simplifying of, 105, 219–25, 252, 255
  software for, 6, 213, 215, 224
  as time-consuming, 5–6, 212–13, 215, 220,
    223–24, 256
financial activities tax (FAT), 180–85, 254–55
financial industry, 137–38, 180–85
financial system, 199, 207
financial transactions tax (FTT), 180–85,
  254–55
Finland, 14, 19, 86, 105, 131, 239
Fiorina, Carly, 95, 214
flat-rate income tax, 44
  advocates for, 8, 91, 95–100, 104, 106, 111,
    253–54
  in eastern Europe, 18, 95, 103–14
  explanation of, 91, 95–114
  problems with, 95–100, 104, 110–11
  of Ted Cruz, 246–48
Flat Tax Revolution (Forbes), 99–100, 108
food taxes, 10, 38–40, 52, 55, 178, 200, 237,
  239–40. *See also* sugar tax
Forbes, Steve, 8, 99–101, 108
Forbes magazine, 99, 224
Foreign Account Tax Compliance Act
  (FATCA), 205–7
Forsberg, Viktor, 104–5, 113–14
Fortune magazine, 162

France, 7, 31, 34, 38, 49, 54, 60, 115, 121,
  198–99, 245
  and charitable donations, 24, 86
  corporate taxes of, 21–22, 145–46, 164
  estate taxes in, 131, 133
  and FTT tax, 181, 183
  and ISF tax, 128–30
  tax avoidance in, 133–34, 139, 142, 151, 207,
    227–28
  taxes on *les riches*, 17, 125–29, 133–34, 139,
    145, 173
  tax revenues of, 14, 79, 128, 134
  VAT rates of, 184, 194, 239–40
Francis, Pope, 118–19
Franklin, Benjamin, 30, 191
fraud, 51, 206, 213, 218
Free to Choose (Friedman), 103
Friedman, Milton, 103, 109, 175
Friedman, Thomas, 187

gas tax, 10, 13, 17, 19–21, 39–40, 187, 234
General Electric, 169
General Motors, 74, 156
George, Henry, 171–76
Georgia, 110
Germany, 17, 71, 102, 106, 113, 164, 147, 181
  BBLR in, 57
  corporate taxes of, 22, 146
  estate taxes of, 131
  and FTT tax, 183
  gas tax in, 20–21
  Nazi era in, 119, 138
  and tax avoidance, 207
  tax breaks in, 36, 89–90
  tax revenues of, 15, 79
  VAT rates of, 239–40
gift tax, 82–86, 130, 246, 254
Gillard, Julia, 190
Gini coefficient, 120, 127
global associations for specific industries, 49–50
global recessions, 112, 116, 182–83, 190, 199
global tax issues, 124–25, 148, 165, 182–83
Global Tax Optimization Program (GTOP),
  142–43
global warming, 185, 188–89
Gonzalez, Rick, 157
goods and services tax (GST), 11, 19, 61,
  228–29, 235–39, 242–48. *See also* value-
  added tax (VAT)
Google, 151–54, 161
government
  borrowing, 33–34, 42, 50
  confidence in, 46–48
  programs, 100, 112–14, 156–58,
    186, 256

services, 33, 63, 72, 96, 126, 150, 174, 218, 235, 244
spending, 23–24, 28–32, 48, 74–79, 81, 106, 126–27, 236, 245, 247
Government Accountability Office (GAO), 147–48, 165, 252
Great Britain. *See* United Kingdom/Great Britain
Great Depression, 121
Great Recession of 2008–2009, 172, 190
  and austerity measures, 34, 52, 112, 127, 129
  bailouts after, 182–83
  and economic collapse, 41–42, 51–52, 235
  and taxes, 41–42, 110, 175
  and wealth, 116, 199, 253
Greece, 15, 33–34, 47, 51, 146, 245
Greenspan, Alan, 246
Gregory, Evelyn, 160–61. *See also Helvering* v. *Gregory*
gross domestic product (GDP), 14, 23–24, 33, 104, 108, 117, 126, 186
gross receipts tax, 228, 247
Group of Twenty, 182
Guth, Petr, 109

Hall, Robert, 96–97
Hand, Learned, 159–61
Hanseatic League, 102
Hatch, Orrin, 77–78
Hayek, F. A., 44–45
health care, 17, 37–38, 44, 51, 63, 69, 114, 118, 157, 176–80, 186, 221
health insurance, 29, 36, 52–53, 63, 81, 126, 133, 209, 218, 246–47, 251
hedge funds, 137–38, 183
Helvering v. Gregory, 159–61
Hines, James R., 56–57
Hollande, François, 127, 133–34, 142, 151
Holmes, Oliver Wendell, Jr., 30, 32, 36
home ownership, 8–9, 36, 40, 52, 75–81, 87–91, 116, 122. *See also* mortgage interest deduction; property: taxes
Hoover Institution, 96–97
Hungary, 15, 18–19, 41, 111, 239

Iceland, 15, 129, 200
Illinois, 141–44, 157, 163
immigrants, 155, 192, 194–95, 229
imports, 34, 50, 65, 187, 189, 193
income
  definition of, 17–18, 52, 222, 255
  distribution of, 44–46, 57
  foreign-earned, 22–23, 81, 143–58, 161–64
  inequality of, 43–46, 115–25, 135, 139
  "ordinary," 137, 160

seven brackets of, 97
"stateless," 150, 154
income tax
  earned income tax credit, 217
  elimination of, 225
  history of, 1–3, 12, 34–35, 45–46, 121, 135, 145, 173, 250
  nonpayers of, 233–34
  rebates of, 41–42
  See also specific types
Income Tax, The: A Study of the History, Theory, and Practice of Income Taxation at Home and Abroad (Seligman), 45
India, 34, 129
inequality, economic, 8, 43–46, 98, 107, 115–25, 127, 135, 139, 172–75, 242, 253–56
inflation, 32–33
inheritance tax, 17, 30, 99, 121, 129–33, 254
insurance, 31–32, 60–61, 181–82. *See also* health insurance
intellectual property, 151–53
interest charges, 9, 33–34, 53, 61, 151, 155, 166, 173, 202, 241
interest groups, 41, 56–57, 62, 66, 68, 225
Internal Revenue Code. *See* tax code
Internal Revenue Service (IRS), 30, 35, 72, 75
  art appraisal office of, 83–84
  commissioners of, 161, 210, 213, 249
  complexity and, 39, 55, 83, 97–98, 130, 194, 209, 213, 215–16, 249
  dislike of, 24, 26, 212
  expenses/revenues of, 214–15, 241, 256
  and filing returns, 222–24, 255
  taxpayer advocate of, 211–16, 220
  underfunded, 161, 163
  See also audits; *specific tax types*
International Consortium of Investigative Journalists, 198–99
International Fiscal Association, 229
International Monetary Fund (IMF), 50–52, 57, 103, 112, 158, 175, 182, 185–86, 237–38
international organizations, 49–52, 56–57, 203
International Tax Handbook, 191–92
Internet, 49–50, 86, 105, 121, 200, 234, 255
Intuit, 224
investment, 36, 50, 55, 57, 167, 254–56
  accounts, 9, 129
  bankers, 119, 137
  in eastern Europe, 105–10
  encouraging of, 41, 241
  houses, 182–83
  income, 111, 124, 136–39, 192–93, 223
  taxes on, 136–39, 173, 233
  See also capital investment

IRA deposits, 9, 69
Ireland, 19, 33, 86, 175
  corporate taxes of, 22, 145–46, 149–50,
    152, 166
  tax reform in, 69–70
  tax revenues of, 14–15
  and U.S. corporations, 147, 149–53, 156–57,
    162, 164
  VAT rates of, 41, 239–40
IRS Offshore Voluntary Disclosure
    Program, 201
IRS Restructuring and Reform Act of 1998,
    211–12
Israel, 15, 20, 89–90, 146
Italy, 14, 17, 29–30, 33, 147
  and FTT tax, 181, 183
  and tax breaks, 78, 86
  tax bureau in, 24–25
  VAT rates of, 41–42, 240

Japan, 30, 33, 71, 131, 147, 187, 228
  corporate taxes of, 22, 146
  deductions in, 86, 89–90
  gas tax in, 20–21
  simple returns of, 7, 220–21, 223
  tax bureau in, 25, 220
  tax revenues of, 15, 17
  and VAT, 238, 240
Jersey, isle of, 157
Jesus Christ, 28, 44, 134–35
job creation, 41–44, 91, 123, 125, 136, 162,
    168–69
Johnson, Paul, 91
Johnson Controls, 156
Joint International Tax Shelter Information and
    Collaboration Network (JITSIC),
    204–5, 207
Journal of Public Policy, 58

Kažimír, Peter, 112–13
Kennedy, John F., 75, 120
Keynes, John Maynard, 50, 54
Kiwis, 58–60, 62, 65
Kleinbard, Edward D., 148
Koskinen, John, 161, 210, 213
Kotlikoff, Laurence J., 169–70

Laar, Mart, 102–4
labor, taxes on, 17, 58, 123, 136–37, 173
labor/labour parties, 43, 60, 91,
    189–90
land, taxes on, 46, 52, 83, 173–76
La taxe sur la valeur ajoutée (Lauré), 228
Latvia, 15, 106, 109
Lauré, Maurice, 227–29, 232

lawyers, 13, 62, 109, 169, 205–6, 211. *See also*
    Mossack Fonseca; tax avoidance
left, the, 43, 80, 107, 109, 112–13, 126–27,
    137–38, 170, 175, 247, 253
Levin, Carl, 148, 162–63
Lew, Jacob, 161–62
Lewis, Al, 158
liberals, 2, 12, 43, 58, 64–65, 68, 78, 127, 188,
    190, 236, 244, 248
life insurance, 61, 78, 80
Lithuania, 106, 109
loans, 29, 51, 69, 70, 155, 166, 181, 221
lobbyists, 41, 57, 67, 70, 89, 168, 177–78, 180,
    183, 224–25, 240, 245, 252
Long, Russell, 74
Luntz, Frank, 131–32
Luxembourg, 15, 164, 183, 203–4
luxury goods, 239

Macau, 194–95
McCain, John, 44, 150–51
McTigue, Maurice, 62, 251
Malaysia, 136, 200, 240
Mankiw, N. Gregory, 170
manufacturers' sales tax (MST), 243–44
manufacturing companies, 11, 107–8, 141–45,
    153, 156, 187
Maori tribe, 58–59
Marlborough wine region, 60
Martin, Lucy, 47
Massachusetts, 35, 45, 64, 223
media, 44, 74, 120, 127, 197–200, 204, 207–8
Medicaid, 63, 79, 157, 174, 234
Medicare, 17, 79, 157–58, 246
medicine, 52, 55, 156–58, 165, 237, 239
Mexico, 19–20, 24, 51, 120, 240
  corporate tax of, 22, 146
  fat/sugar tax in, 38–39, 177–79
  and safe water, 39, 177–79
  tax revenues of, 14, 16
Microsoft, 151, 153–54
Middle East, 34, 152, 155, 167, 187, 191–95
Mikloš, Ivan, 106–8
Monaco, 194–95
Monitor Securities Corporation, 160
mortgage interest deduction, 8–9, 53, 61, 69,
    75–76, 78, 80, 88–91, 100, 252
  eliminated in Britain, 90–91
Mossack Fonseca, 197–203, 205, 207–8
Mulroney, Brian, 243–44
Murdoch, Rupert, 190, 199

NASA, 168, 174
National Bureau of Economic
    Research, 168

National Commission on Fiscal Responsibility and Reform, 56
national parks, 34, 103, 168
National Taxpayer Advocate, 211–16, 220
nation-state concept, 34
Native Americans, 58, 80
Netherlands, 20, 87, 131, 146
    deductions in, 86, 89–90
    and Google, 152–53
    simple returns of, 7, 219–21
    and tax avoidance, 164, 167
    tax reform in, 69–70
    tax revenues of, 15, 17
    and VAT, 10, 235, 240
Nevada, 204
New York Times, 115, 155, 162, 187, 198, 224
New Zealand, 18, 65, 166
    BBLR in, 57–63, 86, 136
    deductions in, 89–90
    GST in, 11, 19, 61, 228, 238, 240, 243
    tax reform in, 57–63, 65, 69, 107, 251
    tax revenues of, 15, 79
Nigeria, 24–25, 35, 47
Nikoloudis, Panagiotis, 47
Norway, 15, 17–18, 20, 79, 87, 120, 129, 132, 146, 240

Obama, Barack, 39, 56, 132, 188, 205, 229
    on corporate taxes, 158, 166
    on economic inequality, 43–44, 117–20, 253
    tax reform of, 88, 125, 137–38, 241
Obermayer, Bastian, 197–98, 207–8
obesity, 38–40, 176–78, 180
Occupy Wall Street, 116–17, 119, 127
Ódor, Ludovit, 107–8, 111
oil, 22, 32, 34, 36, 39, 64, 73, 186–87, 191–93
Olson, Nina, 211–16, 218–19, 221
online purchases, 234
Oregon, 19, 245
Organization for Economic Cooperation and Development (OECD), 20, 77, 89, 128, 228
    on BBLR system, 57, 70
    BEPS plan of, 163
    member countries of, 59, 120, 145
    role of, 50–52
    on tax revenues, 14–18
overall tax burden, 13–18, 46, 126, 148, 165, 175

Packwood, Robert, 68
Panama Papers, 195, 197–208
Paris, France, 7, 31, 115, 126, 133, 181, 204
Paul, Rand, 8, 95
payroll taxes, 41–42, 110–11, 173, 192, 233, 242, 246

Peichl, Andreas, 113
penalties, 39–40, 163, 206–7, 211, 243
Pennsylvania, 180, 182
pensions, 17, 63, 108, 126
Perkins, Tom, 119
Perry, Rick, 8, 95
Pfizer, 156–57, 162
pharmaceutical companies, 34, 156–58
Philippine Cigar Case, 30–32
Piketty, Thomas, 115–16, 121–25, 127–28, 136, 139, 171–73, 183
Poland, 15, 102, 109, 119, 138, 240
political contributions, 36, 70, 74, 123, 138
politics, 36, 48, 62, 102, 116, 131–32
    Georgism movement, 171–75
    polarization of, 12, 63–64, 69, 241–42
    of tax breaks, 72, 86, 90
    of tax rates, 91, 111–12
    of tax reform, 66–68, 91, 224–25
    and VAT, 229–30, 236, 241–48
Portugal, 15, 17, 33, 221
President's Advisory Panel on Federal Tax Reform, 56, 241–43
PricewaterhouseCoopers (PwC), 142–44, 148, 162–63, 252
private sector, 29–30, 42, 122
Progress and Poverty (George), 171–76
progressive income tax, 10, 28–29, 241
    advocates for, 44–46, 54, 62, 114, 125, 135
    and inequality, 135, 253–54
    in other nations, 97, 104–8, 110, 112
    in U.S., 97–98, 100–101, 135–36
property
    rights, 103–4
    taxes, 35, 52–54, 79, 88, 124, 128, 173–76, 191, 193
public programs/services, 27–33, 35, 44, 125–26, 218, 247
Puerto Rico, 153
Putin, Vladimir, 134, 200

Rabushka, Alvin, 96–97
Reagan, Ronald, 12, 64–65, 67–69, 137, 245, 254
real estate, 18, 61, 69, 89–90, 101, 105, 123, 128, 133, 136, 195
recessions, 43, 101, 112, 233. *See also* Great Recession of 2008–2009
Regan, Donald, 65–67, 250
religious organizations, 84. *See also* churches
Republicans, 8, 12, 42–44, 64–68, 77, 91, 95–96, 99, 117, 138, 150, 188, 190, 210, 214, 245–47, 253–54
retail sales tax. *See* sales tax; value-added tax (VAT)

retirement, 9, 24, 36, 52–53, 81, 246
rich, the, 1, 113, 184
  high taxes on, 16–18, 27–29, 34, 97, 120,
    123–29, 173–75, 180, 253
  lower taxes on, 134–39, 253–54
  and tax increases, 43–46, 112
  and tax rate cuts, 62, 69, 91, 117
  tax-reform plan for, 95–96
  top 1%, 18, 44, 67, 116–17, 119, 121, 198
  See also superrich, the; tax avoidance: by the
    rich; tax breaks: for the rich; wealth; *specific*
    taxes
Ridley, Matt, 119
"rifle shot" tax provision, 74
right, the, 43, 107, 126–27, 137–38, 175,
  247, 253
Robin Hood tax, 180, 183–84
Rogers, Will, 28
Romania, 106, 110
Romney, Mitt, 46, 95, 117, 138–39, 234
Roosevelt, Franklin Delano, 159, 171
Roosevelt, Teddy, 135
Russia, 32, 101–2, 106, 109, 111, 129, 134,
  200, 240

sales tax, 11, 69, 230–36
  and BBLR, 52, 55–56, 58
  in eastern Europe, 108, 114
  on financial transactions, 180–85
  local, 19, 69, 230, 234, 242–44, 255
  in other nations, 10, 18–19, 61, 128, 133,
    235, 239
  state, 19, 183, 242–43
  in U.S., 10, 17, 19, 37, 96, 173, 193, 247
  world's highest, 18, 41, 111
  See also value-added tax (VAT)
Sanders, Bernie, 132, 138, 158, 172, 180,
  184–85, 253
Sarkozy, Nicolas, 127, 133
savings, 9, 33, 36, 116, 128–29, 173–74,
  181–82, 233, 241, 255
Scandinavia, 105
schools, 24–25, 29, 63, 117, 175, 237, 239
Schuchat, Frank, 139
Schwarzman, Stephen, 119, 138
Scott, Graham, 11, 60–63, 65
securities, 23, 84, 123, 160, 181–85, 255
Securities and Exchange Commission, 163, 181
seigniorage gain, 33
self-employed, the, 63, 223
Seligman, Edwin R. A., 45, 135
Serbia, 106, 110
single-rate tax. *See* flat-rate income tax
Single Tax (Georgist), 173–76
sin tax, 37–39

Skadden, Arps firm, 154
Slemrod, Joel, 43, 238
Slovakia, 10, 15, 23, 106–13
Slovenia, 15, 94
slumps, economic, 37, 41–42, 51, 101, 103, 107,
  113, 172, 233, 235, 238
Smith, Adam, 37–38, 44–45
Social Security, 103, 126
  in flat-rate tax countries, 110–11, 114
  in other nations, 133, 192, 221
  in U.S., 17, 41–42, 63, 75, 79, 165, 173–74,
    186, 234, 246
soda pop tax, 10, 38–39, 176–80, 185
South Africa, 240
South Korea, 14–15, 17, 19, 21, 24, 36, 77,
  146, 181
Soviet Union, 94–95, 101–6, 109–11, 220.
  See also Russia
Spain, 19, 24, 31, 131, 147, 183
  simple returns of, 221
  tax revenues of, 15, 78
  VAT rates of, 25, 41, 194, 240
  wealth tax of, 129
Starbucks, 164, 166–67
state taxes, 13, 17, 19–20, 35, 52–56, 63,
  69, 88, 131, 147, 156, 193,
  222, 255
Steinmo, Sven, 36
Stiglitz, Joseph, 125
stimulus measures, 42, 52
stockholders, 23, 122, 150, 156–57, 168–70
stock market, 101, 111, 118, 136–37, 141,
  180–85, 254
stocks/bonds, 18, 69, 88, 123, 128, 147, 151,
  160, 195, 203
subsidies, 60, 72, 76, 79, 103
Süddeutsche Zeitung, 197–98. *See also* Obermayer,
  Bastian
sugar tax, 37–40, 176–80
Sullivan, Martin, 169
Summers, Lawrence, 188, 211, 248
Sun Yat-sen, 171
superrich, the, 117, 122, 134–39
Surrey, Stanley, 72, 75–77, 79–80, 82, 86
Sutton, Willie, 128
Sweden, 18–19, 22–24, 86–87, 102,
  105, 126
  corporate taxes of, 146
  economic equality in, 120–21
  and inheritance tax, 132
  simple returns of, 221
  stock trades taxed by, 181–82
  tax revenues of, 14–17
  VAT rates of, 240
Sweers, Michiel, 235

Switzerland, 49, 86, 117, 129, 181
   corporate taxes of, 54, 143, 145–46, 164, 166
   and tax avoidance, 164, 167, 202–7
   tax revenues of, 14–15
   and U.S., 54, 143–45, 147, 156–58, 162–63,
     166–67

Taft, William Howard, 31–32
tax agencies/bureaus, 39, 105, 182, 232
   despised in U.S., 24, 26
   faith in government enhanced by, 46–47
   and ombudsman, 211, 219
   in other nations, 24–25, 35, 219–21, 227–28
   and tax avoidance, 163, 201–2
   See also audits; Internal Revenue
     Service (IRS)
Tax Analysis Center, 166
taxation
   and bad behavior, 37–41, 175–80
   and good behavior, 36–37, 40, 73
   history of, 1–3, 34–35, 45–46, 64–70, 126
   important rule of, 48, 52
   "neutral," 37, 54, 58, 73
   reasons for, 28–32, 35–48, 126
tax avoidance, 73, 213, 215, 232, 241, 252
   and citizenship, 194–95
   critics of, 66, 158–64, 199, 204
   "Double Irish with a Dutch sandwich,"
     151–53, 161, 164
   earnings skimming, 155, 163, 166
   inversion, 154–58, 161–62
   investigations into, 51, 149–51, 154, 162–64,
     198–99, 202–8
   offshore tax havens, 200–202, 205, 207
   profit shifting, 143–45, 148–49, 152–53, 158,
     162–63, 165–70
   by the rich, 54–55, 66, 109, 124, 133, 139,
     197–208
   shell companies, 152, 160, 199–204
   and unfair tax system, 218, 221
   See also corporate income tax: avoidance of;
     Philippine
     Cigar Case; *specific countries*
tax breaks, 9–10, 53–54, 64–65
   advocates for, 56–57, 67–68, 72
   elimination of, 60–61, 68–69, 86–91, 119,
     125, 138, 219, 251–52, 255
   for good behavior, 36–37, 40, 73
   and loss of revenue, 78–82, 85–90
   for the rich, 68, 70–77, 87–90, 98, 122, 125,
     136–39, 252, 254
   tax codes complicated by, 40–41, 222
   tax expenditures as, 74–81
   See also corporations: tax breaks for; tax
     preferences; *specific types*

tax code, 212–13
   anti-complexity clause of, 5, 70, 211, 249
   complexity of, 2, 48, 68, 73–74, 130,
     209–19, 250
   history of, 1–3, 69–70
   in other nations, 219, 221, 255–57
   simplifying of, 55, 214, 218–19, 225, 238,
     241, 255
   unified, 107–8, 228
   See also tax reform
tax collection, 7, 11, 17, 34–35, 47, 55, 83–84,
   166, 214–15, 219, 227–38, 243
"Tax Complexity Lobby," 224–25
Tax Equity and Fiscal Responsibility Act
   (TEFRA), 64
tax expenditures, 74–81, 87–88, 91, 224, 252.
   See also specific taxes
Tax Foundation, 148, 247
tax-free countries/states, 183, 191–95
tax-free items, 237, 251
tax-free savings, 9
tax justice, 45, 135
tax law, 50, 64, 68–69, 148–50
   complexity of, 2, 5–7
   first in U.S., 45–46
   violations of, 158–59
   writers of, 10, 112–13, 123, 209–13, 245, 252
Tax Law Design and Drafting (Thuronyi), 158
Tax Policy Center, 136, 184, 247
tax preferences, 54, 68
   carried-interest, 137–39, 254
   elimination of, 55–57, 66–67, 219,
     251–52, 255
   explanation of, 76–79, 250
   in New Zealand, 59–60, 62
   and tax complexity, 40–41, 48, 55, 225
   See also specific types
tax preparers, 6–7, 213, 215, 217, 219,
   223–24, 252
tax rate
   inequality in, 70, 123, 254
   top, 82–83, 85–86, 107, 160
   top marginal, 17–18, 59–60, 67–70, 76, 124
   See also broad base, low rates (BBLR);
     flat-rate income tax
tax reform, 2, 61, 66–68, 91, 211–12
   and BBLR, 56–58, 125, 218–19, 251–52, 255
   fair type of, 95–96
   of George W. Bush, 56, 88, 132
   in New Zealand, 57–63, 65, 69, 251
   of 1986, 10, 12, 85–86, 250–51, 254, 257
   by rewriting code, 250–51, 255–57
   in Slovakia, 107–8, 112–13
   in U.S., 8, 12, 63–70, 73–74, 125, 241–48
   and VAT, 229, 241–48, 255

Tax Reform Act of 1984, 64
Tax Reform Act of 1986, 12, 68–70, 85–86
tax revenue. *See specific countries; specific taxes*
tax systems, 27, 53–54, 213, 221
   best examples of, 57–63, 73, 106, 251
   complexity of, 5, 9, 26, 40, 48, 55, 64, 68,
     224, 229, 237, 257
   cost of, 214–15, 238
   efficiency of, 3, 241–42
   fair, 3, 28, 46, 55, 111, 114, 125–26, 229,
     237, 253
   goals of, 36, 41, 44, 46
   simplifying of, 2–3, 7, 56, 61, 79, 97–100,
     105, 107, 256
   successful, 2–3, 7–8, 28, 51–52, 126–27, 218,
     251–52, 256
   unified, 107–8, 228
Tea Party, 85
technological advances, 49, 105
terrorism, 187
Thuronyi, Victor, 158
timber, 34, 59–60, 80, 131, 164
Times (London), 119
"tiny tax," 180–85
tobacco tax, 17, 21, 37–38, 40, 176
Tobin tax, 180–83
Tokyo, Japan, 7, 25, 30, 187
Toscana, David, 177
transfer tax, 130
Treasury I (tax reform), 65–66
Trump, Donald, 12, 98–100, 117, 138, 158, 166,
   253–54
trusts, 6, 216
Tsipras, Alexis, 47
Turkey, 15, 20
Tyco International, 156

Uganda, 47
U.K. Office of Tax Simplification (OTS),
   220–21
Ukraine, 109
Ullman, Al, 245
Underwood-Simmons Tariff Act (1913), 1
unemployment, 42, 107–8, 114, 116, 127
Union des Associations Internationales, 50
United Arab Emirates (U.A.E.), 191–92, 194
United Kingdom/Great Britain, 15, 17, 20, 22,
   31, 35, 49, 50, 57, 77, 96, 121, 131, 146,
   157, 179, 200, 243, 255
   charitable donations in, 40–41, 221
   inequalities in, 119, 122
   media of, 198–99
   mortgage deduction eliminated by, 90–91
   simple returns of, 7, 220–21
   and tax avoidance, 159, 166–67

   tax breaks in, 78, 80, 90–91
   tax bureau in, 24–25, 220–21
   tax on stock trades, 181, 183–84
   tax rates of, 10, 19, 166–67
   tax reform in, 69–70, 90–91
   VAT rates of, 41–42, 235, 240, 247
United Nations, 34, 49
University of Tartu, 103–4, 113
Uruguay, 39
U.S. Congress, 7, 42, 80, 99, 113, 181, 194
   accounting arm of, 147–48
   and capital gains tax, 137–39
   charities law of, 84–85
   and corporate money, 63, 144
   and corporate taxes, 165–66, 168–69
   IRS berated by, 26, 161, 209–10
   and pre-filled tax forms, 223–24
   and tax breaks, 9–10, 56–57, 65, 71–76, 78,
     89, 250–52
   and tax code reform, 8–9, 12, 64–70
   on tax complexity, 5, 26, 219, 249
   and tax-ducking inversions, 161–62
   tax evaders investigated by, 149–51, 154,
     162–63
   tax law written by, 1–3, 10, 45–46, 74,
     209–13, 245, 252
   See also bailouts; political contributions; U.S.
     House of Representatives; U.S. Senate
U.S. Constitution, 46
U.S. Customs House, 35
U.S. House of Representatives, 64, 67–68,
   74, 245
U.S. Justice Department, 201, 205–7
U.S. Mint, 33
U.S. Senate, 1, 66–68, 74, 77–78, 150, 154,
   162, 245
U.S. Supreme Court, 30–32, 46, 123, 161
U.S. Treasury Department, 5, 78, 159, 182
   on lowering tax rates, 251–52
   secretaries of, 65–66, 161, 211, 248, 250
   and tax breaks, 71–72, 80–81
   and tax-ducking inversions, 157, 161–62
   and tax expenditures, 75, 87–88
   and tax policy, 245–46
   and tax reform, 65–66, 250

value-added tax (VAT), 10, 19, 25,
   110, 194
   explanation of, 228–38, 241–46
   raising rates of, 41–42, 111, 114
   standard rates of, 183–84, 238–40
   and U.S., 11–12, 229–30, 241–48,
     254–55
   See also goods and services tax (GST)
Vano, Vladimir, 106

Walgreens, 157–58
Wall Street, 10, 65, 70, 180–81, 184, 255
Wall Street Journal, 109, 119, 162–63, 169, 184,
   190–91, 199, 205, 236–37
Wandell, Keith, 156
War of 1812, 34–35
Warren, Elizabeth, 117, 223, 253
Washington, D.C., 30, 69, 84–85, 120,
   131, 136, 156, 169, 184,
   198–99, 224
Washington Post, 116
water (safe, drinking), 39, 177–79
wealth, 110
   wealth tax, 17, 124–25, 128–32,
     173, 183, 192–93

See also gross domestic product (GDP);
   inequality, economic; rich, the;
   superrich, the
Wealth of Nations, The (Smith), 37
Wegelin & Co. (Switzerland),
   205–6
welfare state, 80
widow's mite, 27–28, 135
Wilson, Woodrow, 1
World Bank, 16–17, 23–24, 50–52, 57,
   77, 126, 182
World Health Organization, 49, 176
world wars, 1, 50, 106, 121, 228

Zolt, Eric, 12

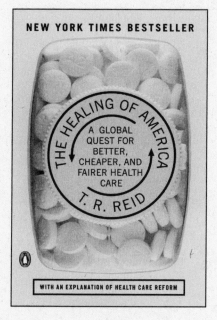

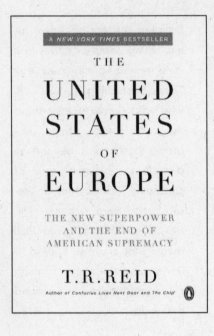